D1765649

3 0116 00417 7117

This book is due for return not later than the
last date stamped below, unless recalled sooner.

ASTON
UNIVERSITY

LIBRARY &
INFORMATION
SERVICES

Aston Triangle
Birmingham
B4 7ET
England

Tel +44 (0121) 359 3611
Fax +44 (0121) 359 7358
email library@aston.ac.uk
Website http://www.aston.ac.uk/lis/

INSIDE THE BUNDESBANK

Hans Tietmeyer
President of the Deutsche Bundesbank (*reproduced with the Bank's permission*).

Inside the Bundesbank

Edited by

Stephen F. Frowen
Honorary Research Fellow
Department of Economics
University College London
and former Bundesbank Professor
of Monetary Economics
in the Free University of Berlin

and

Robert Pringle
Editor, Central Banking

Foreword by Hans Tietmeyer
President, Deutsche Bundesbank

 in association with
CENTRAL BANKING

This edition first published in Great Britain 1998 by
MACMILLAN PRESS LTD
Houndmills, Basingstoke, Hampshire RG21 6XS and London
Companies and representatives throughout the world

A catalogue record for this book is available from the British Library.

ISBN 0–333–69988–2

This edition first published in the United States of America 1998 by
ST. MARTIN'S PRESS, INC.,
Scholarly and Reference Division,
175 Fifth Avenue, New York, N.Y. 10010

ISBN 0–312–21253–4

Library of Congress Cataloging-in-Publication Data
Inside the Bundesbank / edited by Stephen F. Frowen and Robert
Pringle.
p. cm.
Includes bibliographical references and index.
ISBN 0–312–21253–4
1. Deutsche Bundesbank. 2. Banks and banking, Central—Germany.
3. Monetary policy—Germany. I. Frowen, Stephen F. II. Pringle,
Robert, 1939– .
HG3054.I32 1998
332.1'1'0943—dc21   97–42221
                                                              CIP

Selection and editorial matter © Central Banking Publications Ltd 1995, 1998
Individual chapters © Jürgen Becker, Leonhard Gleske, Reiner König and Caroline
Willeke, Peter Schmid, Berthold Wahlig and Carola Gebhard 1995, 1998
and © Hans Tietmeyer, Otmar Issing, Norbert Kloten 1998

Earlier versions of Chapters 2–6 and 11 appeared in the summer 1995 issue of *Central
Banking* and Chapter 8 in the autumn 1995 issue of *Central Banking*.

This book is printed on paper suitable for recycling and made from fully managed and
sustained forest sources.

10   9   8   7   6   5   4   3   2
07   06   05   04   03   02   01   00   99   98

Printed and bound in Great Britain by
Antony Rowe Ltd, Chippenham, Wiltshire

Contents

List of Tables and Figures   vii

Acknowledgements   viii

Foreword by the President of the Deutsche Bundesbank   ix

Notes on the Contributors   xii

List of Abbreviations   xvii

Introduction by Stephen F. Frowen and Robert Pringle   xix

1 The Bundesbank: Committed to Stability
   Hans Tietmeyer   1

2 Bundesbank Independence, Organisation and Decision-
   Making
   Leonhard Gleske   11

3 German Monetary Unification: Domestic and External
   Issues
   Reiner König and Caroline Willeke   20

4 Monetary Policy: Targets and Instruments
   Peter Schmid   32

5 Relations between the Bundesbank and the Federal
   Government
   Bertold Wahlig   45

6 Banking Supervision: Who is Doing What?
   Jürgen Becker   56

7 Recollections of the German Treaty Negotiations of
   1990
   Hans Tietmeyer   68

8 German Unification: A Personal View
   Norbert Kloten   110

9   Ethics and Morals in Central Banking: Do They
    Exist, Do They Matter?
    Otmar Issing   120

10 The Evolution of the Deutsche Mark as an
    International Currency
    Carola Gebhard   139

11 Profiles of Bundesbank Presidents   174

Index   181

List of Tables and Figures

Tables

3.1	Discount rate of the Bundesbank	26
4.1	Monetary targets and their implementation	36
4.2	Basic scheme for deriving a monetary target	39
8.1a	German public sector deficit	116
8.1b	The credibility bonus: foreign financing of the deficit	116
10.1	Inflation rates of selected countries based on consumer price indices, 1980–95	141
10.2	Currencies and weights in the SDR basket	141
10.3	Share of world exports	142
10.4	Currency denomination of German exports	143
10.5	Structure of German foreign trade by currencies and by regions in 1989	144
10.6	Currency denomination of German imports	144
10.7	Currency denomination of exports in other countries	145
10.8	Currency denomination of imports in other countries	145
10.9	Foreign Deutsche Mark denominated investment in Germany, 1980–94	153
10.10	Currency distribution of international bond issues, 1985–94	154
10.11	Shares of major currencies in total foreign exchange reserves, 1975–95	158
10.12	Location of Deutsche Mark denominated foreign reserves	160
10.13	Currencies and weights in the ECU basket	161
10.14	The international role of the Deutsche Mark at a glance	166

Figures

10.1	International Deutsche Mark denominated bonds held by non-residents, 1980–94	155
10.2	Foreign exchange reserves held in Deutsche Marks by country group, 1975–94	159

Acknowledgements

We wish to thank Central Banking Publications for the permission they have kindly given to reprint in this volume updated versions of the essays by Jürgen Becker, Leonhard Gleske, Reiner König and Caroline Willeke, Peter Schmid and Bertold Wahlig as well as the profiles of Bundesbank Presidents. These articles and profiles were originally published in the Summer 1995 Special Issue of *Central Banking* on 'Understanding the Bundesbank'. Our thanks are also due for permission to reprint an updated version of the paper by Norbert Kloten which appeared in the Autumn 1995 issue of *Central Banking*.

The chapter by Otmar Issing is the text of his Henry Thornton Lecture presented in London at the City University Business School on 23 November 1995. We are grateful to Professor G.E. Wood of the Business School for his generosity in allowing us to include the Issing contribution, first published in G.E. Wood and Forrest Capie (eds) *Monetary Economics in the 1990s* by Macmillan, in our book.

The German version of Chapter 7 by Hans Tietmeyer, 'Recollections of the German Treaty Negotiations', was originally published in 1994 in *Tage, die Deutschland und die Welt veränderten*, edited by Theo Waigel and Manfred Schell.

We wish to express out deep appreciation to the members of the German Central Bank Council past and present, and to the Heads of Bundesbank Departments who have contributed to *Inside the Bundesbank*. Above all, we owe a special debt to the Bundesbank President, Professor Hans Tietmeyer, without who support this volume would not have been possible.

We wish, finally, to thank Tim Farmiloe, the publishing director of Macmillan, Sunder Katwala, the editor, and Keith Povey, the editorial services consultant, for the endless skill, resource and care which they have lavished upon this book.

STEPHEN F. FROWEN
ROBERT PRINGLE

Foreword

The monetary policy decisions of the Deutsche Bundesbank are attentively registered, analysed and occasionally also criticised world-wide. What monetary policy can and should achieve is assessed by many observers primarily against the backdrop of short-term financial market interests. Medium and longer-term aspects of monetary policy, its macroeconomic integration and responsibility, sometimes recede into the background. This book addresses itself especially to Anglo-Saxon readers who are less familiar with the historical, legal and institutional basis of German internal and external monetary policy. In the individual contributions both former and active representatives of the Deutsche Bundesbank highlight the goals of the German central bank and its role in the economy as a whole in terms of its duties and functions. Furthermore, the book reports on events in the historical context of German reunification.

The Deutsche Mark is one of the leading international transaction, reserve and investment currencies. In Europe it has, moreover, become the *de facto* anchor currency for the European Monetary System (EMS). The international reputation of the Deutsche Mark is based on its remarkable stability performance. Since the introduction of the Deutsche Mark in 1948, the rate of inflation in Germany, at an average of $2^3/_4$ per cent, has been comparatively low by international standards. As a mirror image of the stability of domestic purchasing power, the Deutsche Mark has appreciated considerably relative to most other currencies. The internal and external stability of the value of the Deutsche Mark is ultimately a reflection and result of a stability culture in Germany which has grown over a period of decades and which has its origins in the painful historical experience of two hyperinflations with their disastrous social and political consequences.

Judging by past experience, monetary stability has no special lobby. It needs to be based on a social consensus which assumes concrete shape in terms of adequate legal and institutional regulations. The German legislature has deliberately and unambiguously committed the Bundesbank to the primary objective of safeguarding the currency. The fact that it is independent of instructions from other bodies in monetary policy matters takes account of the finding that, without the protective shield of independence, central banks are exposed to a latent danger of being called upon to perform tasks which they cannot fulfil with the instruments they have.

Ensuring the stability of the currency can be lastingly successful only if it is understood and accepted as a common task of all those responsible for economic policy. Fiscal and pay policy makers, in particular, are called upon to play their part in anti-inflation policy. In the long run, too great a burden would be placed on monetary policy makers if they wished to correct misalignments in other policy areas. Exaggerated demands on the national product, either by excessive government debt or by a wage policy that does not give sufficient consideration to the trend in productivity, might make it more difficult to discharge the central bank's stability mandate. An expansionary monetary policy does not create competitive jobs, and low central bank interest rates do not solve any structural problems. Indeed, low capital market rates cannot be achieved by a monetary policy decision: they must be earned by a credible stability orientation of all policy areas which convinces the markets.

Monetary policy stands or falls by its credibility. A central bank's monetary policy strategy plays a major part in this. For 25 years the Deutsche Bundesbank's monetary policy has been founded on a basic monetary stance which is geared to the longer term, with an annual monetary target and a medium-term price target. This monetary policy strategy has stood the test and has itself become one of the key elements of the German stability culture. In contrast to many other countries, the empirical basis for successful monetary targeting, a link between trends in the money stock and in prices that is stable over the longer term, still exists in Germany. The public self-commitment associated with the announcement of a monetary target makes monetary policy measures transparent and promotes the acceptability even of unpopular monetary policy decisions.

A policy of consistently ensuring the stability of the currency is not an end in itself but a major prerequisite for economic prosperity and social equity. The difficult process of German reunification was undoubtedly assisted by the stable Deutsche Mark. However, a strong Deutsche Mark is also in the longer-term interests of Germany's partners. As a stable anchor currency in the EMS, it gives the European partner countries the opportunity to participate in the stability of the Deutsche Mark by pursuing an appropriate exchange rate policy.

The following applies to the European currency envisaged in the Maastricht Treaty as well: lasting stability will be achieved only if

safeguarding the value of money is understood as a task and obligation for society as a whole in all of the countries participating in the
monetary union. The strict and narrow interpretation of the convergence criteria of the Treaty, complemented by effective regulations for
a permanent safeguarding of fiscal policy discipline, is intended to
create the economic basis for the European Monetary Union (EMU)
to become a genuine community of stability. Judging by all historical
experience, however, it will also require a more far-reaching political
integration in Europe in the long run in order to survive.

HANS TIETMEYER
President of the Deutsche Bundesbank

Notes on the Contributors

Jürgen Becker has been Head of the Deutsche Bundesbank's Department of Banking and Minimum Reserves since 1987, having joined the Central Office of the Deutsche Bundesbank in 1977 to work in the area of banking supervision and minimum reserves. He previously worked at the Land Central Bank in Lower Saxony and during that period spent seven years as the Bank's Branch Manager. In 1983 he was seconded as Adviser to the Central Bank of the Bahamas and in 1985 became a Member of the Basle Committee on Banking Regulations and Supervisory Practices.

Stephen F. Frowen, Honorary Research Fellow in the Department of Economics at University College London, Senior Research Associate at the Von Hügel Institute, St Edmund's College, University of Cambridge, and External Professorial Research Associate at the Institute for German Studies, University of Birmingham, was formerly Bundesbank Professor of Monetary Economics in the Free University of Berlin. Prior to this appointment he was Visiting Professor of Monetary Economics at the Universities of Frankfurt and Würzburg, and for many years held senior teaching posts at the Universities of Surrey and of Greenwich, following appointments as Research Officer at the National Institute of Economic and Social Research, London, as Economic Adviser to the Industrial and Commercial Finance Corporation (now 3i) and as Chief Editor of *The Bankers' Magazine* (now *The Chartered Banker*). In 1980–1 he served as Special Adviser to UNIDO, Vienna. He has published extensively in monetary and macroeconomics and in banking. He is the editor of many collective works and sits on various editorial boards. In 1993 he was appointed a Commander of the Order of Merit of the Federal Republic of Germany, and in 1996 was awarded a Papal Knighthood.

Carola Gebhard has been Assistant Managing Editor of Central Banking Publications since 1996. Born in Stuttgart (Germany), she began her career in the book trade before studying International Business Economics at the University for Technology and Business Administration of Reutlingen (Germany).

Leonhard Gleske was a Member of the policy-making Central Bank Council of the Deutsche Bundesbank from 1964 until 1989, first as an *ex officio* member as President of the Land Central Bank in Bremen (1964–76) and subsequently as a Member of the Directorate of the Deutsche Bundesbank (in charge of foreign affairs and international monetary issues). He was previously Director for Monetary and Financial Issues at the Commission of the European Economic Community in Brussels (1958–64). From 1969 to 1975 and again from 1989 to 1993 he served as a Board Member of the Bank for International Settlements (BIS), Basle, and from 1990 to 1994 as an Adviser to the Polish National Bank (on behalf of the International Monetary Fund (IMF)). Since 1990 he has been Deputy Chairman of the Supervisory Board of the Bank of Tokyo (Deutschland) AG, Frankfurt, a Board Member of BDO, Deutsche Warentreuhand AG, Hamburg (auditing company), and of J. P. Morgan Funds, Brussels. Professor Gleske is also a member of the Advisory Board of J.P. Morgan GmbH, Frankfurt. In 1985 he was awarded an honorary doctorate by the University of Münster and during the same year became an honorary professor of the University of Mannheim.

Otmar Issing is a Member of the Board of the Deutsche Bundesbank and a Member of its policy-making Central Bank Council. He is also in charge of the Bundesbank's Economic Research Department. He was previously (1973–90) Professor of Economics at the University of Würzburg, holding the Chair of Economics, Monetary Affairs and International Economic Relations, subsequent to a Professorship at the University of Erlangen-Nuremburg (1967–73), where he was also Director of the Institute for International Economic Relations. From 1988 to 1990 he was a member of the German Council of Economic Experts (Sachverständigenrat) and since 1980 he has held a Membership (currently dormant) of the Economic Advisory Council at the Federal Ministry of Economics, being Deputy Chairman in 1987–8. In 1991 he became an elected Member of the Academy of Sciences and Literature, Mainz. His principal contributions cover aspects of monetary theory, monetary policy and international monetary economics. Apart from contributions to learned journals and collective volumes, he published (among his books) two leading textbooks in monetary economics, *Einführung in die Geldtheorie* (*Introduction to Monetary Theory*) and *Einführung in die Geldpolitik* (*Introduction to Monetary Policy*), which went into several editions.

Norbert Kloten was President of the Land Central Bank in Baden-Württemberg and an *ex officio* member of the German policy-making Central Bank Council from 1976 to 1992. He is now a member of the Economic Advisory Council at the Federal Ministry of Economics (Chairman from 1992 to 1996). Other activities include membership of the Board of Academic and Non-Academic Associations and the Trilateral Commission. His Professorship at the University of Tübingen (1960–76) was combined with membership of the German Council of Economic Experts (Sachverständigenrat) from 1969 to 1976, being its Chairman from 1970 to 1976. He has published extensively on the principles of economic policy and in the area of monetary and international monetary economics, on the theory and policy of transition and development, and on the methodology of economics. He holds two honorary doctorates from the University of Karlsruhe (1980) and the University of Stuttgart (1993) respectively, and is the bearer of the Commander's Cross with Badge and Star of the Order of Merit of the Federal Republic of Germany.

Reiner König has been Head of the Department of Economics at the Deutsche Bundesbank since 1991. He joined the Bundesbank's headquarters in 1972, holding various positions in the Monetary Policy and Balance of Payments Division. He gained his initial practical experience at a savings bank and at regional branches of the Deutsche Bundesbank. Dr König holds a PhD in economics from the University of Cologne.

Robert Pringle has pursued a career as an economics editor, publisher, author and consultant specialising in international trade, banking and capital markets. In the 1980s he helped to set up, and was the first Executive Director of, The Group of 30, a well-known 'think tank' based at that time in New York. More recently he has been a Director of Graham Bannock & Partners Ltd, an economic research and consulting group based in London, for whom he managed major research projects for clients such as NatWest Bank, the UK Government and major city institutions. He is the founder of Central Banking Publications, publishers of a range of journals and directories on international monetary subjects and the author of numerous publications on international monetary subjects.

Peter Schmid has been Head of the Money, Credit and Capital Market Division of the Deutsche Bundesbank since 1990. From 1965 to

1971 he was a research assistant *inter alia* for a project on developing countries. He joined the Bundesbank in 1971 and held various positions in the Economics Department prior to his present Headship.

Hans Tietmeyer has been President of the Deutsche Bundesbank since October 1993 and Chairman of the G-10 Central Bank Governors since January 1994. He became a Member of the Board and Central Bank Council of the Deutsche Bundesbank on 1 January 1990 and was appointed Deputy Governor on 1 August 1991, with special responsibility for the Foreign Department and the Department of International Monetary Issues, Organisations and Agreements. From April to June 1990 he was suspended from his duties to become the Personal Adviser to the German Federal Chancellor for negotiations on the State Treaty establishing the inter-German Economic, Monetary and Social Union. After graduating and obtaining his doctorate in economics at Cologne University, Professor Tietmeyer held leading positions with the Federal Ministry of Economics in Bonn for twenty years from 1962 to 1982, which included the headship of the division responsible for basic issues of the economic system and of economic policy, the headship of the directorate responsible for the European Common Market and relations with third countries, and the headship of the directorate responsible for basic issues of economic, business cycle and growth policy; during his term of office with the Federal Ministry of Economics he finally became head of the Directorate-General I, responsible for economic policy, in 1973, a position he held until his appointment as State Secretary in the Federal Ministry of Finance in 1982. As State Secretary from 1982 to 1989, Professor Tietmeyer was personally commissioned by the Federal Chancellor to prepare for the World Economic Summit (SHERPA) and became Chancellor Kohl's personal adviser for the German Treaty negotiations of 1990. Professor Tietmeyer has been awarded the Grand Cross of the Order of Merit of the Federal of Germany, and numerous foreign honours have been bestowed on him. He was appointed Honorary Professor of Economics in the Faculty of Economic Sciences at the University of Münster, and is also a member of the Pontifical Academy of Social Sciences.

Bertold Wahlig is Head of the Legal Department of the Deutsche Bundesbank. He studied at the law schools of the Universities of Mainz and Freiburg, Germany, receiving his law degree after fulfilling the practical requirements of the degree by practising with various law courts, offices and law firms. In 1962 he joined the Legal Department of the Deutsche Bundesbank. He now serves as General Counsel. In addition to his immediate work, Mr Wahlig has attended UNCITRAL meetings and participated in UNCITRAL working groups as special adviser for the Ministry of Justice of the Federal Republic of Germany. Since 1985 he has been a member of the Committee on International Monetary Law of the International Law Association. Mr Wahlig has published a number of articles concerning issues of monetary law.

Caroline Willeke joined the Money, Credit and Capital Markets Division of the Deutsche Bundesbank in 1993 where she works as an economist in the Monetary Analysis Section. She graduated from the University of Bonn with a master's degree in economics and then became an assistant lecturer at the University of Cologne. In 1992 she took her PhD in economics at the University of Cologne.

List of Abbreviations

BIS	Bank for International Settlements
CDU	Christian Democratic Union
CMEA	Council for Mutual Economic Assistance
COMECON*	
CSU	Christian Social Union
ECB	European Central Bank
ERM	Exchange rate mechanism
ESCB	European System of Central Banks
EMS	European Monetary System
EMU	European Monetary Union
FDP	Free Democratic Party (Liberal Party)
IMF	International Monetary Fund
SDRs	Special drawing rights
SPD	Sozialdemokratische Partei Deutschlands (German Socialist Party)

*Formed from the English title 'Council for Mutual Economic Assistance', coined by analogy with the then extant Cominform and the previous Comintern.

Introduction

Stephen F. Frowen and Robert Pringle

The 50th anniversary of the introduction of the Deutsche Mark through the German Currency Reform of June 1948 seems a most fitting occasion for the publication of the present volume. Five decades of a prudent and consistent monetary policy pursued by an independent central banking system in line with its chief mandate of defending the stability of the Deutsche Mark has resulted in Germany possessing one of the world's most stable and successful currencies, which has become not only the European anchor currency but one of the leading reserve currencies as well.

Following Hawtrey's Law that 'it is not the *past* rise in prices but the *future* rise that has to be counteracted' (Hawtrey, 1926, p. 106), the Bundesbank has conducted its price stabilisation policy with considerable foresight and success – not least during the difficult years following the German reunification of 1990 (see Frowen and Hölscher, 1997). And yet, questions are being asked by some whether Bundesbank policy has in fact benefited the German economy at all times. There are those who argue that its policy of suppressing inflation disregards the direct promotion of economic growth and therefore fosters a lower growth path in Germany with a consequential lower level of employment. However, this view overlooks the Bundesbank restraint in that by law (Bundesbank Act of 1957) the stability of the DM must be given priority over all other objectives of Bundesbank policy. But although price stability has in this sense to be the principal objective of the policy-making Central Bank Council, it is also true that the Bundesbank's money supply target is determined by the production potential of the economy and should therefore not be an impediment to economic growth.

Members of the Bundesbank's Central Bank Council certainly have diverse views at times, although once a decision has been taken, it will be defended *vis-à-vis* the public regardless of personal opinions. Adherence to this unwritten but nevertheless powerful code of conduct appears to have strengthened rather than weakened the position of the Bundesbank, and is in sharp contrast to UK procedure whereby the minutes of the meetings of the newly established Monetary Policy

Committee of the Bank of England, which decides on interest rate changes (see Frowen and Karakitsos, 1997), are published in full after a relatively short time interval.

Not surprisingly, discussions about the Bundesbank often generate more heat than light. While it can count on the support of public opinion in Germany, outside Germany's borders it is often portrayed as rigid and even arrogant. This is understandable. The same stability-oriented policies that have brought so much benefit to Germany may not necessarily suit the interests of other countries, at least in the short term. Yet these other countries cannot escape from the side-effects of its policies, even if those effects are sometimes both politically and economically harmful in the short term.

Because of the weight of the German economy and the roles of the Deutsche Mark as an anchor and reserve currency – roles that the Bundesbank did not seek but have developed as a long-term consequence of its sound-money policies – interest rate decisions of its Central Bank Council have immediate and often long-lasting repercussions, not only for other European countries but worldwide. Even a policy of delinking from the Deutsche Mark, as Britain, Italy and other countries have perforce done, can confer only slight protection, and this entails a cost in terms of a higher risk premium in their long-term interest rates. Thus it is natural that government ministers in other countries should often feel frustrated, especially when told by their central bank governors that they cannot cut their domestic interest rates – 'because of Bundesbank policy'.

Yet by the standards that central bankers set themselves, the Bundesbank has been the world's most successful central bank. The Deutsche Mark has lost less of its value than almost any other currency over the past quarter century, and such long-term measures are much more appropriate than the short-term ones beloved of many commentators. Can that be a bad thing for other countries? Surely not. In the long term we would argue strongly that this record is an unalloyed good. The Bundesbank has brought the public good of price stability not only to Germany itself but to a widening ring of other states. These countries have reason to be enormously thankful to successive leaders of the Bundesbank and the collective wisdom of the members of the Central Bank Council for safeguarding the German currency and forging it as an anchor of stability for Europe. Central bankers everywhere acknowledge that the status of their institutions and of their profession have been raised by the

Bundesbank's practical demonstration of the benefits of central bank independence.

Without the benchmark provided by the Deutsche Mark, it would have been much harder for other countries to have reformed their economic policies. Would France have been converted to the *franc fort* policy from the path of continual devaluations without the Bundesbank's example and challenge? If France had continued with the easy-money policies of the 1960s and 1970s, many other European countries would have followed suit. Political and economic turmoil would have resulted. The project to achieve a single market might well not have been realised. Europe would be a different place, and a much worse one.

It is deeply ironic that now, with its prestige riding high, and its gospel of central bank independence spreading round the world, the Bundesbank is due to make the ultimate sacrifice: its immolation on the altar of European integration. By the terms of the Maastricht Treaty it stands under sentence of death. If, with its last breath, it can pass on the torch of monetary stability to a new European System of Central Banks (ESCB), the sacrifice will have been worthwhile. The Bundesbank has certainly done everything possible to ensure that the European Central Bank (ECB), modelled totally on the Bundesbank with an impressive range of central bank instruments, and moreover having even stricter rules by not being allowed to finance the public sector, will follow as consistent a monetarist policy – in the best sense of that much-abused word – as the Bundesbank.

People with doubts will understandably hope that the Bundesbank with all its present powers will still be around at the start of the next millennium. For those it would be gratifying, perhaps, to think that the Statement signed by 155 German-speaking Professors of Economics, calling for 'an orderly postponement' of European Monetary Union (EMU), published simultaneously in the *Financial Times* and the *Frankfurter Allgemeine Zeitung* on 9 February 1998 and receiving world-wide attention, might in some way contribute towards the fulfilment of their hope, although there are powerful voices in Germany and elsewhere being totally opposed to any postponement.[1]

At this historic juncture it is crucially important for more people outside Germany to understand how the Bundesbank actually works. It is simply not enough to have attitudes, whether of affection or hostility. This volume is therefore offered to readers who genuinely wish to acquaint themselves with the multifarious tasks of the Bundesbank and the philosophy on which its decision-making is based.

That is why we have invited leading representatives of the Bundesbank to explain its operations and policies in their own words.

We are happy to be able to include in this volume two papers of considerable historical importance by Hans Tietmeyer and Norbert Kloten respectively on the negotiations leading to German Economic, Monetary and Social Union (GEMSU) of 1990, and a searching paper by Otmar Issing on some ethical problems of central banking.

Note

1. Among those totally opposed to any postponement of EMU is Claus Köhler (himself a former member of the Directorate of the Deutsche Bundesbank and of the Central Bank Council), and Peter Bofinger (a former member of the Land Central Bank in Baden-Württemberg and now Professor of Economics at Würzburg University). For the latter's views, see Bofinger (1998).

References

Bofinger, P. (1998) 'Die Zeit ist wirklich reif für den Euro' (the time is indeed ripe for the Euro), *Frankfurter Allgemeine Zeitung*, no. 35, 11 February, p. 13.
Frowen, S.F. and Hölscher, J. (1997) *The German Currency Union of 1990 – A Critical Assessment* (London: Macmillan; New York: St. Martin's Press).
Frowen, S.F. and Karakitsos, E. (1997) 'An Evaluation of Inflation Targeting in Germany and the UK', *Kredit und Kapital*, vol. 30, no. 4, pp. 501–32.
Hawtrey, R.G. (1926) *Monetary Reconstruction*, 2nd edn (London, New York and Toronto: Longmans, Green).

1 The Bundesbank: Committed to Stability

Hans Tietmeyer

In post-war Germany, there has been a broad consensus about the importance of a stable currency across all political groupings. The bitter consequences of two previous hyperinflations as well as the positive experience gained with the Deutsche Mark and its strength played a major role in this.

In the recent past, however, the public debate has sometimes caused doubts to be raised concerning how far this consensus still goes. Admittedly, there have often been similar disputes in post-war history. One has only to remember the controversy surrounding the Deutsche Mark appreciations in the 1960s, when the relationship between internal monetary stability and external exchange rate stability first became an issue, or the arguments in the 1970s about the spurious alternative of more inflation or more unemployment. Ultimately, however, all these controversies did not seriously jeopardise the consensus on stability; if anything, they tended to strengthen it, in fact.

NEW DISCUSSION ON STABILITY

In the run-up to the introduction of European Monetary Union (EMU) and against the backdrop of very sharp exchange rate changes in the first half of the 1990s, the debate about the importance of monetary stability – at least in some of its forms – seems to have gained a new quality. For example, it is not only the trade-off between inflation and unemployment (which it was thought had been overcome) which has been revived recently in a number of comments made by industry, trade unions, politicians and, not least, post-Keynesian economists. In view of the degree of price stability achieved, adherence to a policy of non-inflationary growth is occasionally even brought into discredit as a deflationary policy. Perhaps even more frequently one hears the proposition that foreign exchange rate stability must purportedly assume priority over internal price stability, exchange rate stability evidently meaning the nominal and not the real (price level-adjusted) stability of exchange rates. A sustained low external value of the Deutsche Mark has not infrequently even been regarded as necessary (or at least beneficial) for the German economy, regardless of its implications for internal monetary stability.

In the recent past, this debate has also increasingly become part of the wider discussion about monetary integration in Europe. It is thus acquiring a new dimension, even going as far as postulating EMU at all costs; in other words, a monetary union which would tend to result in a soft rather than a strong Euro. At any rate, there are a number of participants in the current discussion (in Germany, too) who – without saying it so explicitly, of course – evidently regard the change-over to the Euro as a welcome opportunity of lessening the Deutsche Mark's former external strength. The open or covert advocates of a weakening of the currency on competitive grounds obviously fail to recognise the interrelationship between internal and external stability. They overlook the fact that, in the past, Germany was regularly among those countries with the lowest interest rate level world-wide, precisely because of the stability of its currency. That gave, and continues to provide, a strong competitive edge which cannot be rated too highly, quite apart from the general cost-curbing effects of monetary stability. The fact that such depreciation strategies are at variance with the aim of the Maastricht Treaty and even more so with its interpretation by the Bundestag, the Bundesrat and the Federal Constitutional Court seems either not to be taken into consideration or to be deliberately accepted. The Deutsche Bundesbank's adherence to internal monetary stability has led to it being accused of an undue stability policy bias, or even of being obsessed with stability.

BUNDESBANK IN FAVOUR OF A STABILITY UNION

To avoid any misunderstanding: the Bundesbank is committed to the road to EMU laid down in the Maastricht Treaty. In the relevant bodies at national and European level it is collaborating intensively in solving the complex and by no means easy technical tasks involved: these range from harmonising the hitherto very different monetary policy instruments in Europe, putting in place the organisational and legal framework for the European Central Bank (ECB) and the Euro, to a fundamentally new and modernised payment system. All this work should not be underestimated. The preparations have to be

advanced to a stage which enables the European Central Bank Council to take decisions immediately after it has been established. The
European System of Central Banks (ESCB) has to be fully operational
and functionally viable right from the very first day of monetary
union. And the set of instruments then in force must not put individual banking groups at a disadvantage or jeopardise the benefits of
the decentralised banking structure which obtains, particularly in
Germany, and the dominant long-term orientation of the markets.

As important as this intensive collaboration in the technical preparation of EMU may be, what is of even greater importance is the
Bundesbank's public advocacy of monetary union actually becoming
a permanent stability union, as is provided for in the Maastricht
Treaty and is quite obviously desired by the majority of the population. Although there are occasionally slight differences of emphasis on
individual points, there is complete unanimity within the Central
Bank Council concerning the goal itself. Monetary union must
become a permanent stability union with a strong currency, not
least in order to prevent political conflict which might otherwise
pose a risk at a later date. The Bundesbank is at one in favouring
the creation of the economic and political preconditions which will
ensure that the monetary stability gained through the Deutsche Mark
is likewise permanently maintained following the change-over to the
Euro. It has the authority to do this not only by virtue of the
consensus on non-inflationary growth prevailing in Germany, for it
is also under a statutory obligation to do so. In accordance with
Article 3 of the Bundesbank Act of 1957 it has the legal mandate of
'safeguarding the currency'. Moreover, in accordance with Article 12,
it 'is required to support the general economic policy of the Federal
Government', but only without prejudice to the performance of its
primary duty to 'safeguard the currency'. The Act explicitly states that
the Bundesbank is independent of instructions from the Federal Government in exercising its powers.

PRIORITY OF INTERNAL STABILITY

However, the legal wording 'to safeguard the currency' does not seem
to be totally unambiguous with regard to the question of internal
monetary stability having priority over exchange rate stability. At
the time this law was drafted in 1957, when the Bretton Woods system
of fixed exchange rates was still in force world-wide, internal and

external exchange rate stability was virtually free of conflict. It was not until tensions emerged between the major industrial countries, as a result of domestic policy decisions and priorities drifting apart, that the subject of protecting internal stability policy against external constraints (as it was later called by Karl Schiller) became a matter of key importance. As the 1960s progressed, the Bundesbank in Germany, with the vigorous support of the then Federal Ministers of Economics, Ludwig Erhard and Karl Schiller, committed itself more and more unequivocally to the priority of internal monetary stability. And that has remained the case to the present day, with far-reaching agreement between the Federal Government and the Bundesbank. The Maastricht Treaty even adopted the priority of internal stability *expressis verbis*, in fact. Maintaining price stability has been enshrined in Article 105 as the primary objective of the European System of Central Banks (ESCB). The Bundesbank's primary orientation towards internal price stability is hence fully consistent with the regulations which will apply one day to the ECB.

The Bundesbank has to fulfil its stability mandate, as defined above, in several ways. Its first and most crucial task is to conduct its own monetary policy in line with its anti-inflationary stance. It does have to play its part in achieving the other targets of the Stability and Growth Act of 1967 (high level of employment, external equilibrium and stable and adequate economic growth), but only to the extent that this does not jeopardise its primary goal of price stability. Since there is a large measure of consensus among economists that price stability is not – at least in the medium term – inconsistent with the other targets of the so-called uneasy quadrangle, but is instead a prerequisite for continued growth, high employment and external equilibrium, there should not actually be any conflict in this respect. An anti-inflationary monetary policy also serves other macroeconomic goals, the example of Germany providing ample evidence of this. Although a stable currency alone cannot automatically bring about and safeguard sustained growth and increased employment, it is an indispensable precondition for them. Furthermore, experience has shown that monetary stability also makes a major contribution to social equity (see Tietmeyer, 1993, pp. 25–40). Given the demographic trends, not only in Germany but also in other European countries, this will be even more the case in the future, since private provisioning by the 'ordinary citizens' will become increasingly important.

ROLE AS A GUARDIAN OF MONETARY STABILITY

In the final analysis, however, monetary stability cannot be safe-guarded by an anti-inflationary monetary policy alone. It will always be influenced by the prevailing behavioural patterns in society and by developments in other policy areas. This applies, in particular, to those decisions taken in areas such as fiscal policy, labour market policy, social policy and wage policy, which affect the viability of the economic and social system. Long-term undesirable trends in those areas also tend to jeopardise monetary stability in the short or long run, and then often require monetary policy counter-measures. For that reason, the Bundesbank's role as a guardian of monetary stability must of necessity extend beyond its decision-making powers in the field of monetary policy. It has to draw attention – at as early a stage as possible – to potential risks to stability in other areas and parallel behavioural patterns in the economy or in society. The Bundesbank has always made every possible effort to do this, without interfering in the political discussion of specific details.

The Bundesbank is also especially suited to this more far-reaching function as a guardian of stability on account of the fact that the legislature has kept it largely free of day-to-day political influence and special party and lobby interests by virtue of its being independent of political instructions and by the long-term appointment of the mem-bers of its governing bodies. Being free of short-term party and special interests, the Bundesbank is hence able to raise its warning voice (which it has always done in the 40 or so years of its existence) if it perceives the emergence of national or international risks to monetary stability.

However, the political independence of the Bundesbank by no means implies that it is free of responsibilities. In contrast to many other countries, it is not – for well-considered reasons – accoun-table to the government or to Parliament. Nevertheless, from the very beginning it has placed itself under the obligation publicly to explain and justify its policy as well as its assessment of developments that are relevant to monetary policy. Its target group is the general public, which it addresses through the speeches of the mem-bers of its governing bodies and its diverse publications, especially its Monthly and Annual Reports. The Bundesbank uses all these opportunities to explain its policy and the reasons behind its decisions. It hence puts itself before the forum of public discussion.

THE ROLE OF A MONETARY POLICY ADVISER...

Furthermore, the Bundesbank has been assigned a specific advisory role *vis-à-vis* the Federal Government by the legislature. In accordance with Article 13, the Bundesbank has to 'advise the Federal Government on monetary policy matters of major importance'. This advisory role has often been quite significant in the history of the Bundesbank. It not only played a considerable part in all the discussions on the design and application of the international and European Monetary System (EMS) but, at the request of the Federal Government, the Bundesbank also advised it in connection with preparing for German Monetary Union. Naturally, the political bodies were and remain free to follow the advice given by the Bundesbank or not. In fulfilling its political responsibilities, the Federal Government departed from the Bundesbank's recommendations on individual points (for example, in the selection of the conversion rate for current payments).

...IN THE MAASTRICHT NEGOTIATIONS

The Bundesbank also performed its advisory function in connection with the negotiations on the Maastricht Treaty. As long ago as September 1990, the Central Bank Council drew attention to what it deemed to be the key issues in a memorandum. It said, among other things:

> the participating economies (that is, in the monetary union) will be inextricably linked to one another in the monetary field, come what may. The implications of this – especially for the value of money – will depend crucially on economic and fiscal policy and on the stance of management and labour in all member states.

And then the indispensable benchmarks of a successful stability union are spelled out in detail: from an independent central banking system, with a priority commitment to the target of price stability, via the regulations for lasting budgetary discipline, to the requirements for sufficient and durable policy convergence among the participating countries prior to entry into the final stage.

In addition, Bundesbank representatives, through their work on the EU Monetary Committee in Brussels and on the erstwhile Committee of Central Bank Governors in Basle, contributed to the wording of the Maastricht Treaty in numerous instances. For example, the statute of the ECB was drafted largely by representatives of European central banks in Basle and then adopted, virtually unchanged, by government representatives in the Treaty negotiations. Parallel to the negotiations in Brussels and Maastricht, there were of course also repeated bilateral talks between the Bundesbank and the Federal Government on major aspects of the Treaty.

These intensive and close contacts were and are fully in line with the Bundesbank's statutory mandate to proffer advice. Equally, attention should be drawn to the fact that this does not affect the Government's political accountability. It was not and is not the Bundesbank that conducted or conducts negotiations itself on these subjects. Incidentally, neither was it the Bundesbank that was responsible for the numerical fixing of the so-called fiscal criteria at 3 per cent of GDP for the current budget deficit and at 60 per cent of GDP for the fiscal debt level. To my knowledge, both figures (which in the eyes of the Bundesbank tend to be too generous rather than too strict) were put forward by delegations other than the German one. In the joint estimation of the Central Bank Council, however, it is imperative that, prior to entry into monetary union, 'the budget deficits in all the participating countries should be reduced to a level which is sustainable in the long run and unproblematic in terms of anti-inflation policy requirements'.

After the conclusion of the Treaty negotiations, the Central Bank Council published the following evaluation of the Treaty early in 1992:

> The question of whether EMU is to be established is a political decision... The planned institutional design of the final stage is largely in line with the Bundesbank's recommendations. In particular, the statute of the future European System of Central Banks... It will be of paramount importance for the overall success of the envisaged economic and monetary union that the Community decisions to be taken in... 1998 on the selection of the countries eligible for participation should be geared solely to their stability policy performance.

...IN THE PREPARATIONS FOR EMU

In line with its statutory mandate, the Bundesbank is also advising the Federal Government in the current negotiations on the preparation of monetary union. That applies particularly to the consultations on the legal texts for what is known as the 'secondary legislation' now taking shape in Brussels. And it also applies to the proposal for a European stability pact (which was put forward by the Federal Government and backed by the Bundesbank) to establish the surveillance process for budgetary and debt trends in the participating countries envisaged in Article 104c of the Treaty. That stability pact has nothing to do with any German desire for hegemony. Instead, it is intended to prevent potential conflicts from arising between the future single stability-oriented monetary policy and fiscal policy (especially the fiscal policies of the major member states), thus protecting the smaller member states, in particular, from hardships imposed by the potential misconduct of the larger ones.

Urging 'strict' compliance with the contractual convergence criteria in the selection decision by the European Council on the member states participating in the monetary union beginning in 1999 – as reflected in the evaluation of the Treaty published early in 1992 – is, after all, part of the Bundesbank's function of being both a guardian of price stability and an adviser. The calls made by the Bundesbank (incidentally, in complete agreement with the Federal Government) for a 'strict' interpretation of the criteria laid down in the Treaty are by no means merely legalistic. Just like the Bundestag and the Bundesrat, the Bundesbank regards strict and lasting compliance with the convergence criteria as an essential precondition for the smooth inception and, as far as possible, conflict-free continuation of monetary union. In this context it might be worth mentioning that the Presidency Conclusions of the Dublin Summit of 13–14 December 1996, emphasise that the Council stressed 'that the four criteria of sustainable convergence and the requirement of central bank independence must be strictly applied'.

LASTING CONVERGENCE INDISPENSABLE

References to the fact that today there is not infrequently divergence, rather than convergence, within existing monetary areas disregard the fundamental difference that obtains between a monetary area that is identical to the borders of a nation state, and a monetary union, which comprises several nation states with different regulatory and social systems. After all, in a monetary union extending beyond the frontiers of a single nation state, the common features and compensatory systems which regularly exist within a nation state (such as a common legal and tax system, a dominant central government budget, common social security systems and fiscal and tax compensation mechanisms) are missing. Hence in a monetary union composed of several member states without superordinate national ties, the potentially diverging forces are far greater than in a nation state. It would be a fallacy to suppose that a common central banking system alone can prevent potential divergences in a union comprising several major member states. This is why a monetary union encompassing several nation states entails from the outset a high level of common 'stability culture', in the sense of joint preferences and tried-and-tested capabilities. The degree of lasting convergence achieved and the readiness to maintain lasting financial discipline are intended to document precisely that. Disregarding the significance of the selection criteria and lastingly failing to acknowledge it would imply a lack of strategic perceptiveness, and not vice versa. A monetary union which later turned out to be particularly conflict-prone, let alone fragile, would not only pose economic problems, but it might even turn out to be a serious threat to the European integration process. Drawing attention to these far-reaching political dangers, and thus to the crucial importance of selecting countries in keeping with the criteria, is undoubtedly part and parcel of the Bundesbank's advisory mandate. After all, the monetary union must not be allowed to fail, let alone to become a source of political conflict in Europe.

NOT A 'STATE WITHIN THE STATE'

All in all, the Bundesbank has constantly endeavoured to perform its role of being a guardian and adviser in keeping with its stability target, as laid down by Parliament, and it will continue to do so. In the basic orientation of its policy it knows at the same time that it enjoys a consensus with the vast majority of the population. The performance of these duties by the Bundesbank, like its monetary policy, which is geared primarily to domestic price stability, has nothing to do with any stance as a 'state within the state'. Neither does it have anything to do with a desire for German hegemony in Europe. Quite the contrary; a lastingly sustainable foundation and an anti-inflationary orientation of the monetary union are without any doubt in the best interests of Europe, too.

It may well be that such a stability-orientated guardian and adviser function does not always fit in with the political and tactical aspirations of the political decision-makers. That may even be true at times of our trading partners. But Chancellor Helmut Kohl rightly said publicly not long ago: 'As the Federal Chancellor, I sometimes have problems with individual measures or statements by the Bundesbank. But as a citizen of this country, I am happy that the Bundesbank exists and that it acts in this way'.[1]

Of course, neither the Bundesbank nor its President can claim always to take the right action in all circumstances. On taking office in 1993 I said: 'Even the Bundesbank is not faultless.' Needless to say, that is just as true today, and will remain so in future. But the fact that the Bundesbank carries a substantial measure of 'credibility in anti-inflation policy' in Germany, in Europe and in international circles alike has certainly done Germany and Europe as a whole more good than harm. That verdict has been confirmed time and again by impartial observers.[2] Hence the Bundesbank will continue to feel itself committed to stability in the period ahead.

Notes

1. Verbal remarks by Chancellor Helmut Kohl on the occasion of Dr. Tietmeyer's birthday reception on 28 August 1996.
2. See, for example, Frowen and Karakitsos (1997), pp. 521–9.

References

Frowen, S. F. and Karakitsos, E. (1997) ' An Evaluation of Inflation Targeting in Germany and the UK', *Kredit und Kapital*, vol. 30, no. 4, pp. 501–32.
Tietmeyer, H. (1993) 'The Value of Monetary Stability in the World Today', in P. Arestis (ed.), *Money and Banking: Issues for the Twenty-first Century*. Essays in honour of Stephen F. Frowen, London: Macmillan, New York: St. Martin's Press, pp. 25–40. Also reprinted in H. Tietmeyer *Währungsstabilität für Europa*, Baden-Baden: Nomos, 1996, pp. 29–43.

2 Bundesbank Independence, Organisation and Decision-Making

Leonhard Gleske

The Deutsche Bundesbank's present structure and its legal and institutional operating basis may be said to reflect the troubled history of more than 100 years of German central banking. During this period the German currency broke down twice under the impact of war, inflation and the monetary disturbances following two lost world wars. These traumatic experiences left a characteristic imprint on German thinking in the field of central banking and currency order. Their consequences can still be felt today. The financial shock events culminating in the currency reforms of 1924 and 1948 had important implications for central banking legislation in Germany. In 1924 the Reichsbank, over which the Chancellor had exercised ultimate control since its foundation in 1876, was given a new charter as part of the reorganisation of the German monetary system in 1923–4. The new Banking Act expressly laid down that the central bank was independent of the Government. Supervision by the Chancellor was dropped and lending to the Government severely limited. Under the dictatorial Hitler regime (1933–45), the prerogatives of the Reichsbank were, however, formally abolished and its Directorate was dissolved in 1939, after it had boldly protested against inflationary budget financing.

Soon after the Second World War, renewed efforts were made to set up a central banking system in Germany which would exercise monetary control free from destabilising political interference. In 1948 the Allied military powers in West Germany set up a two-tier central banking structure broadly mirroring the US Federal Reserve System. This consisted of legally independent regional central banks (the 'Land Central Banks'), established by the State Government in each state (Land), and a joint 'umbrella-type' subsidiary of the Land Central Banks (the 'Bank deutscher Länder'). The latter performed

11

the note issue and other central functions on behalf of the regional institutions. This predecessor of the Deutsche Bundesbank was from the start independent of German political bodies, and gained full autonomy from the military powers in 1951.

A FEDERAL STRUCTURE

After protracted deliberations (lasting about six years) within the Federal Government and Parliament (which were newly established in 1949), the German legislature passed the Deutsche Bundesbank Act in 1957. The main issues discussed at that time were the question of its autonomy, and of whether the new central bank should be, in accordance with German tradition in this field, a centralised organisation, or whether it should maintain its federal structure, introduced by the Allied military powers after the war. That had proved to be a good experience. The outcome in this respect was a compromise: the Bundesbank came into being through the amalgamation of the Land Central Banks and the Bank deutscher Länder. The Land Central Banks lost their independent legal status and, while retaining their previous designations as Land Central Banks, they became 'Main Offices' of the Deutsche Bundesbank in the eleven Länder (states) making up the Federal Republic of Germany until reunification in 1990. Contrary to their name, they are not central banks of the states (Länder) but an integral part of the Bundesbank. However, their presidents, together with the members of the Directorate of the Bundesbank, constitute the Bundesbank's supreme policy-making body, the Central Bank Council.

After reunification, the number of states in the now larger Germany increased to sixteen. In order to avoid a similar increase in the policy-making body and with the aim of strengthening the decision-making process, the Bundesbank Act was amended and the number of Land Central Banks was reduced to nine. While, up to reunification, each state had had a Land Central Bank in its territory, there are now five Land Central Banks that cover two or even three states.

The organisational structure of the Bundesbank reflects the federal constitutional structure of the Federal Republic of Germany. In a uniform monetary area, however, monetary policy must itself be uniform. It cannot differ from region to region or take account of special regional features or requirements. But federal forces, in the shape of the Land Central Bank Presidents, as well as centralist forces, in the shape of the members of the Directorate, are duly involved in an appropriate manner in the necessarily uniform monetary policy opinion-forming and decision-making process. This system has stood the test of time, and indeed has become a model for a future European central bank system. This federal structure is also a major factor in the Bundesbank's independence. The Central Bank Council consists of members who reflect different developments in different parts of Germany. They come from different backgrounds; they are nominated by different governments, corresponding to different political currents. Such a Council makes it possible for a central bank to be independent. It is perhaps no accident that the world's most independent central banks have come into being in federally-structured countries: the USA, the Federal Republic of Germany and Switzerland. For all these countries the wish to constrain the powers of the central government and to let regional political forces participate in the political decision-making process has played a central role in history.

The independence of the Bundesbank is based on section 12(2) of the Bundesbank Act. The Bundesbank is independent in exercising the powers conferred on it by this Act. These powers relate almost exclusively to the Bank's monetary policy in its broadest sense, including operations in the exchange market; decisions about a parity or central rate and the margin of fluctuation in a fixed rate system are the domain of the Federal Government, albeit in consultation with the Bank.

HOW MONETARY POLICY IS DECIDED

Monetary policy is thus determined by the Central Bank Council on its own authority. Originally, a provision specifies that the adoption of monetary policy decisions by the Central Bank Council could be deferred for up to two weeks at the request of the Federal Government. The Federal Government has never exercised this power. In any event, the final decision rested with the Central Bank Council. In order to ensure the full independence of the Central bank, as stipulated by the Maastricht Treaty, this provision has been removed from the Bundesbank Law.

The independence of the Bundesbank as stipulated in the Bundesbank Act rests on a social consensus in favour of a policy geared to price stability. The Bank has no obligation to report to Parliament and the Federal Government. There is no formal accountability but, through its publications, press conferences and speeches given by council members, the Bundesbank makes a virtually continuous effort to inform the public and gain political support for its policies.

As to financial and budget independence, the Bundesbank is not subject to supervision of its administrative expenditures and is not obliged to establish a budget. Nevertheless, as a public authority it has to observe the general rules for economical behaviour in public administration. In this respect it is subject to examination by the Federal Accounting Office (*Bundesrechnungshof*), whose report is sent to Parliament for information. In addition, the balance sheet and the profit and loss account are examined by auditors.

COMPOSITION AND FUNCTIONING OF THE CENTRAL BANK COUNCIL

In the central bank system established in 1948 by the Allied military powers and remaining in force until 1957, the Presidents of the Land Central Banks, who were appointed by their respective State Governments, formed the Central Bank Council, the supreme decision-making body in monetary policy. They elected their own chairman, the President of the Central Bank Council; they also appointed the members of the Directorate of the Bank deutscher Länder. But only the President of the Directorate became a member of the Central Bank Council, as its Vice-Chairman. The decision-making process in the Council was therefore based on the participation of members who were appointed by their respective State Governments, while the Chairman and Vice-Chairman of the Council were elected by the Council itself. The Federal Parliament and the Federal Government, only established more than a year after the foundation of the Central Bank System, had no influence on the composition of the Central Bank Council.

This situation changed with the Bundesbank Act of 1957. The Central Bank Council is now composed of the members of the Directorate and the Presidents of the Land Central Banks. The centralist forces in the Council have been strengthened. The Directorate of the Deutsche Bundesbank consists of the President, the Vice-President and up to six other members. The President, or the Vice-President in his absence, takes the chair at meetings of both the Central Bank Council and the Directorate. The members of the Directorate must have special professional qualifications. They are nominated by the

Federal Government and, after consultation with the Central Bank Council, appointed by the President of the Federal Republic for a period of eight years, with the possibility of reappointment. They cannot be removed from office before the end of their term, except for personal reasons and if the initiative comes from themselves or the Central Bank Council.

These rules also apply to the Presidents of the Land Central Banks, who are at the same time *ex officio* members of the Central Bank Council. They are appointed by a procedure similar to that for the members of the Directorate. However, it is not the Federal Government but the Bundesrat (the Chamber of Parliament representing the Länder) which has the right of nomination, following submission of a proposal from the competent Land Governments. Hence the Bundesbank Act prevents the Federal Government from acquiring a dominant position in the appointment of the members of the Central Bank Council. This is a reflection of the federal element in the Bundesbank constitution.

MEETS EVERY TWO WEEKS

Both the Directorate and the Central Bank Council are organised entirely on the collegiate principle, the President of the Bundesbank being *primus inter pares*. The Central Bank Council generally meets every two weeks and takes its decisions by a simple majority of the votes cast. It determines the monetary policy of the Bank. For determining and implementing its policy, the Bundesbank is independent of instructions from the Government. The Bundesbank Council also issues guidelines on the conduct of business and administration and defines the responsibilities of the other governing bodies (that is, the Directorate and the boards of the Land Central Banks) in so far as this is not already done by the Bundesbank Act. In specific cases it may also give instructions to these bodies.

The Land Central Banks are headed by Managing Boards, which consist of the President, the Vice-President and, in the larger Land Central Banks, one further member. The Vice-Presidents and any-other members of the Managing Boards of the Land Central Banks are nominated by the Central Bank Council and appointed by the President of the Bundesbank; they may attend the meetings of the Central Bank Council, deputising for their President, but they have no voting rights.

The Land Central Banks have Advisory Boards, which consist of representatives of the banking sector, of trade, industry and agriculture and of the trade unions. Their function is to confer with the President of the Land Central Bank on monetary policy questions. The Advisory Board is not one of the governing bodies of the Bundesbank but a consultative organ which enables the Bundesbank to maintain contact with the banking sector and its customers in the various Länder (states). The members of the Advisory Board are nominated by the Land Government concerned and appointed by the President of the Bundesbank.

RESPONSIBILITIES OF THE DIRECTORATE...

The responsibilities of the Directorate and the Land Central Banks are regulated by the Bundesbank Act.

The Directorate is the central executive organ of the Bank, and as such responsible for implementing the decisions taken by the Central Bank Council. It directs and administers the Bank, except in matters falling within the competence of the Managing Boards of the Land Central Banks. One of its important tasks is to coordinate the activities of the different parts of the Bundesbank in the fields of administration and staffing.

The following transactions, in particular, are reserved for the Directorate:

• transactions with the Federal Government and its special funds;
• transactions with banks that have central functions in the whole of Germany;
• foreign exchange transactions and external transactions; management of the Bank's gold and foreign exchange reserves;
• open market operations.

...AND OF THE MAIN OFFICES

The Main Offices, known as Land Central Banks, carry out the transactions and administrative tasks occurring in their area on their own responsibility. Although the Land Central Banks have lost their former independent legal status, they have kept their independent powers in administrative matters. The Bundesbank Act expressly reserves transactions with the Land and public authorities in the Land and transactions with banks in their area for the Land Central Banks. The Land Central Banks are responsible for the branch offices the Bundesbank maintains in larger towns and cities (which are known as 'Bank places'). At present there are 164 of these branch offices, including new branches that have been established after reunification in what was formerly East Germany. The branch network has an old tradition in the German banking system, going back to the time when the main channel for creating central bank money was the rediscounting of commercial bills. The rediscount window plays a reduced but still important role in German central banking, but it is no longer the only way to meet the refinancing needs of the banking system. Unlike the Reichsbank, the Bundesbank does not engage in direct lending to business and industry. The present branch network serves particularly to facilitate the supply of notes and coins and the handling of cashless payments.

One of the major responsibilities of Land Central Banks is their participation in the supervision of banks in their respective areas. Bank supervision is regarded in Germany as a government function. It is entrusted to the Federal Banking Supervisory Office in Berlin, which is a governmental agency. However, the Office cannot issue general supervisory regulations without the formal participation of the Bundesbank. The Bundesbank is involved in current supervision by collecting and processing bank supervisory returns. The Bundesbank makes its local branch offices and expert knowledge available for ongoing bank supervision and assists the Supervisory Office in many ways. In practice, bank supervision is thus carried out in close cooperation between the Supervisory Office and the Bundesbank, mainly via the Land Central Banks and their branch offices in each Land. But formal responsibility for decisions in banking supervision remains with the Supervisory Office. This clear institutional separation is regarded in Germany as necessary in order to protect the authority responsible for the formulation and implementation of monetary policy from conflicts of interest that can arise between the tasks of monetary policy and banking supervision.

THE STAFF OF THE BUNDESBANK

The Deutsche Bundesbank, as a corporation under public law, is part of the public service in the Federal Republic of Germany. In the public service, unlike in private industry, there are three different groups of employees with differing legal status, namely civil servants (*Beamte*), other salaried staff (*Angestellte*) and wage earners (*Arbeiter*). The main difference between civil servants on the one hand and other salaried staff on the other is that the legal status of the former (pay, holidays, other rights and duties) is exclusively regulated by Parliament. The working conditions of the other types of employees, on the other hand, are governed by pay agreements.

The interests of the persons employed in the public service are represented at two levels. At the external level, the pay and other working conditions of wage and salary earners are negotiated between the public employers and the public service trade unions, and embodied in pay agreements. When the arrangements for civil servants are being determined by Parliament, the central organisations of the appropriate trade unions are consulted. For instance, the pay increases negotiated for wage and salary earners (as a rule annually) are generally adopted for civil servants as well.

At the internal level, the interests of the people employed in the Bundesbank are looked after by a Staff Council, established at each office. The Staff Council (*Personalrat*) is the elected representative of all employees; its functions and powers are governed by the Federal Staff Representation Act. The idea underlying the Act is that of cooperation between the office and the Staff Council in a spirit of mutual confidence. The participation of the Staff Council is designed as a way of keeping a check on measures affecting employees, but not as a co-management right. There are staff councils at the branches (Local Staff Councils), at the Main Offices (District Staff Councils), and at the central office of Deutsche Bundesbank (Main Staff Council). Each of the groups of employees (civil servants, other salaried staff and wage earners) working at the office is represented according to its size.

16 000 EMPLOYEES

The number of people employed by the Bundesbank is at present close to 16000. Of these 16000, about 6700 are civil servants. Compared with the much larger USA and the much smaller number of staff people employed by the Bank of England, the number of 16000 seems to be quite high. The main explanation is that, contrary, to the USA and Great Britain, the Bundesbank, like most other continental European central banks, maintains a wide network of branches.

Historically, as has been said before, this has something to do with the rediscounting of bills of exchange, which was in the past the main instrument providing central bank money to the banks and the public in general. This instrument still plays a role in Germany but will not continue in its present form in the future ESCB. Under modern conditions and with the growing importance of open-market operations as an instrument of monetary policy, such a large branch network seems no longer to be a necessity; therefore the Bundesbank has already reduced the number of branches by closing mainly the smaller ones, and is continuing to do so. This can be seen also as a reflection of the concentration process in the banking industry itself.

3 German Monetary Unification: Domestic and External Issues

Reiner König and Caroline Willeke

Monetary, economic and social union between the Federal Republic of Germany and the former German Democratic Republic came into force on 1 July 1990. The Deutsche Mark became the sole legal tender in both German states and responsibility for domestic and external monetary policy in the extended Deutsche Mark area devolved on the Deutsche Bundesbank. The State Treaty on which probably the largest currency transaction in history was based had been negotiated in just less than two months. A slower process would certainly have been preferable from a purely economic point of view. In the light of the differing importance of the GDR Mark and the Deutsche Mark, and the widely diverging economic and structural conditions in the two German states, a phased process seemed, in principle, to be appropriate: one in which basic macroeconomic conditions could gradually be brought into line with those in the former Federal Republic and which could ultimately lead to monetary union.[1]

In the face of political pressure, however, there was no time for the normal sequence of reform steps; monetary union between the two German states could not wait until the GDR economy had adapted sufficiently to the performance standard of the Federal Republic. How urgent the necessity for action was can be illustrated by the fact that more than 300 000 citizens had left the GDR between October 1989 and the beginning of February 1990 alone. If this migration had continued, it would have involved unpredictable political, economic and social consequences for both German states. In this situation, the German Federal Chancellor decided to offer the GDR government an immediate start for negotiations on monetary, economic and social union at the beginning of February 1990.

THE CONVERSION OF THE GDR MARK

The question of setting the appropriate conversion rate was a major issue in the discussion on how monetary union should be organised.[2] Uncertainty in this area was great because neither the official conversion rates (differentiated according to the respective field of application) nor the free currency market, which was not very liquid, gave a reliable indication of the 'correct' conversion rate.

The conversion rates more or less had to be 'selected' during negotiations. In these the following (partly conflicting) considerations played a crucial role:

• minimising the inflationary risks arising from the conversion;
• securing the competitiveness of GDR industry;
•· gaining social acceptance by the population of the GDR (and also that of the Federal Republic).

In this context an in-depth look at the adjustment of flows and stocks was absolutely essential as they each revealed different problems.

First of all, the conversion of flows included, in particular, current wage and salary payments, as well as rents and pension payments. Viewed in macroeconomic terms, the agreed conversion rate of 1:1 appeared at the time to be just about justifiable since wage differences between West and East Germany were roughly in line with the discrepancy in labour productivity. Those enterprises which manufactured internationally traded goods, however, were faced with a perceptible appreciation, since the GDR's foreign trade had previously been based on an exchange rate of Mark4.40 to DM1.00; their international competitiveness was therefore weakened. For consumers in the GDR the conversion of flows on balance meant an appreciable strengthening of their real purchasing power. In the case of goods which had previously been heavily subsidised, such as staple foods, price rises occurred, some of which were quite hefty. On the other hand, there was a perceptible decline in prices of many consumer goods produced in East Germany and, furthermore, high quality industrial products from the west were now available.

Second, and of greater significance for monetary policy, was the conversion of stocks. The conversion of bank deposits at the same time determined the scale of the increase in the money stock M3 associated with the extension of the currency area. From the Bundesbank's standpoint the conversion had to take place in such a way that the increase in the money stock could be reconciled with anti-inflation policy requirements. Additionally, since the conversion rate would also determine the amount of their savings, this touched on the question of the introduction of the Deutsche Mark being accepted by the population of the GDR. In the final analysis, it was not possible to look at the conversion of savings deposits in isolation from the conversion of corporate loans. A sharply asymmetrical procedure in the case of bank assets and liabilities was out of the question from the outset; this would have given rise to interest-bearing equalisation claims of the banks on the government on a scale that would have been irresponsible in fiscal policy terms, in order to close the balance sheet gap which would have arisen. From the point of view of the GDR enterprises, however, as drastic a reduction of debts as possible would have been desirable so as not to weaken their competitive situation by excessive debt servicing. There was therefore a considerable degree of conflict between the different interests involved in the conversion of stocks.

Ultimately, a compromise was agreed which, in principle, provided for a conversion of all assets and liabilities at a rate of 2:1. To help secure social acceptance, a basic amount of Mark2000, 3000 or 6000 – depending on the age of the party entitled to make an application – was converted at a rate of 1:1. On average, the conversion rate was 1.8:1, which was roughly in line with the ideas expressed in advance by the Bundesbank.

IMPACT ON THE MONEY STOCK

This currency conversion resulted in an increase of the money stock M3 by DM180 billion, or just under 15 per cent of the West German money stock. In line with the estimates at that time of the relationship of East German to West German production capacities, an expansion of the money stock of around 10 per cent appeared desirable. In assessing the inflationary potential of the conversion, however, a distinction should be made between the initial jump in the money stock level and the permanently effective increase in the money stock resulting from the extension of the Deutsche Mark area. As liquid deposit accounts were the sole investment facility available to GDR citizens, it was to be assumed that offering longer-term forms of saving with attractive interest rates would give rise to above-average monetary capital formation, resulting in the monetary overhang due to conversion receding more or less automatically. Portfolio adjustments of this kind soon occurred, in fact, and by the end of 1990 the ratio of M3 east to M3 west had fallen to 12½ per cent. This trend is likely to have continued initially, particularly as a strengthening of monetary capital formation was perceptible in the new Länder after the turn of 1990–1.[3] On the other hand, however, assuming a ratio of 1:10 for East German to West German production potential proved over time to be excessively optimistic. Seen in this light, the conversion of Marks to Deutsche Marks appears to be quite generous. Nevertheless, it is unlikely that this alone generated any particular inflationary stimuli, not least because the reconstruction of East Germany and the structural adjustment of relative prices following price liberalisation entailed high cash requirements.

THE BUNDESBANK'S MONETARY POLICY IN PRACTICE AFTER THE CURRENCY CONVERSION

Since 1 July 1990 the Bundesbank's area of responsibility has also covered the territory of the former GDR. Since that date its statutory stability mandate has applied to the whole of Germany. The overall economic environment following the extension of the currency area presented a great challenge to practical monetary policy. Economic and monetary union turned out to be an even greater shock to the GDR's industry than had been supposed in the run-up. As a result of the complete liberalisation of the markets and provision with a fully convertible currency, East German enterprises were exposed overnight to international competition, and their products largely turned out to be uncompetitive in that context. Furthermore, its traditional markets broke away with the collapse of the Eastern Bloc. Production and employment declined dramatically within a short space of time. This trend was further intensified by a wage policy which was principally aimed at bringing employees' wages in the new Länder into line with the level in West Germany as quickly as possible, without regard to the fact that a large productivity differential continued to exist between East and West Germany. This behaviour on the part of management and labour further harmed the GDR economy and accelerated its decline.

It was not only wage policy in East Germany which got out of hand, however, but also public finance in West Germany. Cushioning the slump in production and employment in East Germany by transfer payments, financing the necessary infrastructure measures and constructing an efficient administration led to a dramatic rise in public sector debt. Whereas the public authorities had still recorded a slight surplus in 1989, the budget deficit in 1991 was just over 3 per cent of GDP. High deficit spending displayed the effect of a large-scale pump-priming programme in the Keynesian mould. At the same time, there was an exceptionally sharp rise in the money stock. The economy in West Germany was on the verge of overheating. Pay rate rises were a long way above productivity advances, so that aggregate unit labour costs in 1991 and 1992 rose by a total of 8½ per cent, resulting in a marked upsurge in prices.

Similarly to the situation in the 1970s, the Bundesbank was faced at the time with the risk of a higher rise in the price level over the medium term. In this situation a tightening of the monetary policy reins was imperative. For that reason the Bundesbank took forceful counter-measures as early as 1991. Between the start of 1991 and Summer 1992 the discount rate was raised in four stages from 6 per cent to $8^3/_4$ per cent, and the Lombard rate was increased from 8½ per cent to $9^3/_4$ per cent (see Table 3.1).

CRITICISMS FROM SOME EMS MEMBERS

The tight interest rate policy at that time was criticised, especially in some of the EMS member countries. In 1991 and 1992 the Bundesbank was, in fact, faced with an overall economic environment which was different from that of most of the other central banks. At the time of the unification-induced boom in Germany, there were already some clear signs of a slowdown in other European economies, despite the increase in exports to satisfy the pent-up demand for Western goods in East Germany, and inflationary risks receded. The domestic economic situation of those countries made lower central bank interest rates seem appropriate, but such measures were frequently precluded on grounds of exchange rate policy. In the short term the Bundesbank's policy at that time may have placed the EMS partner countries under a certain strain. Looked at in the longer run, however, a monetary policy strictly oriented to stability on the part of the Bundesbank is also in the interests of the other member states. During the 1980s the Deutsche Mark became the anchor currency in the EMS. Other countries benefited from this by pursuing an exchange rate target *vis-à-vis* the Deutsche Mark, thereby 'importing' the success of German monetary policy in terms of stability and credibility. *Furthermore, the aim of developing monetary integration in Europe into a community of stability might have been put at risk by a permanent loss of stability.*

In the first half of the 1990s the Bundesbank was confronted with special challenges not only because of intra-German monetary union, but also because additional special influences made its policy more difficult. These included not least the upheavals in the EMS in 1992 and 1993. This crisis has often been blamed on the Bundesbank's comparatively high interest rates and a general lack of balance in the policy mix in Germany.[4]

At best, this assessment only partly does justice to the facts, however. There had not been a comprehensive realignment in the EMS between January 1987 and September 1992. Many people were already assuming that the exchange rates would be permanently stable, in anticipation of the European economic and monetary union, as it were. This conflicted, however, with diverging trends in costs and prices in the individual member countries. A timely realignment of parities, which would have been appropriate under the rules of the system, foundered on the opposition of those countries which would potentially devalue.

EMS CRISIS

Finally, in September 1992 the need for adjustment which had been building up over a number of years erupted in the case of exchange rates. This might have occurred even earlier, in fact, if the Deutsche Mark had not had a tendency to be weaker in the exchange markets as a result of the strains imposed by unification. With the fluctuation band widened from +2.25 per cent to +15 per cent in August 1993, calm finally returned for a period to the exchange rate mechanism (ERM).

In Autumn 1992 the Bundesbank's anti-inflation efforts were made easier by the *de facto* appreciation of the Deutsche Mark in the EMS. The Bundesbank used the changed underlying conditions to initiate the latest phase of interest rate reductions. In 1993 the Bundesbank pursued a policy of cautiously lowering interest rates in stages. It had to proceed carefully since, despite a sharp slackening of economic activity, inflationary pressures were subsiding only gradually at the time and because monetary growth was quite strong. The effect of a policy of accelerated interest rate reductions, as was suggested to the Bundesbank in some quarters for economic policy reasons, would probably have been counter-productive. Reductions of interest rates that are not justified in terms of the anti-inflation policy environment easily lead to a rise in inflationary expectations and, in its wake, to an increase in the long-term interest rates which are relevant in Germany to financing investment. Such a procedure would not have been helpful to the process of adjustment in East Germany.

The prospects for stability have improved since 1994. The Bundesbank's strict adherence to a non-inflationary course resulted in a sharp decline in the rates of price rises. In 1995 and 1996 they reached 1.8 and 1.5 per cent respectively compared with the previous year, and thus price stability was almost reached in Germany.

Table 3.1   Discount rate and Lombard rate of the Bundesbank

Date applied		Discount rate (%)	Lombard rate (%)	Date applied		Discount rate (%)	Lombard rate (%)
1986	07 Mar	3.5	5.5	1993	05 Feb	8	9
					19 Mar	7.5	9
1987	23 Jan	3	5		23 Apr	7.25	8.5
	06 Nov	3	4.5		02 Jul	6.75	8.25
	04 Dec	2.5	4.5		30 Jul	6.75	7.75
					10 Sep	6.25	7.25
1988	01 Jul	3	4.5		22 Oct	5.75	6.75
	29 Jul	3	5				
	26 Aug	3.5	5	1994	18 Feb	5.25	6.75
	16 Dec	3.5	5.5		15 Apr	5	6.5
					13 May	4.5	6
1989	20 Jan	4	6				
	21 Apr	4.5	6.5	1995	31 Mar	4	6
	30 Jun	5	7		25 Aug	3.5	5.5
	06 Oct	6	8		15 Dec	3	5
1990	02 Nov	6	8.5	1996	19 Apr	2.5	4.5
1991	01 Feb	6.5	9				
	16 Aug	7.5	9.25				
	20 Dec	8	9.75				
1992	17 Jul	8.75	9.75				
	15 Sep	8.25	9.5				

The Bundesbank's monetary policy following German monetary union can therefore be described as being quite successful. It was possible to break the persistent inflationary expectations that set in with reunification with an equally persistent anti-inflation stance on the part of the Bundesbank. A glance at the trend of long-term interest rates underlines this assessment. After the Berlin Wall came down in November 1989, there was a sharp rise in the yield on bonds outstanding (by 1½ percentage points) into the Spring of 1990. In the period that followed, interest rate movements became appreciably calmer, however, and from January 1991 (the peak of the last interest rate cycle) a declining trend set in. Investors' confidence in the Deutsche Mark was therefore quickly restored following a brief phase of uncertainty in the financial markets concerning the further course of developments in Germany. In this context, the credibility acquired by the Bundesbank over a period of decades and its consistent anti-inflation policy were probably key factors in the situation at that time.

STRATEGIC PROBLEMS

The Bundesbank has been pursuing a strategy of preannounced monetary targets for over 20 years in order to achieve the stability target which the legislature has assigned to it. As the central bank is not in a position to have a direct influence over the general price level, concentrating on an intermediate variable which is located between those variables in the transmission process over which the central bank does have direct control, together with the ultimate target, makes the process of monetary management considerably easier. There are a number of reasons that argue in favour of the money stock being the 'natural' intermediate target of monetary policy. The long-run relationship between the money stock and the price level can be regarded as theoretically assured. The money stock, therefore, in principle, represents a suitable nominal anchor for a central bank policy geared to the target of monetary stability. Publicly announced monetary targets are, moreover, also useful to other economic agents as general guidance and, additionally, possess the character of a self-commitment on the part of the central bank.

However convincing these advantages may be in theory, since about the mid-1980s it has proved to be equally difficult to provide empirical support for monetary targets in a large number of major countries.

Since it occupies an intermediate position between the instruments employed by the central banks and the ultimate target of price stability, the money stock as an intermediate target must, first, be sufficiently elastic in terms of interest rates for it to be controlled by using those central bank instruments. Second, a stable relationship to aggregate demand and to price movements is necessary. Changes in the financial system put these two conditions so much in doubt in a number of countries that, in effect, they had to abandon the money stock as an intermediate target.

In Germany, too, the demand for money has at times been subject to quite a number of special influences. In this connection the question should be asked as to the extent to which a part has been played by factors to do with unification or whether there is a permanent dislocation of basic monetary relationships.

ALL-GERMAN TARGETS

At the end of 1990 the Bundesbank announced the first all-German monetary target for the following year which, at 4 per cent to 6 per cent, was unchanged against the previous year.[5] With this the Bundesbank first of all signalled its adherence to a tight monetary policy and, second, demonstrated continuity in its monetary policy strategy. The Bundesbank was indeed well aware of the uncertainties that arose initially from the assessment of the demand for money and of the production potential in East Germany. On the other hand, the economic weighting between West and East Germany alone made it reasonable to expect that the known structural relationships in the Federal Republic would be restored in the longer run, despite the GDR being included in the Deutsche Mark currency area. In the first few years after German monetary union, however, it became increasingly essential to observe the process of adjustment in East Germany on a continuous basis and, when necessary, to act in response to the given situation. The Bundesbank displayed a greater degree of flexibility under these circumstances and used other indicators to supplement its interpretation of monetary trends.

Following a moderate money stock trend in the first half of 1991, monetary growth accelerated markedly in the ensuing period. In 1991 it was just possible to achieve the monetary target; in 1992, however, there was a marked and in 1993 a slight overshooting of the target. That pronounced monetary growth was due to several factors. The high public sector borrowing from banks which accompanied the sharp rise in public sector deficits was closely connected with unification and generated perceptible expansionary stimuli, particularly in 1992 and 1993. Since changes in the level of interest rates, judging from experience, play only a minor role in the public authorities' budget management, this tightening of monetary policy did not have a noticeable impact. The effectiveness of the Bundesbank's interest rate policy was further impaired by large-scale government interest rate subsidies which were granted, in particular, to promote investment in East Germany. Private sector credit demand remained expansionary, despite comparatively high interest rates.

Furthermore, additional special influences, not directly caused by unification, led to the money stock trend being overstated. These included, in particular, the increasing use of the Deutsche Mark as a parallel currency in eastern and central Europe, the new provisions for taxation of interest income, the cutback in tax concessions for the acquisition of owner-occupied residential property and its concomitant anticipatory effects, the inverse interest rate structure up to the start of 1994 and, not least, the currency crises in the EMS.

MONETARY TARGETING REMAINS EFFECTIVE

Since unification it has not been easy for the Bundesbank to keep its interest rate policy always in line with its monetary targets. At times it had to resort to unorthodox means, such as lowering short-term interest rates (thereby increasing the spread between short-term and long-term interest rates) in order to unblock the liquidity log-jam which had arisen during the first few months of 1994. In the strategic sense, however, the Bundesbank's persistence has paid off. After the target had been overshot twice, it was possible for the first time again in 1994 to achieve the monetary target which had been set. During the two following years, however, the volatility of shorter-term monetary growth continued, especially as a result of portfolio shifts. Target undershooting in 1995 was followed by overshooting in 1996. Despite this increased volatility, the monetary targeting strategy has proved to be effective in difficult times, too. Although the accumulation of special factors occasionally had a marked dislocating effect on the money stock trend, the Bundesbank was able to explain the fluctuations largely *ex post* so that problems of credibility did not arise. The policy of interest rate reductions which has been pursued since

September 1992 has basically called into question neither the Bundesbank's stability orientation nor its strategy of setting intermediate targets.

The Bundesbank has never seriously taken into consideration to depart from its tried and tested strategy. It is supported in this attitude by econometric studies which have mainly shown that the long-run relations between the money stock, on the one hand, and between interest rates and aggregate demand, on the other hand, have remained stable, despite the recent short-term distortions.[6] Until the start of stage three of the European Monetary Union the Bundesbank will have to continue to watch trends in financial operations carefully and not subordinate its interest rate policy exclusively – let alone automatically – to a one single indicator, but rather root it in a comprehensive analysis of the national economy.

CONCLUDING REMARKS

The Bundesbank's monetary policy has also proved to be effective after the currency area was extended to cover the former GDR. There has been a return to greater price stability following a lengthy period of persistent inflationary trends. The fact that international investors' confidence in the Deutsche Mark remained unimpaired even after unification is, moreover, likely to have been due not least to the Bundesbank's consistent anti-inflation orientation. Problems remain in the real economy. High unemployment is a cause of particular concern. Its origins are largely of a structural nature, however. Accordingly, the solution to the problems of the labour market lies in the hands of enterprises and of management and labour. Fiscal and social policy should, of course, contribute to improving the general climate and locational conditions of the German economy. A relaxed monetary policy, on the other hand, is not a proven means of easing the structural rigidities on the labour market. Experience shows, rather, that central bank action which is strictly oriented to stability ultimately provides the best monetary conditions for steady growth and a high level of employment.

Notes

1.　An overview of the most important phased plans which were initially under discussion is given by Gawel (1994).
2.　See Deutsche Bundesbank (1990).
3.　A quantitative breakdown of M3 for West and East Germany is, however, possible only up to the end of 1990 as there is no longer a matching breakdown of the banking statistics for the period after that.
4.　See, for example, Hefeker (1994).
5.　In July 1991 the target was adjusted during the target review to between 3 per cent and 5 per cent on the basis of the muted money stock trend in the first half of the year and a downward revision of East German production capacities.
6.　See, for example, Deutsche Bundesbank (1997). 'On the Stability of the Money Demand', *Monthly Report*, Vol. 49, No. 8 (August), pp. 27–9.

References

Deutsche Bundesbank (1990) 'The monetary union with the German Democratic Republic', *Monthly Report*, vol. 42, no. 7 (July), pp. 13–28.

Gawel, E. (1994) *Die deutsch-deutsche Währungsunion – Verlauf und geldpolitische Konsequenzen (Intra-German monetary Union – Development and Monetary Policy Consequences)*, Baden-Baden: Nomos, p. 149 ff.

Hefeker, C. (1994) 'German Monetary Union, the Bundesbank and the EMS Collapse', *Banca Nazionale del Lavoro Quarterly Review*, pp. 379–98.

4 Monetary Policy: Targets and Instruments

Peter Schmid

Viewed over the long term, prices have risen at a considerably slower pace in Germany than in comparable major industrial countries. At the same time the Deutsche Mark has appreciated strongly in the foreign exchange markets and has become the anchor currency in the EMS. This has owed much to the monetary policy of the Bundesbank, which is based on a clear statutory stability mandate, an independent status and a convincing monetary policy strategy.

MONETARY POLICY FUNCTIONS

Safeguarding Monetary Stability as the Primary Function

Pursuant to section 3 of the Bundesbank Act, the primary function of the Bundesbank is to regulate the amount of money in circulation and of credit supplied to the economy, with the aim of 'safeguarding the currency'. This should not be interpreted as meaning that monetary stability, in complete isolation from the overall economic conditions, is to be the sole yardstick for monetary policy makers. But, in the interaction between the various economic policy makers, the Bundesbank is bound by law always to regard its task to safeguard monetary stability as its primary function. In retrospect, this statutory regulation, which dates back nearly 40 years, has been praised for its wisdom since it was adopted at a time when Keynesianism exerted a strong influence on economic policy theory and practice and when using monetary policy measures to achieve full employment was a widely accepted idea. Admittedly, Germany had lived through two periods of hyperinflation as well as the 'economic miracle', with stable prices following the currency reform of 1948. In addition, representatives of the neo-liberal school, with their market economy philosophy in particular, made a significant contribution of their own to the concept of economic policy in which monetary stability enjoyed absolute priority.[1] The modern central bank's specific understanding of its own role, on which the Bundesbank Act is based, also won increasing acceptance abroad over the course of the decades. The experiences of the 1970s, if not before, dispelled the widely held illusion that lastingly higher employment could be secured in return for a slightly higher inflation rate. Rather, monetary stability turned out in the longer run to be the prerequisite for the smooth functioning of the market economy and for sustained economic growth. There are also basic objections to the idea of exploiting a putative short-term trade-off between inflation and unemployment for monetary policy purposes. If they were to do this, monetary policy makers would run the risk of destabilising the economy and of coming under political pressure at times. For this reason there is a widespread consensus among central bankers today that monetary stability should be the primary aim of monetary policy.

Independence of the Bundesbank

The legislators provided the Bundesbank with a high degree of independence from government and Parliament so that it could perform its task unhampered. Although it is required to support the general economic policy of the Federal Cabinet, it must do so 'without prejudice to the performance of its functions'; in addition, the Bundesbank, 'in exercising the powers conferred on it, ... is independent of instructions from the Federal Cabinet' (section 12 of the Bundesbank Act). The impact of central bank independence on its policy and credibility has never been as controversial in Germany as it is in the USA or the UK.[2] This was due, first, to Germany's experience of two periods of hyperinflation triggered by the central bank's financing of government deficits. Second, the notion gained acceptance that monetary stability is a 'public good' for which there is no 'pressure group' in the political arena and which therefore risks being given the lowest priority in the political decision-making process.[3] This applies all the more as the effects of an inflationary policy are not felt immediately but only after a considerable time-lag. An independent central bank is thus better equipped to pursue a successful counter-inflationary policy stance than is a dependent one. Empirical studies on the significance of central bank independence corroborate this belief. These indicate that the higher the degree of central bank independence, the lower are the average inflation and price fluctuations.[4]

MONETARY TARGETING

Origins

The strategy which the Bundesbank pursues in performing its legal mandate may be labelled 'pragmatic monetarism'. While the money stock had always been regarded as an important indicator in Germany, the Bundesbank announced a monetary target for the following year for the first time in 1974. This change-over to monetary targeting was due to the difficulties which the Bundesbank – like other central banks – was facing in pursuing its original strategy and which came to a head in the early 1970s when inflation escalated. A second factor was the collapse of the Bretton Woods system of fixed exchange rates, which created the necessary scope for national monetary targeting. Finally, the advance of monetarist ideas fostered the explicit turn towards monetary targets, although the Bundesbank did not implement these in a mechanistic way.

Concept Underlying Monetary Targets

The Bundesbank's monetary targets are based on the monetarist principle that monetary expansion determines price movements in the medium term.[5] Therefore, the money stock is particularly well suited to play the role of a nominal anchor in a central bank policy stance geared primarily to maintaining price stability. Furthermore, the concentration on a single variable simplifies the process of monetary control. Economic agents are given a general guideline, in the form of the monetary target, which makes it easier to formulate expectations and helps to avoid unnecessary friction. At the same time the monetary target acts as a shield for the Bundesbank – in addition to its independent status – against unjustified demands. On the other hand, the central bank commits itself in this respect and also renders itself accountable. Thus monetary targets offer a chance to build up credibility and to impose a certain discipline on the decision-makers.

Unlike other major central banks and in spite of repeated difficulties, the Bundesbank has adhered to monetary targeting for more than 20 years. Today monetary targeting has become a symbol of Germany's 'stability culture'. This continuity of monetary policy strategy has been facilitated by the stability of the financial sector and financial relationships in Germany. The deregulation and liberalisation of financial markets occurred earlier in Germany than in many other countries. Capital and interest rate controls have long been a thing of the past. The universal banking system which dominates the financial sector and the relatively low inflation rates offered little opportunity or reason to search for loopholes in the form of new financial instruments. As a result, there were no radical changes in the financial system and no erosion of the basic financial relationships. Hence it comes as no surprise that most of the studies conducted on the stability of the demand for money in Germany up to the recent past have shown positive results.[6]

Handling of the Monetary Target

Another reason why the Bundesbank has been able to adhere to monetary targeting is the way it has gone about implementing it.[7] Although the Bundesbank has adopted the monetarist principle according to which inflation is in the long run a monetary phenomenon, in other aspects its strategy differs from strictly monetarist ideas. In spite of the high stability of financial relationships, the Bundesbank has from the start conducted monetary targeting in a flexible way and has never conferred on it an 'autopilot' function. It has never tried to keep the money stock on the envisaged growth path each and every month as this would inevitably have led to considerable interest rate and exchange rate fluctuations and thus to disruptions of economic developments and to unnecessary economic costs. In addition to the money stock, it has evaluated other monetary and real indicators as well. This flexibility is also mirrored in the fact that the Bundesbank has up to now adhered to annual targets which are determined on the basis of the monetary conditions prevailing at the time. It is further reflected by the review of the monetary target undertaken in the middle of each year (with the Bundesbank reserving the right to adjust the monetary target if necessary).

Technical Modifications

In the course of the past 20 years, the Bundesbank has made technical modifications to its strategy on a number of occasions. Particularly significant was the change-over in 1979 from single-figure targets to a target corridor. This took into account first the limited precision with which money stock growth can be controlled over the short term.

Second, the Bundesbank thereby sought to create a certain room for manoeuvre that would enable it to react to unexpected developments as regards prices, business activity or exchange rates during the year without having to abandon the principle of monetary targeting oriented to the medium term. All in all, after the initial testing period during which the target formulation did not prove very viable, the Bundesbank has been fairly successful in meeting its quantitative targets (see Table 4.1).

Table 4.1   Monetary targets and their implementation

Year	Target growth of the central bank money stock or M3* (%)			Actual growth (rounded figures) (%)		
	In the course of the year†	On an annual average	Concretising of target in the course of the year	In the course of the year†	On an annual average	Target met
1975	8	–	–	10	–	no
1976	–	8	–	–	9	no
1977	–	8	–	–	9	no
1978	–	8	–	–	11	no
1979	6 to 9	–	Lower limit	6	–	yes
1980	5 to 8	–	Lower limit	5	–	yes
1981	4 to 7	–	Lower half	4	–	yes
1982	4 to 7	–	Upper half	6	–	yes
1983	4 to 7	–	Upper half	7	–	yes
1984	4 to 6	–	–	5	–	yes
1985	3 to 5	–	–	5	–	yes
1986	3 ½ to 5 ½	–	–	8	–	no
1987	3 to 6	–	–	8	–	no
1988	3 to 6	–	–	7	–	no
1989	5	–	–	5	–	yes
1990	4 to 6	–	–	6	–	yes
1991‡	3 to 5	–	–	5	–	yes
1992	3 ½ to 5 ½	–	–	9	–	no
1993	4 ½ to 6 ½	–	–	7	–	no
1994	4 to 6	–	–	6	–	yes
1995	4 to 6	–	–	2	–	no
1996	4 to 7	–	–	8	–	no
1997§	3 ½ to 6 ½	–				

*Since 1988: M3.
†Between the fourth quarter of the preceding year and the fourth quarter of the current year; 1975: Dec. 1974 to Dec. 1975.
‡According to the adjustment of the monetary target in July 1991.
§Embedded in a two-year orientation for 1997/98 of about 5% per year.

However, in some years the target was missed. This was only partly due to shortcomings in the targeting process and the target formulation. In most cases, the likely failure to meet the monetary target was knowingly accepted in order to combat unforeseen shocks. For instance, the Bundesbank tolerated stronger monetary growth at the end of the 1970s and in the second half of the 1980s, when the Deutsche Mark appreciated strongly in the foreign exchange markets, because the dampening effects on price movements and business activity emanating from that appreciation seemed to constitute a sufficiently strong counter-balance. It responded in a similar way to the uncertainties and distortions of monetary expansion following German reunification.[8]

Since then volatility of shorter-term monetary growth has increased, especially as a result of portfolio shifts. Target overshooting in 1992–93 was followed by undershooting in 1995. In the eyes of the Bundesbank this increased volatility does not entirely cancel out the advantages of monetary targeting, even if it does make it more difficult to attain annual monetary targets. In order to take due account of the increased volatility of shorter-term monetary trends, the Bundesbank has widened the target corridor to three percentage points in 1996. In addition, it has argued that the advantages of monetary targeting become more obvious over the medium term and that its interest policy is primarily geared to the medium-term trends in the money stock.

When it last set its monetary target, the Bundesbank extended the time-horizon to two years, which is long enough to cover the expected 'remaining life of the Deutsche Mark'. This measure should not be mistaken as a fundamental change in strategy and as a preference, in principle, for multi-year monetary targeting. Instead, the Bundesbank has taken account of the changed underlying conditions in the run-up to the third stage of EMU. Uncertainties in the financial and foreign exchange markets may increase, above all, in the interim period, which will begin in the spring of 1998 with the decision on the participants in the third stage of EMU and which will end with the start of EMU on January 1, 1999. Furthermore, a closer coordination of monetary policy among the participating cental banks might be necessary in that period. Against that backdrop the two-year target is intended to create confidence in the continuation of a stability-oriented policy stance. It could also serve as a reference variable for closer coordination. Finally, it creates the conditions that will allow the ECB to carry on as smoothly as possible from the Bundesbank's policy of monetary targeting.

Advantages of Targeting

In retrospect, the Bundesbank's pragmatic approach has proved its worth during such bouts of turbulence. The credibility associated with the continuity of monetary targeting has contributed to the fact that the Bundesbank's determination and capacity to safeguard the value of money in the medium term has never been doubted, not even when the monetary target was overshot. At the same time, adherence to monetary targeting subjected the Bundesbank to the salutary requirement to justify itself, sustained a keen awareness of the implications of monetary growth for price movements, and precluded major monetary aberrations. For these reasons monetary targets make sense even if they cannot always be met. They are similar to a compass, which not only helps the traveller to keep on course but also to correct an erroneous course. In this respect, the fact that the monetary targets have sometimes been missed has not caused the principle of monetary targeting to be questioned either by policy consultants or the general public.

Formulation of the Monetary Target

In order to emphasise the monetary target's indicative function, the Bundesbank does not formulate the target in an abstract fashion but rather derives it from a small number of key economic variables. The procedure is simple, transparent and underlines the medium-term orientation of monetary policy. The monetary growth target set for the year ahead is the sum of the estimated growth of the overall real production potential in the coming year, the rate of price increases defined as being acceptable in the medium term and the estimated rate of decline in the trend velocity of circulation of money. For the Bundesbank the production potential means the output that can be achieved on the basis of the existing technology, capital stock and labour potential given normal utilisation of productive resources. Since the middle of the 1980s it has set the medium-term price assumption at 2 per cent maximum and in doing so has taken account in particular of statistical inaccuracies in measuring the inflation rate. In the context of the present two-year orientation the medium-term price assumption was lowered to between 1½ and 2 per cent in response to the continued progress in price stabilisation and the favourable outlook for prices. To offset the decline in the long-term trend velocity of circulation of money, the Bundesbank includes an add-on of (currently) one percentage point. The sum of these factors yields the potential-consistent growth rate of the money stock as an annual average (see Table 4.2).

Table 4.2 Basic scheme for deriving a monetary target

(Yearly averages)	
1. Growth of (real) output potential	(+)
2. Medium-term price assumption	(+)
= Nominal growth of output potential	
3. Additions/deductions for the long-term trend in the velocity of circulation	(±)
= Potential-consistent monetary growth	

Since 1979 this figure has been translated into a four-quarter target running from the fourth quarter of the base year to the fourth quarter of the following year. In this context the Bundesbank also takes due account of the monetary situation in the base quarter. Since 1996 the four-quarter target has been formulated as a target corridor with a fluctuation margin of three percentage points.

Broadly-Defined Aggregates

The Bundesbank has from the start based its monetary target on a broadly defined monetary aggregate. Initially this was the central bank money stock, and since 1988 it has been the money stock M3 (currency, sight deposits, shorter-term time deposits and savings deposits at three months' notice). In broadly defined aggregates, interest rate induced shifts between the individual monetary components (which are rather marked in Germany) are of no or only minor importance. Therefore, the movement of such monetary aggregates is much steadier than that of narrowly defined aggregates. The relationship between monetary expansion and the overall expenditure trend can thus easily be identified. At the same time the intended course of monetary policy can be deduced fairly clearly from the trend in the target aggregate.

Although financial innovations in Germany, as already mentioned, have not brought about any insidious erosion of basic financial relationships, they have nevertheless left their mark. Such developments as the growth of shorter-term bank debt securities at the beginning of the 1980s, the expansion of domestic non-banks' Euro-deposits, a certain change in the monetary character of short-term savings deposits and the recent establishment of money market funds have continually posed new challenges as regards the 'correct' definition of the money stock. In the last few years, a host of distorting special factors, particularly changes in tax legislation which affected the demand for money and credit, have been added to this. The Bundesbank responded to these changes and shocks with restraint. In 1988 it switched from the central bank money stock to the money stock M3, as the former's 'currency bias' increasingly led to misdirections. Since then the Bundesbank has adhered to M3, but it has supplemented this aggregate with the extended money stock M3, an auxiliary indicator which includes liquidity holdings in the Euro-market and in money market funds not included in M3. The Bundesbank monitors this aggregate closely so that it is forearmed against possible major shifts in the demand for money.

No Alternative to Monetary Targeting

Adherence to monetary targeting is further bolstered by the fact that no equivalent alternative is discernible. Exchange rate targets are out of the question for Germany, as its currency plays an anchor function in the EMS. Interest rates and the interest rate pattern show no clearcut connection with price movements; therefore, they cannot be used as a nominal anchor for price stability. For inflation targeting, comprehensive knowledge about the correlation between monetary policy instruments and the ultimate goals of monetary policy are required. Although the first results obtained using this strategy are quite good, the negative experience gained in the field of monetary policy prior to the 1970s, when intermediate monetary targets were generally dispensed with, calls for caution. For the Bundesbank, these concepts are at most second-best solutions for the scenario in which basic financial relationships have broken down. Therefore, they represent no real choice in Germany. On the contrary, a change-over to an alternative strategy for no compelling reason could lead to considerable agitation.

IMPLEMENTATION

Indirect Management via the Money Market

The Bundesbank exerts indirect control over the money stock. Its ideas on monetary management are rather 'conservative'.[9] They are aimed at influencing the credit supply of banks and non-banks' demand for money and credit indirectly through changes in bank liquidity and the interest rate mechanism in the financial markets. It is in the nature of this monetary management approach that the necessary adjustments in the markets take time and are predictable only to a limited extent. Therefore, the Bundesbank moves tentatively towards its goal by using its instruments flexibly. In line with the various phases of the monetary policy transmission channel, the Bundesbank's monetary management approach can be briefly characterised as follows:

Monetary Transmission

1. As regards its instruments, the Bundesbank decides upon suitable individual measures which are aimed at establishing the desired money market conditions.
2. As regards the money market, the Bundesbank sets appropriate short-term operational targets for bank liquidity and money market rates which appear conductive to achieving the annual monetary target and the aspired key economic target variables in the longer run.
3. As regards the intermediate target, which is embodied in the annual target for the growth of the money stock, the Bundesbank examines on a more or less continuous basis throughout the year whether, when and to what extent deviations of monetary growth from the target path are to be corrected through adjustments of conditions in the money markets and the other financial markets.

Instruments

Rediscount and Lombard Policy

The traditional monetary policy instruments in Germany are the rediscount, Lombard and minimum reserve policies; by contrast, open market policy has gained major importance only since the end of the 1970s. In its discount business, the Bundesbank buys trade bills from the credit institutions at the discount rate which it has defined.

This rate is generally somewhat lower than the money market rates and therefore contains a certain 'subsidy element'. As a consequence, the total amount of rediscount credit available to each bank is limited by rediscount quotas. Lombard loans are granted by the Bundesbank against the collateral of certain securities and Debt Register claims. In contrast to rediscount credit, they are not intended as a 'permanent source of funding' but rather as bridging loans for very short-term liquidity shortages. Consequently the Lombard rate is always higher than the discount rate.

Open Market Policy

Particularly since the mid-1980s there have been marked shifts of emphasis in the provision of central bank money. Since then, the Bundesbank has adopted a more flexible approach to money market management, mainly through the use of securities repurchase transactions. The reason for this was, above all, the growing global integration of financial markets which suggested the need for greater elasticity of money market rates than was obtainable through the rather cumbersome method of changes in the discount and Lombard rates. In the past few years, securities repurchase agreements are offered to the banks at weekly intervals with maturities of 14 days in the form of either variable-rate or fixed-rate tenders. This instrument is reversible at short notice and gives the Bundesbank the initiative in determining the supply of central bank money. For some time now the Bundesbank has been using this channel to provide the bulk of its central bank money. Rediscount lending, which was previously the main source of funds, today serves only as a basic instrument of funding. Although securities repurchase transactions are not a substitute for day-to-day money, securities repurchase rates today largely determine the trend in the day-to-day money market rate. The Lombard rate, which had acted as the respective key variable under the old coarse-tuning approach, now merely functions as an interest rate ceiling.

Minimum Reserve Policy

On the demand side for central bank money, the Bundesbank's array of monetary policy instruments includes minimum reserve requirements. Their character has changed a great deal over time. Initially, it was the effects on bank liquidity of this instrument which were to the fore. Particularly during the Bretton Woods system, the Bundesbank often tried to skim off external inflows of funds by raising the reserve ratios. Today, minimum reserves rather have a general regulatory function: they define the framework within which the other instruments are used. The minimum reserve requirements ensure that banks' demand for central bank money is sufficiently stable; moreover, as they must be complied with only as a monthly average, they serve as a liquidity buffer in the money market which offsets sudden fluctuations in the demand for liquidity. This exerts a steadying influence on interest rate movements. At the same time the central bank is freed from the need to intervene constantly in the money market, thereby running the risk of being 'towed along' by the banks. However, the stabilisation function is assured without the banks' needing to maintain minimum reserve balances which far exceed their working balances. The Bundesbank has therefore lowered the reserve ratios perceptibly in the last few years and has also simplified the minimum reserve system, thus largely reducing the distortionary effects on competition associated with this administrative instrument.

The Bundesbank's flexible approach to money market management has proved effective. 'Unproductive' rate fluctuations are rare and, in addition, they are limited by the Lombard rate at the top end and – if appropriate – by offers of very short-term Treasury bills at the bottom end. In the Bundesbank's view, the German experience suggests that the ECB would be well advised to adopt a similar monetary management approach in line with market conditions, one in which open market policy, in the form of operations reversible at short term, form the centrepiece of the provision of central bank money and in which minimum reserve requirements ensure a stable need by banks to maintain central bank balances.

Notes

1. See Eucken (1952), p. 255 ff.
2. See Caesar (1980) for details of the debate on the pros and cons of an independent central bank.
3. Regarding the difficulty of organising general interests, see Olson (1965).
4. See, for instance, Alesina and Summers (1993).
5. Regarding the correlation between monetary growth and price movements in Germany, see Deutsche Bundesbank (1992); Deutsche Bundesbank

(1997), especially Annex 2: 'The leading indicator properties of the money stock'.
6. See Gerlach (1994); Issing and Tödter (1995).
7. On the Bundesbank's implementation of monetary targeting, see also Schlesinger (1985).
8. See in this context Chapter 3 in this volume.
9. On the Bundesbank's monetary control see Deutsche Bundesbank (1994).

References

Alesina, A. and L.H. Summers (1993), 'Central Bank Independence and Macroeconomic Performance: Some Comparative Evidence', *Journal of Money, Credit and Banking*, Vol. 25, No. 2, pp. 151–62.

Caesar, R. (1980), 'Die Unabhängigkeit der Notenbank im demokratischen Staat – Argumente und Gegenargumente' ('The independence of central banks in democratic countries – arguments for and against'), *Zeitschrift für Politik*, Neue Folge (new series), Vol. 27, pp. 347–77.

Deutsche Bundesbank (1992), 'The correlation between monetary growth and price movements in the Federal Republic of Germany', *Monthly Report*, Vol. 44, No. 1 (January), pp. 20–8.

Deutsche Bundesbank (1994), 'Money market management by the Deutsche Bundesbank', *Monthly Report*, Vol. 46, No. 5 (May), pp. 59–74.

Deutsche Bundesbank (1997), 'Review of the monetary target', *Monthly Report*, Vol. 49, No. 8 (August), pp. 17–32.

Eucken, W. (1952), *Grundsätze der Wirtschaftspolitik (Principles of Economic Policy)*, Berne and Tübingen: Franke and Mohr.

Gerlach, S. (1994), 'German Unification and the Demand for German M3', *BIS Working Paper No. 21*, Bank for International Settlements (BIS), Monetary and Economic Department, Basle.

Issing, O. and K.-H. Tödter (1995), 'Geldmenge und Preise im vereinigten Deutschland' ('The money stock and prices in unified Germany'), in D. Duwendag (ed.), *Neuere Entwicklungen in der Geldtheorie und Währungspolitik (New Developments in Monetary Theory and Monetary Policy)*, Schriften des Vereins für Socialpolitik, Neue Folge (new series), Vol. 235, Berlin: Duncker & Humblot, pp. 97–123.

Olson, M. (1965), *The Logic of Collective Action – Public Goods and the Theory of Groups*, Cambridge, USA: Harvard University Press.

Schlesinger, H. (1985), 'Zehn Jahre Geldpolitik mit einem Geldmengenziel' ('Ten years of conducting monetary policy with a monetary target'), in W. Gebauer (ed.), *Öffentliche Finanzen und monetäre Ökonomie*, Festschrift für Karl Häuser zur Vollendung des 65. Lebensjahres (*Public Finance and Monetary Economy*, commemorative volume in honour of the 65th birthday of Karl Häuser), Frankfurt am Main: Fritz Knapp Verlag. pp. 123–47.

Tietmeyer, H. (1993), 'The Value of Monetary Stability in the World Today', in P. Arestis (ed.), *Money and Banking: Issues for the Twenty-First Century. Essays in Honour of Stephen F. Frowen*, London: Macmillan, pp. 25–40.

5 Relations between the Bundesbank and the Federal Government

Bertold Wahlig

In a nutshell, the relationship between the Deutsche Bundesbank and the Federal Government is characterised by the fact that the Bundesbank, in exercising its monetary powers, is independent of instructions from the Federal Government, but is required to support the Federal Government's general economic policy, without prejudice to the performance of its priority functions. This relationship between the government and the central bank served as a model when the framework for European monetary union was drafted; one of the main points on which the members of the European Community agreed when drawing up the framework for monetary union and the ESCB in the Maastricht Treaty was that the ECB and the national central banks should be independent of instructions from Community organisations and institutions, and from governments or other bodies of the member states. For the German representatives the independence of the future ECBS and the commitment to price stability as an overriding priority was an indispensable component of European monetary union. Overall, major characteristics of the German central banking constitution are to be found in the Maastricht Treaty and, in particular, in the Statute of the European System of Central Banks. I should like to provide a more detailed description of the relationship between the Deutsche Bundesbank and the Federal Government under the following headings.

1. What, from the German point of view, is understood by central bank independence, and which factors argue in favour of granting a central bank independence?
2. What can be inferred from the German constitution concerning the position and functions of the Bundesbank?
3. How does the Bundesbank Act regulate cooperation between the Federal Government and the Bundesbank in the fields of economic and external monetary policy?

4. How is cooperation between the Federal Government and the Bundesbank regulated in the area of international monetary policy?

Sentence 2 of section 12 of the Bundesbank Act stipulates that, in exercising the powers conferred on it by the Act, the Bank is independent of instructions from the Federal Cabinet. This makes fully explicit the *institutional* or functional independence both of the institution itself and of its decision makers in discharging the Bank's monetary policy functions. This institutional independence must be joined by instrumental independence: that is, the central bank must be equipped with an array of instruments suitable for performing its functions, and must be entitled to make use of them solely at its own discretion. Particular mention should be made in this context of the imposition of a limit on lending to public authorities, as has hitherto been regulated by section 20 of the Bundesbank Act (which provided for limited ceilings for short-term cash advances, and of the basic prohibition of overdraft facilities or any other type of credit facility to the public sector under Article 104 of the EC Treaty). This provision necessitated an amendment of the Bundesbank Act upon entry into the second stage of monetary union and led to the repealing of the powers to grant cash advances to the Federal and Länder Governments. A central bank would not be able to control the money stock autonomously if it were compelled to engage in public sector financing to an extent which it regarded as unacceptable. Institutional and instrumental independence requires safeguarding by means of a high degree of *personal* independence on the part of the decision makers. A major factor in this is that the decision makers have terms of office which are of sufficient length – if possible, lasting longer than one legislative period – and that it is not possible to terminate the appointment of a central bank manager who is out of favour.

POTENTIAL CONFLICT BETWEEN MONETARY AND EXCHANGE RATE POLICY

A fundamental dilemma with regard to independence is posed by the potential conflict between monetary policy and exchange rate policy as long as responsibility for these is in different hands. Looked at realistically, this must be expected until further notice, as is shown by the arrangements governing European economic and monetary union. A central bank which is obliged to make unlimited interventions in the foreign exchange market on account of an exchange rate system laid down by the government runs the risk of losing control over monetary policy. The Bundesbank had painful experience of this constraint on monetary policy, for instance, during the period when it was obliged to make unlimited interventions *vis-à-vis* the US dollar under the Bretton Woods system of fixed parities, thus having to create money far in excess of what was acceptable in monthly policy terms. Even under the EMS it has again become obvious that unlimited intervention obligations may adversely affect the central bank's control of money creation; that was the reason why it was necessary to widen the margins of fluctuation in the intervention system. In view of the potential impact of exchange rate arrangements it is therefore envisaged that the Council of the European Community will be able to reach formal agreements on an ECU exchange rate system *vis-à-vis* non-Community currencies in the future European monetary union only after having consulted the ECB 'in an effort to arrive at a consensus which is consistent with the aim of price stability'.

Central bank independence is generally understood to mean freedom from government instructions. This must, however, also include freedom from the instructions of Parliament. In order to preclude any misconceptions: central bank independence cannot be construed as a limitation of Parliament's legislative powers unless such limitations derive from the constitution. By contrast, the conduct of monetary policy in line with the statutory mandate must likewise be independent of instructions from Parliament.

WHICH FACTORS ARGUE IN FAVOUR OF GRANTING A CENTRAL BANK INDEPENDENCE?

The fact that the partners in the European Community have accepted the German model to such a great extent shows that it is no longer necessary to undertake the laborious task of convincing others of the advantages of an independent central bank. Confirming its basic conviction in the matter of central bank independence, in 1992 (in connection with the ratification of the Treaty on European Union) the German legislature itself unanimously approved an amendment to the Constitution which ensures that the functions and powers of the Deutsche Bundesbank can be transferred only to an independent

ECB. In assenting to the Treaty on European Union, all those involved acted on the firm assumption (backed up by all available empirical evidence) that the central bank's independent position will make it much easier to implement a monetary policy geared to stability. Furthermore, in view of the painful experience of hyperinflation after the First and Second World Wars and the radical currency reforms which followed them, the Deutsche Bundesbank has always had the firm backing of general public opinion in the matter of independence. The Deutsche Bundesbank has always felt obliged, however, to win support for this conviction by conducting a policy geared to monetary stability and, through the success of its anti-inflation policy, has played a major part in reinforcing this conviction. These lessons have also been confirmed time and again of late in economic studies. Recent studies, whether it be those of Alesina and Summers (1993) in Harvard or Cukierman (1995) in Tel Aviv, have provided further empirical evidence of the advantages of central bank independence in pursuing a consistent anti-inflation policy. In these studies the Bundesbank is at the top of the ranking in terms of organisational independence, on the one hand, and the success of its anti-inflation policy, on the other.

WHAT CAN BE INFERRED FROM THE GERMAN CONSTITUTION CONCERNING THE BUNDESBANK'S POSITION AND FUNCTIONS?

Concerning the establishment of a central bank, sentence 1 of Article 88 of the German Constitution states briefly: 'The Federal Government shall establish a central bank and bank of issue as a Federal Bank (Bundesbank).'

The Constitution thus assigns to the Federal Government the mandate of establishing a central bank and bank of issue and, at the same time, provides a guarantee of the existence of a Federal bank (Bundesbank) with the characteristics defined by the Constitution.

The institution to be created is to be established as a bank (that is, as a credit institution), which must be entitled to conduct the banking business essential to its function as a central bank and bank of issue. Monetary policy decisions by the Central Bank Council, such as setting official interest rates or minimum reserve regulations, do not implement themselves but must be put into effect through banking transactions, such as discounting bills of exchange and entering into open market operations, and by carrying giro accounts for holding minimum reserves. Intervention in the foreign exchange market presupposes powers to buy and sell foreign exchange.

The Constitution assigns to the institution which is to be established the function of being a currency bank: that is, a central bank which has to manage the currency and has the exclusive right to conduct monetary policy. This implies that the legislature is required to place at the direct disposal of the Bundesbank the range of monetary policy instruments which enables it to manage the amount of money in circulation and to safeguard the currency.

The Federal bank to be established is, finally, to be set up as a bank of issue. This term means that the Bundesbank must have the right to issue banknotes as legal tender. As it is scarcely possible to imagine a currency bank without a monopoly over the issuing of banknotes, Article 88 of the Constitution calls for a monopoly over the issuing of banknotes for the Bundesbank (but not, however, for the issuing of coins).

On the other hand, the brief first sentence of section 88 does not state expressly that the currency bank to be established must be independent. Even so, in the literature on the Constitution there have been a number of attempts to derive the Bundesbank's independence from the Constitution itself. Reproducing this constitutional discussion here in detail, however, would go beyond the scope of this chapter.

In constitutional reality, at any rate, the Bundesbank's independence is safeguarded by public opinion. In the wake of Maastricht, it is now quite inconceivable that the Bundesbank's independence could be curtailed by law, seeing that the member states are themselves required to grant independence to their respective national central banks.

HOW DOES THE BUNDESBANK ACT REGULATE COOPERATION BETWEEN THE FEDERAL GOVERNMENT AND THE BUNDESBANK?

The Federal Government – and, following it, the Bundestag – had the courage in the mid-1950s to grant the Bundesbank, established with effect from 1 August 1957, a large measure of independence in the performance of the monetary policy functions assigned to it. At the same time, however, they were shrewd enough to provide for a demarcation of functions and responsibilities, and for the institutional arrangements necessary for all parties involved to cooperate smoothly.

Section 3 of the Bundesbank Act assigns the following function to the Bank: 'The Deutsche Bundesbank regulates the amount of money in circulation and of credit supplied to the economy, using the monetary powers conferred on it by this Act, with the aim of safeguarding the currency, and sees to the execution of domestic and external payments.'

The Bundesbank is thus entrusted with monetary policy (in the wider sense of domestic monetary and credit policy) and is required to safeguard the currency with the instruments at its disposal. Safeguarding the currency is, at the same time, also a matter for the government. As one of the aims of economic and fiscal policy, Article 109 of the Constitution and section 1 of the Economic Stability and Growth Act require the Federal Government and the Länder Governments to safeguard overall economic equilibrium, and thus also price stability. In order to link the Bank's monetary policy with general economic policy, sentence 1 of section 12 of the Bundesbank Act requires the Bundesbank 'without prejudice to the performance of its functions...to support the general economic policy of the Federal Cabinet'.

In other words, the Bank not only must respect the economic policy decisions of the Federal Government but also work actively to implement them, using the instruments which it has at its disposal. However, the obligation to give support is subject to the proviso that the Bank has its own duty to discharge; the obligation to provide support exists only as long as and to the extent that this is compatible with the Bank's prime function. In considering whether these conditions are met, the Bank acts at its own discretion and is just as free of instructions as when exercising the powers conferred on it by the Bundesbank Act, as provided by sentence 2 of section 12 of that Act, which is the key provision regulating the Bank's independence.

In section 13, however, the Bundesbank Act also provides an institutional framework for cooperation between the Federal Government and the Bundesbank:

- The Bank shall advise the Federal Cabinet on monetary policy issues of major importance;
- The members of the Federal Cabinet are entitled to attend the meetings of the Central Bank Council. They have no right to

vote, but may propose motions and demand that decision-taking be deferred for up to two weeks. In addition, the Bank's by-laws provide that the Federal Minister of Economics and the Federal Minister of Finance are to be invited to attend every meeting of the Central Bank Council by the process of sending them the agenda. In practice, these ministers receive not only the agenda but also the preparatory documents;

• Finally, the Federal Cabinet should invite the President of the Deutsche Bundesbank to attend its deliberations on important monetary policy issues.

The obligation, incumbent on the Bank under the Bundesbank Act to advise the Federal Government on monetary policy issues of major importance (unlike the obligations to furnish the Federal Government with information) does not depend on a request to this effect being made by the Federal Government. This means that the Bundesbank is not dependent on suggestions or prior statements by the Federal Government, but may approach the Federal Government on its own initiative. Indeed, it must do so when, in its estimation, advice to the Federal Government is required. It is not without good reason that the Bundesbank Act did not make such advice dependent on an explicit request by the Federal Government; otherwise, it might be possible to prevent the Bundesbank from providing unsolicited advice by not requesting it.

The Deutsche Bundesbank has invariably taken its duty to advise the Federal Government very seriously and, accordingly, has expressed its views on all matters that it considered important from the standpoint of monetary policy, doing so in the form it deemed appropriate in each situation. It discharged this duty even when it knew, or could assume, that the timing or content of its advice might not be welcome.

On the other hand, the norm for the various Federal Cabinets has been to attach great importance to the views expressed by the Bundesbank on questions of monetary policy. Federal ministers have frequently taken part in the discussions of the Central Bank Council in order to exchange the views held on both sides and to coordinate, as far as possible, the measures of the Federal Government and the Bundesbank. This type of cooperation has always been frank and beneficial to both sides.

THE RIGHT TO DEFER DECISIONS

The result has been that, thus far, no member of the Federal Cabinet has had to exercise the right granted under section 13(2) of the Bundesbank Act to defer a decision by the Central Bank Council for up to two weeks. The prior notification of the questions to be considered and resolved and the thorough discussion of the sometimes divergent views of the two sides have always rendered a formal procedure of this kind superfluous.

The legislature, for its part, at that time also looked into the question of whether it should make arrangements for the eventuality of a conflict between the Federal Government and the Bundesbank, but decided against this in consideration of the fact that it would not be possible to make generally valid institutional arrangements in the Bundesbank Act for the event of conflict. Ultimately, a decision by Parliament would be the only solution. The report of the responsible Bundestag committee made the supplementary observation that, in the event of the conflict of principle, the parties involved would be at liberty to effect a 'dramatisation' of the conflict (which evidently meant mobilising public opinion), which should then be conducted publicly, be subject to the scrutiny of public opinion and, if possible, lead to an agreement.

In addition to the basic standard for cooperation laid down in sections 12 and 13, the Bundesbank Act contains a number of rules in matters relating to both operations and staff which secure for the Federal Government some influence over the Bundesbank. There are also some rules on interaction outside the Bundesbank Act, such as in the Banking Act which regulates banking supervision, and in the Act to Promote Economic Stability and Growth. For instance, the Bundesbank is represented *inter alia* in the Business Cycle Council for the Public Sector, which was formed under the 1967 Act to Promote Economic Stability and Growth. That Council deliberates on measures to prevent disruptions of overall economic equilibrium. It likewise attends meetings of the Financial Planning Council, which makes recommendations on coordinating financial planning between the Federal Government, the Länder Governments and the local authorities. Finally, outside the context of formal cooperation there is an ongoing exchange of views between the Bank and the Federal ministries regarding draft legislation.

HOW IS COOPERATION BETWEEN THE FEDERAL GOVERNMENT AND THE BUNDESBANK REGULATED IN TERMS OF INTERNATIONAL MONETARY POLICY?

Whereas the Bundesbank Act clearly assigns functions and responsibilities in terms of domestic monetary policy, and contains precise ground rules governing cooperation, the functions and powers of the Federal Government and the Bundesbank in the field of external or international monetary policy are only in part explicitly defined by the legislature. Such definitions are to be found, in particular, in respect of the Federal Government's membership of the International Monetary Fund (IMF). In terms of international law, it is the Federal Republic of Germany which is a member of the IMF and which is thus responsible for the rights and duties arising from membership. This means, for example, that it is primarily the Federal Government that is entitled to the special drawing rights (SDRs) allocated by the Fund, however, and that the inpayment and other financing obligations are incumbent on the Federal Government. As the Bundesbank manages the German monetary reserves, it was an obvious step to integrate the Bundesbank in the financial obligations *vis-à-vis* the IMF and, on the other hand, to transfer the financial claims on the IMF to the Bundesbank. Since 1978 the IMF Act has therefore provided for the financial obligations arising from the Federal Government's membership of the IMF to be met by the Bundesbank, and the assets to which the Federal Government is entitled on account of its membership to devolve on the Bundesbank. First, this relieves the Federal budget of the relevant inpayment obligations to the membership quota and, second, it enables the Bundesbank to show the SDRs which have been allocated and the drawing rights within the reserve tranche as assets of its own among the monetary reserves in its balance sheet. The IMF Act also provides for the Governor for the Federal Republic of Germany in the IMF, his deputy and the German executive director to be appointed by the Federal Government in agreement with the Bundesbank.

THE IMF ACT

The IMF Act does not contain an explicit ruling on the question of who has the right to issue declarations to the IMF on the setting or amendment of currency parities, or the selection of a different exchange rate system. As the Act does not regulate this point, it follows that the Federal Government is so entitled, by virtue of its membership of the IMF. This is the generally accepted opinion, and is not disputed by the Bundesbank. It is likewise undisputed that declarations of such basic monetary policy importance must be – and have always been – subject to thorough consultation and coordination between the Federal Government and the Bundesbank. Outside the EMS there is at present no generally or globally valid parity for the Deutsche Mark, but only a common understanding among the Western industrial nations that erratic exchange rate fluctuations should be countered without fundamentally opposing market forces.

Things are different, albeit also more complicated in legal terms, with regard to the EMS. This is not a case of a binding exchange rate regime having come into being by virtue of a decision by the Federal Government, but rather that the Federal Government and the Bundesbank together, by participating in various Community acts, have played a part in the creation of the EMS. For instance, the Federal Government participated in the political foundation of the EMS by means of the European Council resolution of 5 December 1978, as well as the EEC regulations on the composition of the ECU and the functions of the European Monetary Cooperation Fund. On the other hand, the EMS also owes something to the Agreement between the central banks of the EEC member states on the operating procedures of the EMS, which was signed by the Deutsche Bundesbank as a contracting party. Later ideas that governments have had on changes to the EMS have therefore in all cases entailed an amendment of the central bank agreement.

THE MAASTRICHT TREATY

The necessary linking of monetary policy, which is the responsibility of the central bank, to the responsibility for fixing the exchange rate regime is incidentally also reflected in the Maastricht Treaty. Article 109 of the EC Treaty expressly requires the Council of Ministers, when setting exchange rates (*vis-à-vis* non-Community countries), to seek a consensus – in consultation with the ECB – which is consistent with the target of price stability. The ECB has to follow the general 'guidelines' of the Council of Ministers on exchange rate policy only insofar as this does not have an adverse impact on the priority target of stability.

The Maastricht texts (which, according to the proposed timetable, will in fact take precedence over the Bundesbank Act in a few years' time) provide a good basis for a stable European currency. The success of European monetary integration will hinge upon the stability orientation of the ESCB gaining broad public acceptance in the participating countries. The history of the German central bank shows that monetary stability is possible on a durable basis only against the backdrop of a 'stability culture' which is backed by all groups in society.

References

Alesina, A. and Summers, L.H. (1993), 'Central Bank Independence and Macroeconomic Performance: Some Comparative Evidence', *Journal of Money, Credit and Banking*, vol. 25, no. 2 (May), pp. 151–162.
Cukierman, A. and Webb, S.B. (1995), 'Political Influence on the Central Bank: International Evidence', *The World Bank Economic Review*, vol. 9, no. 3.

6 Banking Supervision: Who is Doing What?

Jürgen Becker

MAIN DEVELOPMENTS IN BANKING SUPERVISION IN GERMANY AFTER 1945

In the Federal Republic of Germany, as in virtually every other country with a banking system organised along free-market lines, the banking system is subject to special government regulation and supervision, for credit institutions occupy a special position within the economy as reservoirs of capital, as suppliers of credit to enterprises, households and public authorities and as agencies of monetary policy.

After the end of the Second World War banking supervision in Germany was initially the responsibility of the Länder Governments. There was no uniform regulatory framework throughout the Federal Republic of Germany until the adoption of the Banking Act of 10 July 1961, which simultaneously provided the legal basis for establishing the Federal Banking Supervisory Office.

The credit institutions' expanding volume of business made it necessary after a few years to modify the set of prudential instruments. Triggered by the bankruptcy of the Herstatt Bank in 1974, surveillance was extended, *inter alia*, to cover foreign exchange trading, and the scope for speculative activities was restricted by the adoption of Principle Ia. The radical transformation of the financial markets which began in the 1980s and the concomitant growing internationalisation of banking business necessitated a fundamental reorientation of banking supervision. The previously predominant national perspective needed to be replaced by a uniform, internationally-oriented approach to developing and designing banking supervisory standards and procedures to enable regulators to respond appropriately to the changed risk situation in the banking sector. As a result, the consolidation principle was introduced world-wide and in 1988 uniform capital standards were agreed. At the same time this created a level playing field in the international financial markets.

At the international level the work of the Basle Committee on Banking Supervision, as well as the EC Directives, have had a major bearing on national legislation. Thus, as part of the harmonisation efforts undertaken within the EU over the past years alone, several central banking supervisory directives have been adopted which have prompted (or will do so in the near future) several amendments of the Banking Act.[1] As a whole, the adjustments to the banking supervisory framework over the past few years have occurred in rapid succession. In the coming years, therefore, the focus will lie on fine-tuning the various new regulations.

LEGAL FOUNDATIONS AND OBJECTIVES OF BANKING SUPERVISION IN GERMANY

The legal basis for banking supervision in the Federal Republic of Germany is the Banking Act. According to the substantiation by the legislators, the Act is designed to achieve three main aims:

- to provide a general system of order in the banking industry;
- to maintain the viability of the banking sector; and – as far as possible –
- to protect the banks' creditors against losing their assets.

In seeking to realise these aims, the banking regulators and supervisors pursue a liberal philosophy based on free-market concepts which, as a matter of principle, does not envisage any direct interventions in banks' business policy decisions. Instead, the entire responsibility for decisions rests with the credit institutions' managers. The activities of credit institutions are restricted solely by regulations covering their organisation and conduct of business, by quantitative parameters (for example, concerning lending) and by information and disclosure obligations *vis-à-vis* the supervisory bodies.

In addition to these general banking supervisory regulations there are also special provisions for individual categories of credit institutions, such as public credit institutions, mortgage banks, investment companies, building and loan associations and risk capital investment companies.

WHO IS DOING WHAT?

Agencies of Banking Supervision

In the Federal Republic of Germany banks are supervised by the Federal Banking Supervisory Office in cooperation with the Deutsche Bundesbank. Other agencies, such as executive bodies, auditing firms[2] and the audit associations of the banking industry, are integrated into the supervisory system. Finally, the banking associations are always consulted on any changes to the supervisory regulations. Moreover, the associations play an important role as an effective adjunct to the government supervisory agencies; in particular, by providing privately organised deposit guarantee schemes.

The Federal Banking Supervisory Office is a superior Federal authority which comes under the jurisdiction of the Federal Minister of Finance and is based in Berlin. As the Federal Banking Supervisory Office does not have any field offices of its own, the Bundesbank provides the links to the individual credit institutions at a local level via its network of about 160 branch offices throughout the Federal Republic of Germany. Ninety per cent of the costs incurred by the Federal Banking Supervisory Office have to be borne by the banking industry.

Definition of Responsibilities

Federal Banking Supervisory Office and Bundesbank

The respective responsibilities of the Federal Banking Supervisory Office and of the Bundesbank in the field of banking supervision are clearly defined by law. The Federal Banking Supervisory Office is the primary regulatory agency in Germany. However, the Federal Banking Supervisory Office and the Bundesbank cooperate closely. Pursuant to section 7 of the Banking Act, the Bundesbank and the Federal Banking Supervisory Office 'shall communicate to each other any observations and findings which may be of significance for the performance of their functions'. Their areas of competence are specifically defined as follows.

- Sovereign tasks, such as granting and withdrawing bank licences, the ordering of special audits, the issuing of instructions to a bank's management in special cases and the issuing of other administrative acts, are the responsibility of the Federal Banking Supervisory Office.

- Prior to issuing general regulations, the Federal Banking Supervisory Office must consult the Bundesbank. The degree of the latter's involvement depends on the extent to which the regulations in question affect the Bundesbank's range of functions as the central bank. The Bundesbank's rights of involvement range from mere consultation to the requirement to reach agreement with the Bundesbank. For example, when issuing Principles Concerning the Capital and Liquidity of Credit Institutions, the Federal Banking Supervisory Office has to reach agreement with the Bundesbank.
- In terms of regulatory practice, the Bundesbank is extensively involved in the ongoing supervision of credit institutions and hence of the entire banking system. That is one of the foremost areas of its participation in supervisory activities.

This division of labour ensures that the Bundesbank maintains its independence with regard to its basic function of conducting monetary policy and also that no conflicts can arise between monetary policy interests and banking supervisory interests.

Other Individuals and Institutions

Apart from its statutorily prescribed cooperation with the Bundesbank, the Federal Banking Supervisory Office may also draw on other individuals and institutions for assistance in its work. These are primarily auditors and the audit associations of the banking industry. As a matter of principle, the Federal Banking Supervisory Office and the Bundesbank do not perform on-site inspections, and neither do they have their own teams of auditors to audit banks' annual accounts except in the case of Model Testing and examinations of the Minimum Requirements of the Trading Business. Instead, the credit institutions are examined by independent external auditors of the banks' own choosing. As a rule, the institutions of the savings bank and cooperative bank sectors are examined by audit teams belonging to their respective association.

Federal Government/Federal Minister of Finance

The Federal Government can issue regulations if acute dangers are posed to the economy as a whole by financial difficulties encountered by banks (for example, by means of a moratorium or the suspension and resumption of banking and stock market business pursuant to sections 47 and 48 of the Banking Act). The Federal Minister of Finance further has the power to issue regulations designed to uphold the general order of the banking system. For example, the Federal Minister of Finance can declare business not specified in the Banking Act as banking business and thereby extend the provisions of the Banking Act to such business.

INSTRUMENTS AND IMPLEMENTATION OF BANKING SUPERVISION

In order to achieve the twin prudential objectives of protecting the financial system against systemic risk and protecting creditors against losing their deposits, the banking supervisors have at their disposal a range of instruments which is briefly outlined below.

Licensing

Market access to the banking sector requires a special licence from the Federal Banking Supervisory Office. Anyone who meets the legal requirements has the right to obtain such a banking licence. No examination is made of whether there is a public need to set up a particular institution. The prerequisites for obtaining a banking licence relate, *inter alia*, to the quality of the bank's management (at least two full-time managers who must be adequately qualified and trustworthy), to the minimum capital requirements (ECU5 million if the institution wishes to accept deposits from the general public) and to certain organisational stipulations. *An assessment of the share-holders* is also made; these – like the managers – must be 'fit and proper'. This applies not only when the bank is first licensed but also subsequently and following every change in the ownership structure.

Rules Governing Ongoing Business Activity

The instruments available for supervising the ongoing business activities of a credit institution include, first and foremost, the *Principles Concerning the Capital and Liquidity of Credit Institutions*. In order to limit their counter-party exposure, credit institutions must have liable capital which amounts to at least 8 per cent of their weighted risk assets (Principle I). In addition, price risks arising from open foreign currency positions, certain interest rate risks and other price risks must not exceed in the aggregate 42 per cent of the liable capital (Principle Ia). This limit system for market risks will be superseded by the new Principle I. Based on the relevant Basle and European provisions, banks (and other financial institutions) have to hold capital against the credit and market risks. The banking supervisors monitor the banks' liquidity on the basis of the Liquidity Principles II and III, which limit the extent of maturity transformation.

Apart from Principle I, other special provisions apply to *lending business*. A major provision concerns the incurrence of large exposures, such as the granting of loans which exceed 15 per cent (and, from 1 January 1999, 10 per cent) of the liable capital. An individual large exposure may not exceed 40 per cent (and, from 1 January 1999, 25 per cent) of the liable capital (there is a transitional period up to 1 January 2002 to enable compliance to be achieved). All large exposures, taken together, may not exceed 800 per cent of the liable capital. The legislators have defined certain decision-making, reporting and organisational requirements for such business and have imposed limits on the granting of large loans so as to ensure adequate loan diversification.

Loans to managers, etc., i.e. to persons or enterprises having close personal or capital ties with the credit institution, may be granted only on the strength of a unanimous decision by all managers of the credit institution, and only with the explicit approval of the supervisory body.

One important source of information, both for the banking supervisory authorities and for the lenders themselves, is the monitoring of loans of DM3 million or more by means of a central credit register pursuant to section 14 of the Banking Act. This section stipulates that credit institutions and insurance enterprises must report to the Bundesbank any loans granted by them or derivative transactions of DM3 million or more (the latter with their credit equivalent amount). On the basis of the reports submitted, the Bundesbank adds together the total indebtedness of each borrower on its credit register, broken down by credit category, along with the number of lenders involved, and in turn passes this information back to the credit institutions concerned.

Even though the task of processing the reports, which currently number approximately, 440 000 (the total volume of loans of DM3 million or more notified at the end of the first quarter of 1997 came to around DM7653 billion), with each quarter being relatively time-consuming for both the banks and the Bundesbank, it nevertheless provides credit institutions with valuable insights into the aggregate volume of and current changes in loans granted to any one debtor. However, in an era of growing internationalisation, the credit register suffers from the drawback that it is largely restricted to the national sphere. Nevertheless, as part of the international harmonisation of banking supervision laws, cross-border solutions are already being discussed, at least within the framework of European prudential legislation, and in a number of EU countries a first exchange of information is being carried out between the existing central credit registers.

Notable *organisational regulations* outside lending business principally include rules on the content and form of internal audits and the minimum requirements for the trading activities of credit institutions which, among other things, lay down additional qualitative requirements with regard to the banks' risk management.

Another instrument of supervision are the *returns and reports* which credit institutions have to submit continually to the Bundesbank and to the Federal Banking Supervisory Office. The banking supervisory authorities always proceed from the assumption that the data submitted are correct. It should be pointed out, however, that one of the tasks of external auditors is to check the accuracy and completeness of submitted reports. The reports concern lending business (such as the disclosure of large exposures) and Principles I to III, as well as certain personnel, organisational, legal and financial changes at banks (for example, the appointment of a manager, the establishment of a branch or the acquisition of a participating interest). Furthermore, each credit institution has to compile and submit a monthly return enabling the supervisory agencies to identify current changes in the banks' business activities. The data-gathering instruments also include a credit institution's annual accounts and various auditor's reports (audit of annual accounts, audit of safe-custody accounts, audit of the deposit guarantee scheme).

These data and reports form the basis for the decisions of the Federal Banking Supervisory Office. In this context the comments submitted by the Bundesbank are important since, owing to its local knowledge and its function as the central bank, it possesses an extensive insight into the banking industry. The Bundesbank usually acts as a filter which selects facts and figures of interest for supervision purposes and passes these on to the Federal Banking Supervisory Office. The bulk of all data relevant for prudential purposes is received and processed by the Land Central Banks.

One *important piece of information for (potential) bank customers* is demanded by section 23a of the Banking Act. A credit institution which is not a member of a deposit guarantee scheme must explicitly inform its non-bank customers of this fact.

Right of the Banking Supervisors to Request Information and Make Audits

The banking supervisory authorities are empowered to request information from a credit institution at any time on their own initiative. Pursuant to section 44 of the Banking Act, the Federal Banking Supervisory Office and the Bundesbank may demand information from credit institutions or their managers on all business matters and may also insist on the presentation of books and records. The Federal Banking Supervisory Office is further empowered to carry out audits of a credit institution even if there is no special reason for them. The Federal Banking Supervisory Office can also commission auditing companies or the Bundesbank to carry out such audits. The Bundesbank is regularly involved whenever banks' foreign exchange transactions are to be audited. In addition, the Federal Banking Supervisory Office is authorised to obtain cross-border information (in the case of internationally structured groups of credit institutions) and to carry out corresponding audits. Conversely, the Federal Banking Supervisory Office is required to assist, on request, a foreign banking supervisory authority domiciled in an EC member country within the legally defined framework.

Measures in Special Cases

As a necessary complement to the prudential functions described above, the Banking Act confers on the Federal Banking Supervisory Office sovereign powers of intervention in special cases in respect of credit institutions. Insufficient capital or liquidity can constitute such special cases. Other circumstances which can trigger such exceptional supervisory measures are the risk that a credit institution may fail to meet its obligations to its creditors or the threat of bankruptcy. The possible sanctions listed in the Act are graded according to the particular circumstances. They include limiting the size of dividend payments and loans, issuing instructions to the bank's managers, appointing supervisors, prohibiting the acceptance of deposits, imposing a ban on sales and payments, the dismissal of managers and – as the ultimate sanction – the closure of the bank.

If a bank becomes insolvent or overindebted, its managers must notify the Federal Banking Supervisory Office immediately. An *application to institute bankruptcy proceedings* in respect of a bank's assets can only be made by the Federal Banking Supervisory Office.

THE ROLE OF EXTERNAL AUDITORS IN IMPLEMENTING SUPERVISORY REGULATIONS

Auditors of credit institutions perform a dual function in Germany. On the one hand, they are appointed by banks to examine the annual accounts in accordance with the Commercial Code. On the other hand, they help to implement the prudential regulations by ensuring that these are complied with in the course of auditing the annual accounts of banks.

The supervisory bodies themselves do not perform on-site inspections except in the case of Model Testing and examinations of the Minimum Requirements of the Trading Business. They therefore rely on the reports and statements of private auditors. The minimum contents of the auditor's report are set out in the Auditor's Report Regulation to ensure that the banking supervisors are provided with sufficient information. Auditors are required to make detailed statements on the extent to which each credit institution has complied with the prudential regulations. One sanction which the Federal Banking Supervisory Office can use (preventively, if need be) is to reject the auditor chosen by the bank if he or she is deemed to be unsuitable.

Other statutory obligations apply to auditors of credit institutions. Thus, in addition to examining the annual accounts, they must also assess the credit institutions' 'financial circumstances'. Pursuant to section 29 of the Banking Act, auditors must immediately notify the Federal Banking Supervisory Office and the Deutsche Bundesbank of any developments or circumstances that come to light during the audit which might 'endanger the existence of the credit institution or gravely impair its development, or which indicate that the managers have seriously infringed the law, the articles of association or the partnership agreement'. This requirement confers a special importance on auditors and the audit associations of the banks as 'auxiliaries' of the banking supervisors. The banking supervisory authorities ensure the quality of audits and other reports by evaluating bank audits soon after they are made and by conferring with the responsible auditor in the event of missing or unclear statements.

DEPOSIT GUARANTEE SCHEMES

The system of banking supervision in Germany, based as it is on market principles, is necessarily complemented by deposit guarantee schemes in order to avoid any run on the banks in the event of the insolvency of a credit institution, and in this way to reinforce the stability of the banking system. If any bank in Germany is threatened with insolvency, the banking association to which that institution belongs is usually called in so that, in conjunction with the deposit guarantee scheme, the case in question can be dealt with as smoothly as possible, whether through the insolvent bank's take-over by another bank or through the liquidation of the institution and the payment of compensation to its creditors.

Virtually all credit institutions domiciled in Germany which conduct deposit business belong to one of the deposit guarantee schemes set up on a voluntary basis by the banking associations. The deposit guarantee schemes levy contributions from their members as an emergency fund for use in cases of distress. The deposit guarantee scheme established for the commercial banks aims primarily at protecting depositors in the narrow sense, as the collapse of the bank is taken as read. The schemes operated by the savings bank and cooperative bank sectors are designed to avert member institutions' insolvency and thus provide indirect protection to creditors.[3]

The Liquidity Consortium Bank also contributes towards depositor protection. It was set up on the initiative of the Bundesbank. It incorporates all the German categories of banks. The task of this special institution is to provide temporary assistance in the form of short-term bridging loans to banks which experience liquidity difficulties but which basically are sound. The aim of this assistance is to prevent chain reactions throughout the banking industry triggered by the insolvency of a bank which could also imperil sound institutions.

SUMMARY

The Germany banking system is one of the most stable in the world; it is internationally competitive and records high levels of earnings. To date there have been no instances in Germany of crisis-like developments, as have occurred in some other countries owing to speculative bubbles in the real estate or share markets, with serious repercussions for the entire economy.

Naturally, this positive overall picture is not ascribable solely to the banking supervisory authorities. It is probably due to a number of factors, including the orientation of the German banking system to the universal banking principle, the fairly conservative mentality of German banks and the early liberalisation of the German financial sector. On the whole, the German system of banking supervision has proved effective hitherto. This applies both to the division of labour between the Federal Banking Supervisory Office and the Bundesbank and to the introduction of measures aimed at regulating the banking sector.

This positive track record is an incentive to the banking supervisory authorities to continue to play their part in future in ensuring the stability of the financial system by means of rules and procedures which, while adequately covering risks, do not cramp the markets' style. The dynamic growth of financial markets and their global integration require some new qualities and thinking in quite different dimensions, including on the part of banking supervisors.

One example of this is the document submitted by the Basle Committee on Banking Supervision on the 'Amendment to the Capital Accord to Incorporate Market Risk'. However, here too the precept 'safety first' applies. That means that the quality of the risk models must be tested and guaranteed before they are put into practice. Enlightened banking supervisors keep an open mind on such new developments if they are conducive to enhancing the stability of the financial sector as a whole.

This stability of the financial sector as a whole is also promoted in the recent consultation document 'Core Principles for Effective Banking Supervision' issued by the Basle Committee on Banking Supervision. In this document 25 elementary principles are published, which must be fulfilled so that an effective banking supervision is possible. These principles reflect the fundamental standards necessary for an effective banking supervision in every country of the world.

Notes

1. The Second EC Banking Directive, the Own Funds Directive and the Solvency Ratio Directive were reflected in the Fourth Act Amending the Banking Act; the Consolidation Directive and the Large Exposures Directive were essential inclusions in the Fifth Act Amending the Banking Act, which came into force on 31 December 1995. The Capital Adequacy Directive and the Investment Services Directive will be translated into German law in the wake of the Sixth Act Amending the Banking Act, which is in legislative preparation. The Deposit Guarantee Directive, which has likewise been adopted by the EC, will be translated into German law in the coming Seventh Act Amending the Banking Act. The 'BCCI Directive', which was adopted in 1995, has already been largely implemented.
2. Although about 12 500 auditing companies exist in Germany, the work of auditing the annual accounts of credit institutions is confined to a relatively small group of 500 smaller and medium-sized firms and around ten large accounting firms.
3. See 'Deposit protection schemes in the Federal Republic of Germany', Deutsche Bundesbank, *Monthly Report*, July 1992.

7 Recollections of the German Treaty Negotiations of 1990[1]

Hans Tietmeyer

It was on the evening of 26 March 1990 that my telephone rang. The Federal Finance Minister, Dr Theo Waigel, was on the line. He came straight to the point. 'Mr Tietmeyer, we need you in Bonn again. It's an historic assignment. On behalf of the Federal Government, I would like to ask you to chair the negotiations on intra-German monetary, economic and social union, which are of such importance to our country.' I was greatly taken aback, and asked for 24 hours to think it over. It had been barely three months since I had moved from the Federal Ministry of Finance to the Board of the Bundesbank. On the one hand, of course, the assignment was tempting. On the other, I had to give due regard to the constraints imposed by my new position. I made a reply to that effect on the following evening. My agreement in principle was subject to certain conditions; I would be able to accept the assignment only if I could be temporarily released by the Bundesbank for the purpose, if the assignment would be subject to a strict time-limit, and provided that it did not conflict with my position at the Bundesbank. The decision on this would lie with the Bundesbank. The minister immediately contacted the President of the Bundesbank, Mr Karl Otto Pöhl. Just two days later the Central Bank Council approved a motion to this effect by Mr Pöhl, referring to the function of advising the Federal Government provided for in the Bundesbank Act. Following this, both the Bundesbank President and the Federal Finance Minister agreed that I would be seconded as the Federal Chancellor's personal adviser until the conclusion of the negotiations.

In a telephone conversation, the Federal Chancellor expressed his pleasure at the solution which had been found. A few days later he informed me during the course of a lengthy discussion in Bonn of his ideas on what the substance of the treaty should be and on the time-scale. The GDR's economic situation was, he said, so critical and the expectations of the people there were so great that the envisaged monetary and economic union would have to be implemented before the summer holidays. Political responsibility for the negotiations would rest with the Federal Minister of Finance; it was intended that I should chair the discussions of experts in preparation for the final political negotiations.

In order to document to the general public the fact that I belonged to the Bundesbank, the institution set up a provisional office for me at the Land Central Bank branch in Bonn. The office was to be headed by Mrs Habrunner, who has been my secretary for a good many years.

Although I had become quite familiar with basic issues of economic, monetary and social policy and their diverse international implications by virtue of almost 30 years of working, first of all in the Federal Economics Ministry and thereafter in the Federal Finance Ministry, as well as through a variety of international assignments, I had little experience up to that point of the GDR's economic and monetary policy and of dealing with its authorities. My work hitherto had principally been concerned with the Federal Republic's economic and fiscal policies, as well as with cooperation with other Western countries and international organisations. Intra-German issues and relations had not previously been among my immediate range of duties. For that reason, I had also never negotiated with GDR authorities until the Berlin Wall was breached. The first time that I came into contact with representatives of the GDR was at the beginning of December 1989, in connection with the negotiations on the restructuring of 'welcome' money, at which time I was still minister of state in the Federal Ministry of Finance.

Naturally enough, I had been paying keen attention to the political developments in the GDR, especially since the early Autumn of 1989. I well recall the annual meeting of the IMF in Washington at the end of September, during which a constant stream of new reports arrived on the growing number of refugees in the Federal Republic's embassies in Hungary, Czechoslovakia and Poland. After our return to Bonn we followed the escalation of developments from day to day with keen interest and concern. However, the hopes that the intra-German border would become more open and that there would be liberalisation were accompanied by growing worries as to whether there would be a peaceful solution, bringing greater freedom to the people of the GDR. I remember 9 November, the day the Wall was breached, especially vividly, even though I was able to witness events only on television. There was a spontaneous demonstration in the

Bundestag that evening, when the German national anthem was sung. From that date onwards, the political landscape in the GDR changed day by day, with the formation of the new Modrow government, the ten-point programme formulated by Chancellor Kohl, the resignation of Honecker's successor, Egon Krenz, and the creation of the round-table discussions, to mention just a few of the staging posts. At my official farewell as minister of state and long-standing 'sherpa' (commissioner for the preparation of the global economic summits) in the Palais Schaumburg on 20 December 1989, the Federal Chancellor had just returned from the remarkable gathering in front of the *Frauenkirche* in Dresden. This popular demonstration had made a very deep impression on him; the large crowd's call for unity had become increasingly vociferous.

The idea of a monetary and economic union between the Federal Republic and the GDR was being discussed ever more intensively in German politics as early as the turn of 1989/90. At first, however, the focus was on various types and forms of phased plans. At the Bundesbank, too, initial analyses and discussions had begun as early as January 1990. As in other specialist circles, these deliberations mainly concentrated on the possible ways of bringing the GDR economy and the GDR currency more closely into line with the West German economy and the Deutsche Mark in a phased process. The key factor in this was the prevailing expectation at that time that two German states would continue to exist for some considerable while. In parallel to the studies on the phased solutions that might be conceivable, initial consideration was also given as early as late January/early February, however, to the economic and monetary implications of the possibility that the GDR might be prepared to relinquish its economic and monetary sovereignty.

Above and beyond that, in other quarters, too, initial consideration was already being given to the still distant prospect of early political reunification. I still well remember, for example, a meeting of the *Kirche und Staat* (Church and State) discussion forum that was held in Cologne during the first few days of February with Mr Stolpe, who was consistorial president at that time, and a number of other church representatives from the GDR. Mr Stolpe first described the political and economic situation of the GDR from his point of view. In much the same way as some SPD members of the Bundestag, he urged a speedy monetary union (to be guaranteed by the Federal Republic), but with the GDR largely maintaining its sovereignty. A solution of this kind seemed to meet with a certain measure of sympathy, especially among the church representatives who were present. For my own part, I made it clear in the discussion that there could be no question of a 'monetary guarantee' by the Bundesbank as long as the GDR abided by the assumption of its sovereignty in monetary and economic policy. A rapid monetary union or – to be more precise – a rapid extension of the Deutsche Mark currency area to include East Germany would only be possible if the GDR were prepared to relinquish its autonomy in economic and monetary policy and to transfer these responsibilities to the appropriate bodies of the Federal Republic. At that time, Mr Stolpe and the other GDR church representatives evidently felt this to be impossible and unacceptable to the GDR government.

The surprising public offer of an intra-German monetary and economic union that was made by the Federal Chancellor on 6 February 1990 brought about a fundamental shift in the course of developments up to that point. In the light of the fact that the economic situation in the GDR was becoming increasingly critical, the Federal Chancellor (who had met the Prime Minister, Modrow, in Davos just a few days previously), after consultation with the senior members of the GDR coalition, offered a monetary union subject to the condition that the GDR would irreversibly adopt the policies of the social market economy and that the Bundesbank would be able to determine and control the circulation of money in East Germany. The Federal Minister of Finance had drawn attention to the possibility of such a model in a public statement just a few days before. After the Federal Cabinet had officially approved this offer in the presence of the Bundesbank President, Pöhl, it was submitted to Modrow during his visit to Bonn on 14 February. The reaction of the GDR representatives was unenthusiastic, however. The GDR government at that time was evidently not prepared to do more than engage in exploratory expert discussions. They were more interested in a stabilisation of the East German Mark by means of Bundesbank guarantees and, above all, in generous financial assistance from Bonn; but, without a prior agreement on the overall framework, this was something that was rejected by the Federal Government. The Modrow government was not prepared, however, to relinquish its monetary and economic sovereignty. In the debate in the Federal Republic, too, there were influential commentators at that time who voiced misgivings about the Federal Chancellor's offer. One only has to call to mind the Special Report of the Council of Economic Experts of 14 February, in which undue haste in monetary policy was described as an 'unsuitable course' and a 'misguided approach': a position that it, admittedly, later qualified and partially revised. Pöhl, too, had initially pointed to reservations from an economic point of view.

What became known as the 'expert talks', which followed the Modrow visit and which were held in February and the first half of March – headed on behalf of the Federal Republic of Germany by my successor in the Federal Ministry of Finance, the Minister of State, Dr Köhler, and with the extensive participation of the Bundesbank Vice-President, Dr Schlesinger – turned out, however, to be very useful for the later negotiations. At the very least, they played a major part in clarifying ideas and in the exchange of information and data. The overall outcome was that the West German participants began to realise ever more clearly that the GDR's economic and financial situation was far less favourable than had been assumed hitherto; this was due to the low productivity of its industry and agriculture, the heavy burden of debt being borne by enterprises and housing and the greater-than-expected external indebtedness.

The situation in the GDR changed fundamentally in political terms, however, following its first free elections on 18 March 1990. The surprising result made Lothar de Maizière the front runner for the office of the first Prime Minister of the GDR to be elected by a free Parliament. Above all, that accelerated the unification process, since the election results made it clear that there was a predominant desire among GDR residents for early economic and monetary union as well as political unity. In economic and monetary policy terms, it was now important to develop the previous expert talks between the Federal Republic and the GDR into substantive negotiations. In a total of three plenary sessions and various meetings of special working groups, there had by that time been success in elaborating an initial economic, financial and legal stock-taking; consultations on specific provisions of a treaty had not taken place, however, owing to the Modrow government's hesitancy and limited political authority. Such consultations were precisely what was now called for, however.

In view of his diverse international commitments, Köhler asked to be released by Waigel from his position as head of the West German delegation. Because of this, I was officially appointed head of the West German delegation by the Federal Chancellor at the beginning of April (after consultations in the coalition), and was entrusted with coordinating such preparations as were still required on the part of the Federal Republic. Three factors were of advantage to me in this work. First, besides the interim report with the stock-taking of the previous expert talks, a rough draft of the envisaged treaty already existed in the Federal Ministry of Finance. This rough draft was the outcome of intensive preparatory work by the responsible officials of the Federal Ministry and the Bundesbank under the direction of the Ministerialdirektor, Dr Bruno Schmidt-Bleibtreu. This was a valuable starting point for the ensuing discussions with the GDR delegation and our own continuing deliberations. Second, there was the additional fact that I was personally well acquainted with the senior staff members of the Federal Ministry of Finance and the other ministries and, on account of the many years I had worked in Bonn, I was familiar with the way the ministries in Bonn interacted with each other, and with the rules that had to be observed in that process. A third positive factor was the close personal cooperation with the Federal Chancellery from the first day onwards. I had known the head of the Federal Chancellery, the Federal Minister, Dr Seiters, for some considerable time, particularly from our weekly talks as ministers of state, and the responsible departmental head, Ministerialdirektor Dr Ludewig, had formerly been a member of my department in the Federal Ministry of Economics. In terms of professional skills and the personnel involved, everything needed for success was therefore already in place.

The substance and time-scale laid down by the Federal Chancellor formed the broad outline of the envisaged contractual agreements which I discussed during the first few days of April with Waigel and the staff members of the Federal Ministry of Finance. I also had in-depth discussions on specific individual questions that seemed important to me not only with Schlesinger and the staff members of the Bundesbank, but also with representatives of the other Federal ministries. The more deeply I became involved in the subject, the more sceptical I became at first as to whether it would be possible to keep to the time-scale envisaged by the Federal Chancellor. As he saw it, the monetary union was to come into force as early as 1 July 1990, a date that was also reflected in the East Berlin Coalition Agreement of 12 April for the new GDR government. In order to put an end as soon as possible to the disquiet that had arisen, above all among GDR residents, since the beginning of April, the Federal Chancellor was, in fact, urging that the conversion rates be fixed, if at all possible, as early as the beginning of May. Unrest and public protests had mainly occurred in the wake of a confidential statement by the Central Bank Council of 29 March, which was intended only for the Federal Cabinet, but had been leaked to the media and publicised. In that statement the Central Bank Council had advocated a general conversion of all debt relationships in the ratio of 2:1, but had considered a conversion of natural persons' savings deposits up to an amount of 2000 Marks per GDR inhabitant in the ratio of 1:1 to be acceptable. This statement generated a wave of protest among GDR residents, who demonstrated – influenced not least by a large number of election statements made by West German politicians belonging to both the coalition and the opposition – in favour of a general 1:1 conversion. This unrest in the GDR was fostered by prominent West German politicians at the time, going so far as to talk of a 'breach of promise' if the conversion ratio of 2:1 advocated by the majority of the Central Bank Council were to be implemented.

The Federal Chancellor reaffirmed his previous thoughts on the time-scale during the course of an in-depth discussion we had on 5 April. At the same time, he promised me all possible support in the talks and negotiations. In the ensuing coalition discussions it was decided that I would head the delegation, which would be composed as follows: the Ministers of State, Dr Klemm and Dr Köhler (Federal Ministry of Finance); the Minister of State, Dr von Würzen (Federal Ministry of Economics); the Minister of State, Jagoda (Federal Ministry of Labour and Social Affairs); and the Vice-President of the Deutsche Bundesbank, Dr Schlesinger. In addition, depending on the subject matter, ministers of state from other ministries were to be consulted. Thus, at a later stage, Dr Lautenschlager (Federal Foreign Office) and Dr Kittel (Federal Ministry of Food, Agriculture and Forestry) took part at times in the internal consultations of the West German delegation, as well as occasionally in the talks with the GDR delegation itself. Because of the increasingly obvious key significance of the legal issues, expecially with respect to questions relating to ownership, the Minister of State from the Federal Ministry of Justice, Dr Kinkel, participated at my request in nearly all of the later rounds of talks, and played an increasingly important role in them. Apart from the envisaged deadlines and the composition of the delegation, the coalition talks at the beginning of August, which were chaired by the Chancellor, included the discussion of a number of concrete issues; for instance, embedding the intra-German talks in the parallel two-plus-four negotiations being conducted by the Foreign Ministry, the regulation of Council for Mutual Economic Assistance (CMEA) trade, EC-related issues, problems of social policy, and questions of ownership. The details of the planned monetary union were set aside for the time being, however, especially what were known as the modalities of the conversion and the conversion rates.

After the senior coalition representatives had laid down initial basic guidelines for a number of topics, I had several detailed discussions in the next few days with Seiters and my former fellow permanent secretaries on the concrete strategy for the new round of expert talks and negotiations. These were concerned first and foremost with the possible substance and form of the envisaged State Treaty. In addition to the necessary monetary policy agreements (replacing the GDR Mark by the Deutsche Mark, specifying the conversion modalities and regulating the competence of the Bundesbank), my thoughts were aimed from the very first at laying down provisions for the future economic system of the GDR that would be as clear-cut as possible. This was because an extension of the Deutsche Mark area seemed to me to be acceptable only if the GDR largely adopted the economic system that had been tried and tested in the Federal Republic. Besides the incorporation of the main points into the treaty itself and the adoption of the most important Federal German laws, the concept of a 'guiding principles' law (based on Ludwig Erhard's model of 1948) as proposed by the Federal Economics Ministry seemed to me to be the right approach.

However, I was aware from the outset that transferring the relevant economic legislation would not, in itself, be enough. Agreements would also have to be reached on eliminating the internal and external monopolies and on the preconditions for developing competitive structures in the GDR. Apart from that, I did not like the term 'monetary union' very much as, in my view, it did not make the aim of the negotiations sufficiently clear. It was not a matter of merging two currencies but rather of introducing the Deutsche Mark and simultaneously abandoning the East German Mark, and thus of extending the West German currency area to the GDR. But in the run-up to the GDR elections on 18 March the term 'economic and monetary union' had already become so ingrained as a result of public statements made by the political parties that a change of terminology was no longer possible. The inclusion of the third element of the envisaged union, namely social union, was also firmly established politically. The later coalition partners had presented this tripartite monetary, economic and social union to the GDR electorate as a programme, and the voters had made their decision. It therefore came as no surprise that this 'three-dimensional' union emerged as a key point in the GDR coalition agreement of 12 April. From the very start, therefore, there was no scope, for political reasons, for deliberations on our part which were aimed at an initial postponement of the social union. I personally regretted this since a social union which developed gradually (in respect of labour and collective bargaining law, for instance) would probably have been better able to cushion the impact of some of the later economic shocks. All efforts to defer at least some parts of the highly advanced industrial and social legislation for a transitional period met with no success, mainly owing to diverse opposition and interventions on the Western side. It was also clear from the outset that the treaty would have to include provisions to protect the environment, although these should not be allowed to impede the necessary economic transformation process. Transitional arrangements for the GDR's commercial transactions with the CMEA countries were also obviously necessary. It was already apparent that the settlement system based on the transferable rouble was nearing its end, but, in the interests of both sides, it was crucial to find acceptable transitional arrangements. The USSR had made it known through diplomatic channels that it attached particular importance to appropriate provisions guaranteeing that existing arrangements would be respected.

Having collaborated for many years with the EC, I was fully aware of the extremely sensitive nature of all issues connected with relations between the two parts of Germany and our EC partners and the agencies of the EC. For that reason, I attached importance from the outset to the EC Commission, in particular, being briefed as fully as possible on the West German negotiating strategy. As early as 9 April, I travelled to Brussels with Dr Ludewig, a top ministry official, and explained our negotiating approach and strategy in a detailed discussion with President Delors and subsequently informed the *chefs de cabinet* of the responsible EC commissioners. We gave an undertaking to keep the Commission posted about the progress of the talks so that any conflicts with Community law and Community policy would be avoided from the outset. Jacques Delors, the President, was pleased by this, as was the Vice-President, Christophersen, who was responsible for economic and monetary policy in the Commission at that time, and to whom I spoke on the following day in Bonn. The practice of regularly informing the Commission was maintained subsequently and the permanent contact with the responsible directorates proved to be very useful. In this way it proved largely possible to avoid misunderstandings and to find a speedy solution to any problems that arose.

In East Berlin the negotiations on the formation of a coalition government were meanwhile well advanced. Following intensive talks, the CDU, CSU, SPD and FDP had largely come to terms on the basic elements of a coalition agreement. The first Prime Minister of the freely elected government was to be the candidate of the largest party in government, the CDU deputy, Lothar de Maizière. After consulting the Chancellor, I flew to Berlin before the coalition negotiations had been officially concluded in order to establish initial contact with the Prime Minister-designate. We met at the CDU headquarters in the Charlottenstrasse on 11 April, where an initial personal discussion between just the two of us took place. Mr de Maizière told me he agreed with the Chancellor that the economic, monetary and social union must come about as soon as possible. For my own part, I told him that I would do all I could to achieve a sustainable basis for the treaty as quickly as possible. But I added that, in the interests of both sides, the envisaged solution must not impair the stability of the Deutsche Mark. Besides economically acceptable conversion arrangements, the prime need was for an unambiguous ruling as to responsibilities for the Bundesbank's policy. In that very first discussion, I said that the involvement of the GDR Staatsbank, which he proposed, was unacceptable from the Bundesbank's point of view. The delegation of GDR representatives to the Central Bank Council was likewise out of the question as long as the two states were not united. Given the prevailing intra-German situation, the Central Bank Council thought it necessary to maintain its existing decision-making structures and to establish its own provisional administrative office in Berlin with around 15 branch offices in the GDR. Although Mr de Maizière noted this, he was clearly hesitant in responding. We agreed that this would have to be settled during the negotiations. When Mr de Maizière then mentioned the preparations for his government's policy statement, I urged him to include an absolutely candid analysis of the GDR's political and economic situation in that statement. I said that this would be the only way he would be able to defend himself in future against accusations that it was not the former system but the new policies that were responsible for the expected difficulties. Although he listened to this piece of advice, he did not act upon it in the way that I had imagined. With the benefit of hindsight, in particular, I regard this as a regrettable omission.

Just a few days later – on Easter Saturday – I again travelled to East Berlin with Dr Ludewig. Following a brief discussion alone with Mr de Maizière, there was a first in-depth substantive discussion with

Mr Krause and Mr Reichenbach. While Klaus Reichenbach was earmarked for the post of Minister attached to the Prime Minister's Office according to the coalition agreement, Günther Krause was to take on the role of the parliamentary state secretary with responsibility for relations with the Federal Republic over and above his key function as chairman of the CDU parliamentary group which, since the March election, was the largest government grouping in the GDR People's Chamber. I had taken some documents along to the discussion in which I had briefly listed what I regarded as the major benchmarks for the monetary union and the conversion rates. Using these papers, which were based on the figures of the overall monetary balance sheet of the GDR which had since become known to us, I tried to convince my discussion partners, in particular, that their aspiration to convert money balances in the ratio of 1:1 would lead to an unacceptable bloating of the money stock and would also lead to extremely high equalisation claims on the government. This was not easy for my two discussion partners to accept, especially since a commitment had already been undertaken in the coalition agreement to effect a conversion of this kind as well as a large-scale remission of enterprises' debts. Looking back, however, I am convinced that both men realised from that day onwards that a conversion of the entire money balances in the ratio of 1:1 and a simultaneous large-scale remission of enterprises' borrowing was out of the question. They did, of course, describe the expectations that had arisen in the East German population with regard to a general 1:1 conversion – especially in view of the election statements made by many West German politicians (though not the Chancellor) – and, in particular, they pointed out the problems that would be caused, especially for small savers, by a different conversion ratio. Furthermore, they declared emphatically that converting all current payments, especially wage and salary payments, in the ratio of 1:1 was vital (a notion which many politicians in Bonn likewise took for granted). In this discussion, Dr Ludewig and I pointed out the implications of such a conversion for the competitiveness of the already jeopardised GDR economy and for future employment. I therefore urged our partners to reconsider their position. Mr Reichenbach and, above all, Günther Krause (who even in this first talk was emerging increasingly as the spokesman) made it plain, however, that this position, enshrined as it was in the GDR coalition agreement, was of crucial importance for the GDR side. Nevertheless, I gained the impression that our arguments had provoked a degree of reflection on the part of Günther

Krause, in particular. We agreed to discuss these questions further in the delegation talks and negotiations that were to begin shortly. First of all, however, the Prime Minister had to be elected by the People's Chamber, and the new government in East Berlin had to be officially installed. Before the start of the talks, the new Prime Minister, Lothar de Maizière, wanted first to deliver his government's policy statement and to await the debate on it. This was scheduled for the week after Easter. It was not possible to put together the GDR delegation before that.

I myself used the Easter week to hold a series of individual talks with the leaders of the parliamentary groups in the Bonn coalition and with the relevant ministry officials in order to clarify the positions of the West German representatives for the subsequent talks and nego-tiations. Both Dr Dregger and Count Lambsdorff showed a great deal of understanding for the conversion arrangements felt to be necessary by Mr de Maizière's staff. It was already becoming clear to me in these discussions that most West German politicians in the coalition groups as well as in the opposition – as was confirmed to me in a number of discussions – took it for granted that there would be a large-scale conversion in the ratio of 1:1 and were scarcely able to conceive of any other solution. Even at that stage, I was forced to accept that there was hardly any chance of implementing the conver-sion of wages and current payments in the ratio of 2:1 as deemed necessary by the Central Bank Council for what, in my view, were convincing economic reasons.

Alongside the discussions on the possible conversion modalities, the consultation process on the draft treaty which had been prepared by ministry officials was stepped up in the week after Easter. At my suggestion, the head of the Federal Chancellery, Minister Seiters, invited the departments involved on 19 April to a preparatory discus-sion for the consultation with the Chancellor that was scheduled for the weekend. In the preliminary talks, which were attended by the ministers Genscher, Schäuble and Blüm, as well as the responsible secretaries of state, it became apparent that the 'elements of a draft treaty' prepared under the direction of the Federal Minister of Finance met with substantial approval. The preamble, which spoke of a first significant step towards the creation of national unity pursuant to Article 23 of the Federal German Constitution, was given a more precise form and reworded in the light of the two-plus-four talks, which were now being continued and led by the foreign ministers. At the time, the Federal Foreign Office was still afraid that the four partners would react negatively to an overly explicit reference to the goal of political reunification and accession persuant to Article 23 of the Constitution. Changes and reformulations were made on other matters, too. Two points from this discussion, in particular, have stayed in my memory: besides foreign trade, structural and agricultural issues, ownership problems were discussed for the first time. Even at that stage, it was becoming clear that this subject (on which there were differences of opinion within the Bonn coalition, too, at that time) was going to play a key role during the further course of the unification process. The second controversial subject concerned social affairs and labour issues. The discussion revolved, in particular, around whether it would be possible to transfer the Federal Republic's highly developed system to the GDR in one step without unduly hampering its economic development. I expressed my concerns in this respect at the time. At first the decision remained open, however.

These and other subjects were then discussed in greater depth the following weekend in ministerial talks at the Federal Chancellery chaired by the Chancellor. This was the first discussion of the basic approach to adapting the pension system in the GDR and to the possible ways of funding this. There was agreement from the outset that it was desirable to introduce the Federal German pension system as soon as possible. The Chancellor, in particular, was very keen for pensioners in the GDR (who, through no fault of their own, had been deprived of the fruits of their labour under the GDR system) to be able to share the advantages of the West German system in the near future. On the other hand, it was important to keep the associated financial expenditure within bounds. This discussion also brought to light some problems of compatibility in the area of pensions. In the GDR there was both a system of normal pensions and a special pension scheme for certain groups of persons. An arrangement of this kind contrasted sharply with our system in the West which mainly grants individual income and contribution-related pension claims. This subject was to play a prominent role in the later negotiations. In respect of ownership issues, it was decided that a distinction should be made between determining the future system of ownership in the GDR, on the one hand, and the restitution claims arising from expropriations, on the other. Whereas the former subject would have to be regulated as clearly as possible in the treaty, the latter would require further in-depth consultation owing to its highly sensitive nature both in the GDR and on the part of the Soviet Union, and on account of its constitutional implications. The Chancellor charged Dr Kinkel, then the Minister of State, with studying the issues connected with expropriations in the GDR.

In East Berlin the discussion on the government's policy statement had meanwhile come to an end. The new members of the government were now familiarising themselves with their new duties and posts. We therefore had to wait further in Bonn for the official start of the delegation talks and negotiations. The Chancellor thus asked Dr Schäuble to fly with me to see Mr de Maizière to discuss our future course of action.

In his book, *Der Vertrag (The Treaty)*, Dr Schäuble has reported on this discussion in the evening of 23 April in the Prime Minister's office in East Berlin (Schäuble, 1991). It became clear to me at this point that the new leadership in East Berlin was evidently only now beginning to recognise the full implications for the East German economy's competitiveness of the rapid conversion to the Deutsche Mark which they wanted so much. Up to that point I had assumed that those people who were so adamantly demanding an immediate monetary union with a general 1:1 conversion rate were – at least in basic terms – aware of the economic consequences of suddenly opening up their economy to competition on the world market. This was apparently by no means the case, however. At all events, the new Prime Minister expressed his concerns to Dr Schäuble and myself about the future competitiveness of the GDR economy. All this was nothing new to me. It had been clear to economists on the Western side, at any rate, all along that monetary union would, at a stroke, eliminate the existing sheltered areas for the East German enterprises, and that the outcome would be a radical restructuring with far-reaching implications for production and employment. While it is true that we in the West were largely unaware of the internal state of the GDR economy up to that point (the studies published by research institutes and other bodies were not very instructive), the many decades of isolation from the world's markets and political interference had inevitably led to waste and misallocation of resources on a major scale. However, even with a very different rate of conversion, it would only have been possible to cushion some of the impact of the radical adjustment given the very limited international competitiveness of East German products. In theory, the only solution would have been to maintain the intra- German border as a trade and customs border for years to come. This was precisely what Lothar de Maizière wanted to avoid, however, and precisely what the policy makers in Bonn wanted to avoid as well (for good political and also economic reasons, I believe). No one wanted a new Berlin Wall which – apart from everything else – would have created not only political but also economic uncertainty about the future.

It was thus in this discussion that Mr de Maizière more clearly broached the subject of financial assistance for the first time: a subject which was to play an increasingly important role later on. Furthermore, he informed us that he had meanwhile decided to appoint Dr Günther Krause, the parliamentary secretary and chairman of the CDU parliamentary group, as the leader of the GDR delegation. The then GDR minister of finance, Professor Romberg, who had chaired the initial expert talks on behalf of the GDR and also took part in some of these discussions, was clearly peeved. He had probably expected to be given that task himself, but had to accept the decision. Apart from that, the GDR delegation was to include the permanent secretaries and senior civil servants of the relevant GDR ministries (finance, economics, labour and social affairs) as well as a representative of the Staatsbank. Mr de Maizière agreed to start the talks and negotiations in two days' time in East Berlin. In preparation for this first round of talks I presented him with a working paper which contained the basic elements of the draft treaty we had drawn up. He promised to study this working paper carefully and to pass it on to the GDR delegation. On the return flight to Bonn, Schäuble and I were in agreement that a great deal of work would still have to be done during the official talks and negotiations that were about to begin to bring the prevailing hopes and expectations on the GDR side down to earth.

Two days later, on 25 April, the official talks between the two delegations began at the Prime Minister's official residence in East Berlin. Mr de Maizière, who himself opened the meeting, began by stressing the historic significance of the talks and negotiations that were now starting and then introduced the GDR delegation led by Günther Krause; its members included, in particular, the permanent secretaries Dr Walter Siegert (Ministry of Finance), Mr Alwin Ziel (Ministry of Labour and Social Affairs), Mr Wenzel and Mr Grabley (Ministry of Economics) and Professor Stoll (Staatsbank), who were later joined by other officials. Professor Kaufhold of the GDR Ministry of Agriculture, and Professor Supranowitz, the Prime Minister's authorised representative for talks on property issues, also took part in some of the subsequent talks.

The timetable and modalities of the talks were settled in this first discussion. We had also expected an initial general discussion on the substance of the envisaged State Treaty without, at that stage, going into the details. The GDR delegation was apparently not yet prepared for this, as I was soon to discover following the comments made by the leader of the delegation, Dr Krause, which were couched in very general terms. Günther Krause told me later that he had received our working paper from Prime Minister de Maizière only minutes before the start of the first round of talks. There was therefore only a very general exchange of ideas and a meeting that – from my own point of view – was not especially productive. For both delegations it was not much more than an opportunity to get to know one another personally. We nevertheless agreed to continue our talks in two days' time. As for the working paper which I had handed to the Prime Minister two days previously, I had deliberately chosen a form which, while it contained the first draft of the treaty that had been prepared largely under the aegis of the Federal Minister of Finance, left some points open. I was keen to avoid – or at least lessen – the impression of a *diktat* from Bonn which, unfortunately, had arisen in the preceding days as a result of the original draft unfortunately being leaked to the press. It was precisely for that reason, too, that (after consulting the Chancellor) I had handed the text of the working document to Prime Minister de Maizière two days previously. By doing so, it was possible to avoid an emotive reaction that might otherwise have occurred. Günther Krause told me later that the East Berlin side was glad to have been presented with such a draft text in that way.

In the second round of talks on 27 April 1990 (likewise held in East Berlin), there was a first reading of the draft treaty which had been submitted by us as a working paper. At the start of the talks, Günther Krause declared that the GDR representatives were able to accept the draft as a basis for the negotiations. There were, however, a number of amendments which they felt were necessary. He then presented a second working paper with relevant formulations. Already in that first reading, we were able to reach agreement on a number of amendments. The first of these was that the term 'social union' was included in the title of the treaty alongside 'monetary and economic union' at the request of the GDR side. We also reached agreement relatively quickly on new or amended formulations for a number of other points. Above all, however, we noted where the GDR delegation had additional wishes or material objections concerning the draft text we had prepared. These concerned the desire for an explicit recognition of 'common property in various forms', for instance, as this was consistent with the realities of the situation in the GDR (a notion that was unacceptable to us and which, for that reason, occupied us on several occasions in later rounds of talks). Furthermore, the GDR side was hesitant – evidently with regard to the ongoing talks in the GDR on a new constitution – about the commitment to a free, democratic and social system (with explicit reference to the Constitution of the Federal Republic) envisaged in the draft treaty. The GDR representatives also attached great importance to the treaty enshrining not only statutory provisions to be brought into line in the GDR but also changes in the Federal Republic. The GDR delegation, moreover, pressed – as Mr de Maizière had done previously in his discussion with me – for the Staatsbank to be involved as an intermediary and/or to be given its own executive function in currency-related matters. It became quite obvious even in this first round of talks that attitudes to both the social union and the settlement of financial issues were still some distance apart. The discussion of the currency conversion rates and modalities did not take place in this larger forum, however. Günther Krause and I had already agreed before this second round of talks that the discussion on this should be held only by a small group of central bank representatives and permanent secretaries (excluding staff members) as part of the next round of talks that was now scheduled to take place in Bonn. The Bonn talks had been agreed for the beginning of the following week.

There was still much to settle before then in Bonn itself, however. The possibilities and limitations of any compromise draftings of the treaty text were discussed in individual and group talks with the various departments. On the day prior to the round of talks in East Berlin, the head of the Federal Chancellery, Seiters, had already invited the heads of the state chancelleries of the Länder to attend an initial informatory discussion. It was on this occasion that I briefed the Länder representatives on the basic features of the treaty we had proposed. The Länder representatives expressed their gratitude for this information. In such a large forum it was not possible at that point to go beyond a general discussion of the substance of the treaty. If I am not mistaken, no one seriously expected more than this at that stage of the negotiations. Immediate Länder interests were not affected anyway in terms of the topics that were then up for discussion.

Very intensive discussions were taking place at this time in Bonn in preparation for the talks on the conversion rates. I had invited Dr Schlesinger and the permanent secretaries of the Federal Ministries of Finance, Economics and Labour who were directly involved to attend a confidential discussion in the late afternoon of Sunday, 29 April. We discussed the pros and cons of the various possible conversion rates once again very thoroughly. Dr Schlesinger and I, in particular, advocated a conversion of money balances and claims in the basic ratio of 2:1, a position which, later on, also gained political approval (albeit with generous exemption amounts and only after some resistance had been overcome). However, all those involved in Bonn regarded this solution as practicable only if significantly higher amounts than the 2000 GDR Marks mentioned by the Central Bank Council could be converted in the ratio of 1:1. As far as the conversion of current payments (wages, pensions, and so on), was concerned, there was a great deal of sympathy for the Bundesbank's position (which likewise advocated a 2:1 conversion), especially on the part of representatives of the Federal Ministry of Finance, the Federal Ministry of Economics and the Federal Chancellery. In the light of political opposition in the GDR and the public commitments made by leading government and opposition politicians in Bonn, however, conversion in a ratio other than 1:1 was considered unrealistic. This was a key point for Mr Schlesinger and myself, however, which we did not wish to give up just like that. Although the level of wages in the GDR was distinctly lower than in the Federal Republic, the differences in productivity between East and West were evidently greater still. Furthermore, it was likely that much of the industry in the GDR would increasingly become obsolete now that the Berlin Wall had been opened up, and that an incentive for new investment would have to be created. This was recognised by my former colleagues in the Federal Ministry of Finance and in the Federal Ministry of Economics as well as by Dr Ludewig. Nevertheless, they also regarded conversion rates other than 1:1 for current payments to be no longer practicable given the expectations that were already fairly entrenched in East Berlin and the prevailing political opinion in Bonn. In view of this situation, I proposed that at least wages and pension payments should be converted retroactively at their level on 1 January 1990. In this way, the sharp increases in wages in the first few months of 1990, in particular, would not be taken into consideration; they would have to be renegotiated and a new decision made on them. This idea met with quite some sympathy in this largely specialist forum. We agreed to explore this possibility further.

On the morning of the following day (30 April), the third round of talks with the GDR delegation began in the small cabinet room of the Federal Chancellery. For most members of the GDR delegation the setting was just as new as the one in East Berlin had been for us. In this round of talks, which lasted two days, considerable progress was achieved in the course of intensive detailed consultations. In a preliminary discussion, Günther Krause and I had agreed that the common guiding principle of our negotiations would be that the stability of the Mark must not be jeopardised. I am grateful that he accepted what was for me the basic orientation not only at the outset but also continued to acknowledge its validity during the negotiations whenever I referred to it. It was also important for me that he expressly reaffirmed this joint principle on repeated occasions before the television cameras.

In the plenary sessions of the two delegations, the main points of discussion were the sets of issues that were mentioned in the draft treaty itself. Besides the members of the negotiating delegations, other officials from the Ministries of Finance and Economics also took part in the discussions of the relevant issues involved. There was a new version of the draft treaty. The amendments agreed in East Berlin had already been incorporated; more extensive desired amendments, on which there was still no agreement, were placed in square brackets (in accordance with international negotiating practice). The points of contention related, in particular, to the preamble, the future system of ownership, the constitutional principles, the list of statutory provisions to be amended, relations with the CMEA countries, the structural adjustment of trade and industry and of agriculture, environmental protection, the system of labour law, the social security funds and, above all, the financial provisions. The discussions were particularly intensive and contentious in relation to questions of the labour, legal and social security systems. Whereas, following the GDR representatives' basic acceptance of the social market economy, the questions relating to the economic system – with the exception of the issues of ownership – were now mainly concerned with agreeing the precise wording, major differences in attitude were still apparent in this round of talks in respect of the labour, legal and social security systems. In particular, the then permanent secretary in the GDR Ministry of Labour and Social Affairs, Alwin Ziel, was emphatic in urging that at least some of the 'social achievements of the GDR' should be preserved and that they should be combined with, or added to, the regulations and systems obtaining in the West. Some part in this may well have been played by the fact that close contacts existed between his ministry and the opposition in Bonn. At certain points it was discernible that an attempt was being made to use the State

Treaty to influence the debate on social policy issues in Bonn in a manner that suited the opposition. Günther Krause, who was quick to realise this, made it clear that he was unable to support this course of action. Despite intense discussions, conducted on behalf of the Western representatives mainly by Mr Jagoda, who was a permanent secretary at that time, there were still many unsettled questions in that round of talks in the fields of labour and social law.

The problems of adjustment for agriculture and for trade and industry in the GDR posed by the economic and monetary union were also the subject of intense, albeit less contentious, discussions in Bonn at that time. It became increasingly clear to all involved that, with the removal of the economic border and the introduction of the Deutsche Mark, profound and far-reaching structural adjustment problems would arise in both areas. Following decades of isolation and politically-determined integration in the CMEA system, economic and monetary union would expose the GDR economy overnight to global competition and to the EC agricultural system. Furthermore, due regard would have to be given to the fact that responsibility for approving any support measures would largely rest with the EC. We therefore agreed to set up two special working groups which were to study methods and instruments for easing the structural adjustment of trade and industry, on the one hand, and of the agriculture and food industry, on the other. The two working groups were entrusted with drawing up a strategy within ten days.

In this Bonn round of talks there was, moreover, a fundamental debate on one subject that had evidently played a significant role in the East Berlin coalition discussions: the part to be played by private ownership in the new economic system and, in particular, the possibility of buying land. The GDR delegation had initially proposed that, besides private ownership, the phrase 'common ownership in various forms' should be included in the principles of the social market economy in Article 1 of the Treaty. With this formula, the GDR government evidently wished to enshrine the possibility of retaining so-called 'people's property', or national ownership, at least for a transitional period. This was unacceptable to us. Günther Krause evidently had fewer problems with this personally, but was under pressure in terms of the East Berlin coalition agreement. It only proved possible to come up with an appropriate wording for Article 1 of the State Treaty in the further course of the consultations, following lengthy and, on occasion, very animated discussion. In this round of talks, it was already becoming clear, however, that the other positions on the problem of ownership enshrined in the GDR coalition agreement would continue to cause considerable difficulties, especially the handling of the expropriations undertaken by the GDR state and the ban on selling land envisaged for a transitional period of ten years. The Chancellor had already informed me prior to this that Prime Minister de Maizière wanted, as far as possible, to maintain personal responsibility for this range of issues and did not want them to be settled in the State Treaty on Monetary, Economic and Social Union. The Chancellor had therefore asked Dr Kinkel, the Permanent Secretary, to negotiate on these issues with the Prime Minister personally or with his appointed representative in parallel with our treaty negotiations. As this group of issues touched, at least in part, on the substance of the treaty, however, I had agreed with Dr Kinkel that he would keep me constantly informed of his talks, which he did at all times. On the occasion of the official rounds of negotiations, we regularly conferred in detail in a small group on the progress of Dr Kinkel's talks, particularly as Mr Krause was very interested in this subject as head of the CDU parliamentary group in East Berlin.

Even during the initial detailed discussions on this set of issues, it became clear to me that the problem of ownership could become a stumbling block for the GDR's economic development. This was true not only of the restitution ruling for expropriations under GDR law that we on the Western side regarded as necessary, but also of the ten-year ban on land sales regarded as necessary by the representatives of the GDR. The hereditary tenancy right with the right of first refusal to purchase envisaged in the GDR coalition agreement could not be an adequate basis for the required investments, their funding, and the necessary provision of collateral for this. It was, moreover, obvious that only a speedy settlement of the restitution claims on property would be able to create the necessary basis for the investment decisions required on a broad front. We therefore discussed this subject often and in depth during the following weeks. I had doubts from the outset whether the principle of 'restitution instead of compensation' advocated by Dr Kinkel (no doubt with sound constitutional arguments) would be able to take adequate account of economic requirements. These issues were ultimately settled in direct negotiations between Mr de Maizière and/or his special appointed representative and Dr Kinkel, however; the result is enshrined in the joint declaration on the settlement of undecided property questions of 15 June 1990. Only the subject of private investors acquiring ownership of land was discussed further in the treaty negotiations. No agreement was reached in the first round of Bonn talks, however; only some model solutions were discussed.

Of particular importance during this two-day round of talks on 30 April and 1 May were the all-night discussions in a small group on the conversion arrangements for monetary union. The Chancellor had told me immediately after he had returned from his Easter holiday that everything must be done to put a speedy end to the speculation on the conversion rates. He therefore urged that an agreement on the benchmarks of the conversion arrangements be reached, if at all possible, by the beginning of May. After we had studied the various possibilities once more in the preliminary discussion within the West German negotiating delegation on Sunday, I prepared a draft that evening, together with Mr Ludewig, of the subsequent twelve-point declaration. On the basis of this draft we then discussed the points at issue in a small group with Mr Krause and Professor Stoll during the night of 30 April/1 May. During this discussion, it became clear for the first time that the GDR was no longer insisting on a conversion ratio of 1:1 for all private savings and on a sweeping remission of loans to GDR enterprises. Mr Krause signalled that he might agree to a general conversion of money balances and claims of 2:1, provided that persons permanently resident in the GDR would be able to change per capita amounts of at least 4000 to 6000 GDR Marks in the ratio of 1:1. This per capita amount was, additionally, to be on a sliding scale depending on age. For the amounts converted in the ratio of 2:1, savers were, nevertheless, to be granted a securitised right to a stake in state-owned assets. What was indispensable, however, was a conversion of 1:1 for all current payments such as wages, salaries, bursaries, rents, leases, pensions, and so on. In contrast to previous statements, this position signalled flexibility for the first time with regard to the conversion arrangements. In the long night's discussion we carefully went through all the details on the basis of a draft that I submitted for the declaration of the two governments. Decisions on our part could, in any case, only be taken in the coalition discussion scheduled for the following evening under the chairmanship of the Chancellor and attended by the President of the Bundesbank. Besides the conversion rates and the exemption amounts, two other points played a major role. At our insistence, Mr Krause ultimately agreed that the securitised right to a stake in the previous state-owned assets (which the GDR delegation regarded as indispensable compensation for 'nominal conversion losses' suffered by owners of financial assets) would only be considered if there was anything left after the state assets had first been used for the structural adjustment of the nationally owned enterprises and for replenishing the GDR state budget. Today, following the balance of the Treuhand agency's operations and the large losses that are becoming apparent, it is clear that the arrangement reached at that time no longer has any real basis in reality. The other contentious point concerned the per capita allowance from the state budget, envisaged in the GDR coalition agreement, to compensate for the termination of product and payment subsidies and the associated rise in consumer prices. By emphasising that all experience indicates it is impossible to eliminate a general subsidy of this kind once it is in place, we largely succeeded in defeating this proposal. Only in the case of recipients of low pensions and for students did the GDR reserve the right to compensate victims of social hardship.

On the evening of 1 May, I reported in the round of coalition talks chaired by the Chancellor on the progress achieved in the preliminary discussions on the conversion modalities, and submitted the draft for the subsequent twelve-point declaration that had been revised with Mr Krause. After a thorough discussion, the coalition forum consented to a general conversion of money balances and claims in the ratio of 2:1. The per capita amounts of cash and bank balances to be converted in the ratio of 1:1, called for by the GDR, were accepted as 2000, 4000 and 6000 GDR Marks, depending on age. There was likewise consent to the conversion of current payments in the ratio of 1:1, which the representatives of the GDR regarded as indispensable. My proposal to at least backdate this conversion to 1 January 1990 enjoyed initial support, but met with increasing resistance during the course of the discussion. Although the arguments put forward were mainly of a technical nature, such as a lack of documentation, complex conversion procedures and so on, there was, in truth, probably a belief that it would not be possible to force a conversion of this kind on the East German population. The participants in the discussion merely agreed to set 1 May 1990 as the reference date in order to at least remove the incentive for further increases in current payments up to the conversion deadline. Overall, the text we had negotiated for the joint declaration of the two governments (the twelve-point declaration) was approved by the coalition meeting with only a few minor stylistic amendments.

As had been agreed, I telephoned Mr Krause during the night to inform him of the outcome. This was because a cabinet meeting chaired by Mr de Maizière was due to take place in East Berlin on the following morning. During the course of the morning the news came that the GDR basically consented to the outcome set out in the twelve-point declaration. There was merely some telephoning back and forth, for which Dr Seiters had to be called upon, with regard to some of the wording. This mainly concerned the precise definition of the hardship compensation for specific groups of persons, which was deemed necessary by the representatives of the GDR. Parts of the GDR coalition wished to retain greater leeway in this respect. The text was nevertheless ready around midday. The GDR government and the government of the Federal Republic of Germany declared therein that the Treaty on Monetary, Economic and Social Union was to come into force on 1 July 1990 and specified the key points of the currency conversion on which the two sides had achieved agreement. In the early afternoon of 2 May, Seiters and I presented this declaration to the press in Bonn, who were evidently surprised by the speed at which agreement had been reached. A major breakthrough had been achieved with this twelve-point declaration. Whereas the response domestically – in both East and West Germany – was predominantly positive, there were a number of negative reactions, mainly in the international press. In contrast to Germany, abroad the conversion rates were mostly deemed to be too generous.

That same evening I flew to Berlin again, where a meeting of the Central Bank Council was scheduled for the next morning. At this meeting Dr Schlesinger and I informed the other members of the Central Bank Council of the details of the agreements made so far and of the stage that had been reached in the deliberations on the text of the treaty.

The fourth round of talks between the two delegations began in East Berlin on the afternoon of 3 May. The focus this time was on the preamble, articles on the political and legal framework, environmental issues and social policy. Before this, however, there had to be a definitive settlement of the question of how the Bundesbank was to exercise its competence in the GDR in future. A decision was becoming increasingly urgent in view of the short period of time left until 1 July as well as the necessary technical and organisational preparations for the currency conversion and the subsequent exercising of the Bundesbank's functions. In the Bundesbank's opinion, involving the Staatsbank, which Mr de Maizière had proposed during our first discussion, was out of the question. Along with other colleagues on the Bundesbank board, I had had considerable misgivings from the outset about an arrangement of this kind. On account of my experience of the various authorities concerned, it was obvious to me that involving an existing administrative body could – intentionally or unintentionally – easily create fissures. As experience shows, changing the direction of a long-standing administrative body by issuing directions from above is invariably a protracted process. We were therefore bound to insist that the Bundesbank be allowed to set up its own organisation in the GDR so that it would have full operational capability from the very first day of monetary union. Although this position had been noted by the representatives of the GDR, they had not yet made a definitive statement on it. In this round of talks – and in the presence of my fellow Bundesbank board member Mr Gaddum, who was standing in for Mr Schlesinger – I therefore restated the Bundesbank's requirement in the form of a definitive demand. For Professor Stoll (Staatsbank), in particular, this must have been an unpleasant situation, since the Staatsbank must, naturally enough, have been hoping that it would be involved. When Mr Krause realised that this point was not negotiable from our point of view, he acquiesced and consented to the Bundesbank establishing its own structure. I assume that he had consulted Mr de Maizière on this point beforehand. I was aware that, for the GDR side, this was a major yielding of sovereignty. They would have to accept a Federal authority setting up its own branches on their territory and exercising its powers there without the GDR having any kind of veto.

At that moment, if not before, it became obvious to all those involved that the road to German unity could only be a short one in political terms, too. We were unable to accept the proposal put forward by the GDR delegation in this discussion to set up a number of Land Central Banks on the territory of the GDR immediately, the presidents of which were then to become members of the Central Bank Council. As long as there was no unity at the state level, there could be no GDR involvement in appointing the governing bodies of Federal authorities. We therefore agreed to set up a 'provisional administrative office' in East Berlin, to be headed by a member of the board of the Deutsche Bundesbank. The provisional administrative office was to be able to establish up to 15 branch offices on the territory of the GDR. The Staatsbank was to provide the appropriate buildings for the provisional office itself and for the branches. In this agreement there was general unanimity that a provisional arrangement of this kind would exist only until political unity had been achieved. After that, a permanent Bundesbank structure comparable to that of the West German Länder would have to be found (an arrangement that was subsequently enshrined in the second State Treaty). At the request of the GDR delegation, however, the Bundesbank consented at that time to considering, as far as possible, applications from former Staatsbank staff in setting up the administrative office and the branches. The selection of personnel was to remain solely a matter for the Bundesbank, however.

This agreement on 4 May was especially important and urgent because it was only from that day onwards that the Bundesbank was able to undertake the concrete technical and organisational preparations for the currency conversion and the establishment of the administrative office and the local branches. The logistical plans that had already been prepared at the Bundesbank now had to be implemented within a period of just over six weeks. The only way to master this demanding task was the 'sponsorship solution'. In other words, the Land Central Banks in West Germany adopted responsibility for the individual East German branches and ensured that they were equipped with staff and material as well as supplied with currency. The Land Central Banks and their presidents performed this task with great dedication. This was the only way in which this gargantuan logistical task, which later earned praise from many quarters, could be accomplished without major upsets.

A number of individual statements were revised or amended during the second reading of the draft treaty, which began following the agreement on this issue. Several points of special political significance were also discussed, however. It was thus possible to achieve substantive agreement with the GDR delegation on the wording of the preamble that had been revised together with the Federal Foreign Office, subject to the concluding talks scheduled for the next few days as part of the two-plus-four talks. Besides the positive reference to the 'peaceful and democratic revolution' in the GDR in the Autumn of 1989, the GDR delegation was particularly keen to stress that the creation of the monetary, economic and social union represented 'a first significant step towards the establishment of national unity pursuant to Article 23 of the Constitution of the Federal Republic of Germany'. In this way its close connection with the establishment of national unity was to be made clear and the road to accession pursuant to Article 23 of the Constitution firmly established. Following the Federal Foreign Minister's (Genscher) announcement of the successful conclusion of the two-plus-four talks a few days later, this part of the text was to stand definitively.

In these Berlin talks, an agreement was reached on the formulation of the principles determining the social market economy. The GDR delegation had initially wanted to have 'common ownership in various forms' mentioned in addition to private ownership, whereas we rejected any mention of the term 'common ownership'. It was therefore only following lengthy discussion, in which Dr Kinkel was intensively involved, that we arrived at an agreement. The words 'common ownership' were not mentioned. Nevertheless, a form of wording was included to the effect that 'the statutory authorisation of special forms of ownership for the participation of public authorities or of other legal entities in economic transactions is not excluded', a formula which was in full conformity with existing law in the FRG. Overall, it was possible to agree on a text for Article 1(3) which, for the first time, officially enshrined the social market economy as the common economic system of both parties to the treaty, thus giving it a semi-constitutional reinforcement, a fact that was acknowledged in appropriately positive terms by a number of experts in subsequent political commentaries.

A lot of time was also taken up, in particular, by discussion of the necessary legal adjustments within both the GDR and the Federal Republic. The specific legislative changes that were necessary had to be listed and studied in the envisaged schedules to the treaty, a task that could be mastered only with the intensive cooperation of the responsible departmental officials and of the Federal Minister of Finance, in particular. It was especially important from my point of view that, following in-depth consultation, we were able to agree on a joint protocol of principles in the discussion of the negotiating delegations itself. These enshrined the basic guidelines for economic, legal and social policy by analogy with Erhard's Law of Basic Principles of 1948. I personally argued most vigorously in favour of this protocol of principles.

Some difficulties arose in this round of consultations in the discussion of various aspects pertaining to the constitution. Up to that point, the GDR delegation had been reluctant to accept an express reference to the provisions of the West German constitution and to formulate specific constitutional changes for the GDR. The underlying reason for this reluctance was evidently the constitutional debate within the GDR itself, where – triggered by the draft constitution of the Round Table – there were deliberations on a new GDR constitution or a revision of the West German constitution pursuant to Article 146. Apart from these questions of principle, the GDR delegation also had particular misgivings about some of the specific wording we had submitted.

I especially recall the concern that was expressed several times that there would be a large-scale influx of persons of German descent from Eastern Europe if the GDR were to be 'placed under an obligation' – as envisaged in our draft – to allow unrestricted immigration, as far as possible, for all Germans. We subsequently agreed on the formula 'freedom of movement for Germans in the entire currency area' which, of course, implicitly embraced the immigration of Germans from eastern Europe via the Federal Republic. The discussion on environmental protection was also striking. Whereas our own draft tended to be criticised in West Germany as being not far-reaching or detailed enough, it went too far, if anything, for the GDR delegation, or at least in terms of its substance. It was feared that an immediate transfer of the safety and environmental protection regulations applying to new plants and facilities in the Federal Republic would represent too great a burden on enterprises. We succeeded in convincing the GDR delegation, however, that, for the continued operation of existing plants and facilities, the requirements in question would not have to be met immediately but only 'as soon as possible'. Since both sides – irrespective of the material issues – wished to give greater weight in the treaty to environmental protection in the broader sense, we agreed to revise the text once more for the concluding round of negotiations.

In this round, too, the discussions on the principles of the social security system were particularly difficult and contentious. At the centre of the discussion this time were, on the one hand, the future organisational structure of the social security system and, on the other, the exemption from liability to social security contributions for the self-employed. Despite in-depth deliberations, no agreement was achieved in this round of talks. Regrettably, this was also the case for the principles of the institutional organisation of health and pension insurance. There were still a great many unsettled questions on that score for the concluding round of discussions scheduled for the following week. On the late afternoon of 4 May, we ended this round of talks and flew back to Bonn from Berlin-Schöneberg in a Bundeswehr aeroplane with the West German delegation, which included a large number of officials from various departments.

There was a great deal of work waiting in Bonn, for the negotiations were to be concluded, if possible, in the coming week. On the Saturday and Sunday a series of bilateral and multilateral preliminary talks took place to clear up specific points in the light of the latest stage reached in the negotiations. Besides the difficult problems of social security and labour law already mentioned, these mainly concerned problems of structural policy, the future of the Treuhand agency and questions of financial assistance. To these was added a political hot potato: the prevention of fraud with regard to the currency conversion. It was this subject, above all, which proved to be a particularly thorny one, since the Bundesbank (especially Professor Schlesinger) refused – with good reason – to burden the process of currency conversion, and hence the Bundesbank agencies and banks involved in it, with excessive controls. On the other hand, it was, of course, a very sensitive matter politically. The responsible Federal departments on the West German side as well the GDR government wanted to take precautions against the conversion process being abused either by individuals or political institutions in order to gain an unfair advantage. After much toing and froing, an agreement was reached later on in the concluding round of talks that a special regulation should be included in the provisions on monetary union and the currency conversion, under which the government of the GDR was to ensure that its criminal prosecution authorities would be able to examine and, if necessary, freeze accounts in cases where there were adequate grounds for suspicion. Working closely with the Federal Minister of Justice and the GDR Ministry of Finance, the Federal Ministry of Finance prepared a specific procedure for scrutinising conversion balances. The particular details of this were no longer a matter for our negotiations on the treaty, however.

On Tuesday, 8 May, at the request of Dr Dregger, I presented a summary, at the meeting of the CDU Bundestag group, of the stage the treaty negotiations had reached. The many questions and comments showed that the Members of Parliament were extremely interested in this information. Although there were also a number of critical comments on individual points, the line of the negotiations up to that point met with general approval.

The Chancellor had issued an invitation to detailed talks within the coalition government for the following day (9 May). All the main questions that were still unsettled and the future time schedule were discussed on the basis of the paper prepared by Dr Ludewig and myself. The coalition group gave its approval to the submitted compromise formulae on the majority of passages in the text that were still unsettled. There were some discussions of a very fundamental nature on a number of issues, however. One discussion which I vividly recall arose following a short report by Permanent Secretary Kinkel on the parallel talks he had been conducting on the unsettled issues relating to ownership claims. Dr Kinkel first made clear that the GDR government was not prepared under any circumstances to reverse the expropriations that had been undertaken under the Soviet law of occupation between 1945 and 1949. The key factor in this was the intervention of the Soviet government, on the one hand, and concern about public order in the GDR in the light of the new structures of ownership which had arisen in the interim and their utilisation. Despite some objections – especially from the FDP – Dr Kinkel stressed that he saw no possibility of changing this position. As to the expropriations that had occurred under GDR law after 1949, he vehemently supported the principle of 'restitution instead of compensation' and said that there could and must be no other solution despite potential economic as well as political problems in the GDR. Dr Kinkel gained the coalition's consent to this position. I have already mentioned my own misgivings about that decision, even though I had a lot of sympathy for that line on the basis of free market philosophy, of course. Negative feedback was evidently needed first in order to arrive later on at the prioritising of investment.

Another subject that played a major role in this coalition meeting were the GDR's external relations and other commitments (the payment of costs for the stationing of Soviet troops, for example). There was unanimity that the external commitments *vis-à-vis* the CMEA countries within the transferable rouble system should, as far as possible, be maintained. It was already becoming apparent, however, that the system of the transferable rouble was to cease by the end of the year along with the CMEA itself. The conversion rate for the transferable rouble into Deutsche Marks from 1 July 1990 onwards had to be settled without delay, however. The coalition meeting consented to a conversion in line with the general conversion rate of 2:1, which meant a change in the rate of the transferable rouble from 4.67 per GDR Mark to 2.34 per Deutsche Mark. In subsequent talks in Moscow Mr Krause won the Soviet side's consent to this, even though, he informed me, this was achieved only following tough discussions. As the costs of stationing Soviet troops were still to be met by the GDR at that time, an arrangement between the Federal Republic and the GDR was not necessary. It was not until the second State Treaty and the accession of the new Länder to the Federal Republic that this question would be settled at the level of the Federal Republic. By contrast, it was decided in the coalition meeting that the holdings of the Soviet troops in the GDR in GDR Marks were to be converted in line with the general conversion ratio of 2:1. In order to counter abuses by individual members of the Soviet army, the coalition meeting gave its approval to the involvement of the Soviet troops' field bank, in line with a proposal made by Professor Schlesinger and myself, based on discussions with the Staatsbank and the GDR Finance Ministry. In this way it was possible to solve the thorny problem of alleged 'black market money' being exchanged by individual soldiers and officers.

The coalition meeting also discussed the question of the structural adjustment of business enterprises and of agriculture in the GDR. The reports of the working groups that had been set up had not yet been submitted, however. The meeting therefore dispensed with a thorough discussion of the details. A critical reception was rightly given to the proposal to levy import taxes for a transitional period on a number of goods on a graduated scale, or to introduce commercial protective measures with quota limits, which the GDR Ministry of Economics had meanwhile brought into the discussion. The Federal German delegation was asked to discuss this range of issues again thoroughly with the GDR in the concluding round, but to reject administrative and fiscal protectionist measures. The unresolved issues relating to the social union and labour law, some of which were of a quite fundamental nature, were also discussed in this coalition meeting.

The following timetable was laid down for proceeding further: the next (and, it was hoped, concluding) round of negotiations between experts was to take place the following weekend. Before that, however, the chairmen of the responsible Bundestag committees, the representatives of the Länder chancelleries and the Bundestag committee on 'German Unity' were to be informed of the progress achieved in the discussions. Following the concluding round of negotiations at expert level, the negotiations with the GDR were to be officially concluded during the following week by a final round at ministerial level, so that the signing of the Treaty could be scheduled for Friday, 18 May 1990.

This very ambitious timetable determined the framework of the concluding negotiations. From now on, the countdown was running for the concluding round. My next few days were filled, first, with giving informatory talks at various meetings with representatives of the Bundestag and the Länder, and, second, with the concrete preparation for the concluding fifth round of talks at the weekend. The marathon round began in Bonn on Friday, 11 May at ten o'clock in the morning and ended well after midnight on Sunday. I had already agreed with Mr Krause by telephone that – with the exception of settling the financial issues, which were to be reserved for the ministers of finance – we would have to arrive at a definite outcome in these talks. First of all, the preamble, the basic articles and the provisions on monetary union were dealt with in a third and final reading. Happily, there was no need for lengthy deliberation on these points. In terms of the actual issues, there was also no longer any animated debate on environmental protection. With comparatively few difficulties, we agreed on the basic substance of the environmental protection article which, in addition to the GDR's specific commitments, was to list the basic principles held by both parties to the treaty. Mr Krause agreed to adopt the term 'environmental union' that was desired by environmental politicians in Bonn. The definitive wording of the environmental article remained open, however, as I had not yet received approval from the Ministry of the Environment. We agreed to coordinate the final text by phone during the next few days.

There was a particularly intensive and, at the same time, difficult discussion concerning the issue of 'structural adjustment of enterprises'. The working group which we had set up under the direction of the two economics ministries had submitted a written report on this subject. The report studied the methods and instruments which might facilitate the structural adjustment of enterprises to the conditions of the social market economy during a transitional period. The outcome of this took the form of proposals by the working group for fiscal and financial measures to promote investment generally, selective measures for enterprises capable of being restructured, measures for re-skilling, training and further training, measures for creating an economic infrastructure in line with market conditions, and temporary preferential treatment in awarding public orders; all of these measures were subsequently put into practice with the assistance of the Federal Government (although, in most cases, this was only after political union had been established). The discussion within our circle concentrated mainly on the question of whether (and, if so, which) trade policy measures might be considered. The GDR Ministry of Economics wanted to introduce protective measures for its own economy, at least for a transitional period; under consideration were import quotas or levies, or import duties on various graduated scales according to the type of goods. The intention was to make it easier for East German enterprises to adjust to the new competitive conditions.

Despite all the free market arguments which militated against it, I regarded the basic idea behind the proposal of an import duty for a limited period as being not entirely unreasonable, as this was, in fact, an attempt, to correct what was obviously too favourable a conversion rate for wages. Two points appeared to cause particular difficulty, however: first, the GDR side was considering the imposition of import duties only on selected individual goods and by different amounts. On the other hand, I was unable to imagine how it would be possible to monitor this without retaining customs clearance at the old intra-German border. We discussed these two points, in particular, at some length, without reaching an ultimate agreement. The more we went into the details of this proposal, the clearer it became that measures of this kind could scarcely be put into effect without maintaining intra-German border controls. The GDR delegation decided to forgo a decision on this measure – at least in connection with the drafting of the treaty – but reserved the right to continue negotiating on this point with the Federal Ministry of Economics and to come back to it at a later date (after 1 July). For the treaty, we agreed on a procedural rule. The GDR government undertook to reach agreement with the Federal Government before introducing structural adjustment measures. The fact that detailed structural adjustment measures were not laid down in the treaty itself was later heavily criticised by the opposition. For my own part, I remain convinced that the treaty would have been overburdened if such measures had been included. What was crucial was that it established the principles to be observed for structural adjustment measures and a procedure for agreeing on the concrete formulation of the measures.

There was a similarly difficult discussion in the concluding round on the subject of adjusting the agriculture and food industry to the conditions of the social market economy and to EC market regulations. An expert group – in this case under the direction of the Ministries of Agriculture – had submitted a written report on this range of issues, too, which dealt, in particular, with price reform, the external protective system, intra-German trade and the adjustment measures considered necessary from the experts' point of view. This report indicated the methods and instruments which were to assist the fundamental reorganisation of the agriculture and food industry and its integration into the West European system. The data on the requisite financial assistance in this report were especially detailed and generous; it was evident that the GDR agriculture experts had been very quick to learn from the practice of their West German counterparts. Following in-depth discussion and consultation, we concentrated for the treaty only on formulating the basic strategy deemed necessary by both sides and on establishing the principles.

The actual implementation of the transitional solution and the financial assistance, however, were left – as in the case of the structural adjustment of enterprises – to a subsequent agreement between the two governments.

The concluding discussion on the social union, too, was especially arduous and tough. This had to do not only with the already problematical arrangements for the social security funds and health care, but also with labour and collective bargaining legislation. The GDR had, in fact, abandoned its original ideas of maintaining some special GDR labour regulations for a transitional period, and had declared its willingness to adopt the Federal Republic's system of labour law; with a view to the difficult transition period of the next few years, however, we had suggested temporarily permitting certain exceptions in the case of termination procedures and expressly allowing for the possibility of in-house agreements on wages for a transitional period in addition to collective pay agreements. West German union leaders had obviously found out about this. At any rate, there was an intervention at the Federal Ministry of Labour and at the Federal Chancellery. It was evident that there had been controversy on this within the GDR government, too. At all events, in the final round Günther Krause declared very forcibly that, in the light of the objective of achieving full political unity in the near future, even limited-period special arrangements were unacceptable, however justified they might be in economic terms. I personally regretted this sharp reaction. In my view, the process of structural adjustment in East Germany would have been made easier by such transitional regulations for a limited period.

There were, however, to be tough negotiations in the final round, too, in the field of social security: the influence of West German advisers from some Länder ministries was clearly discernible in the GDR position. To the last there were heated discussions, especially on compulsory social security contributions for all, possible exemptions, the authorisation and establishment of occupational pension schemes, the retention of minimum pensions, the authorisation of private health insurance enterprises and of new health care structures. We owe the fact that we arrived at a joint outcome in the end mainly to Günther Krause, who repeatedly urged his delegation to reject special arrangements for the GDR. His basic approach was that the GDR wanted early political unity and therefore wished to adopt the regulations of the Federal Republic. It should be mentioned in this context that Jagoda, the Permanent Secretary from the Federal

Ministry of Labour, did not give way during the many hours of difficult negotiations, and resolutely upheld the Federal Government's position.

In that final round we had an intensive discussion for the first time on finance, an area which came within the remit of the permanent secretaries Dr Klemm and Dr Siegert. Although we had, naturally enough, already discussed the general principles of fiscal policy and tax policy and – for me sometimes surprisingly – achieved a large measure of agreement, I always had considerable doubts myself whether the speedy construction of a tax and fiscal administration and the immediate application of the highly complex West German tax law, to which the GDR side had consented, would be possible. In the meantime, however, the representatives of the tax department of the Federal Ministry of Finance had achieved a large measure of agreement on all these issues with the representatives of the GDR Ministry of Finance. Although my doubts were registered, there was a belief that it would be possible to overcome the problems following a comparatively brief period of transition. Up to that point the arrangements concerning the GDR's borrowing, the allocation of debt and the Federal Republic's cash transfers had been excluded from the negotiations. I had informed Mr Krause that these parts could only be settled definitively in the concluding negotiation between the two ministers of finance. After Waigel had presented his ideas during the last coalition meeting and these had met with basic assent, however, Dr Klemm was now in a position at least to present the broad outline and structure of the arrangement envisaged by the Federal Government. The plans of the Federal Ministry of Finance amounted to laying down the borrowing authorisations of the GDR central, regional and local authorities in the treaty itself (including the assumption of guarantees and other warranties), and to make any excess spending dependent on the consent of the Federal Minister of Finance. The debt incurred by the central budget of the GDR at the time of the subsequent political accession was then to be offset against the assets administered by the Treuhand agency or apportioned to the Federal Government and the new Länder on a fifty-fifty basis. In addition to this, substantial financial assistance to the GDR was to be stipulated in the treaty itself. These proposals were not new for Dr Siegert (from the GDR Ministry of Finance) since in-depth discussions had already been held on this between the two ministries of finance, on which I had, of course, regularly been kept informed. In the negotiations between the delegations we were, in the final analysis, only able to take note of this; the relevant decisions had to be taken by the ministers of finance in the concluding negotiation.

There was another especially difficult point to settle before we could conclude our expert talks, however. Although there was agreement that there should be a separate joint declaration on the settlement of the unresolved property claims, which could not be included in the treaty, and on which Dr Kinkel was conducting parallel negotiations with the authorised representative of the GDR Prime Minister, an arrangement had to be found for the treaty itself by which, first, those state-owned enterprises that were to be converted into incorporated companies would be provided with state-owned land, and, second, private investors would be given previously unavailable opportunities of acquiring ownership of land. On the occasion of our concluding talks we negotiated very thoroughly and at great length – with some degree of dispute, too – on the provision which, in the concluding phase, was attached to the treaty as Annex IX. In particular, this was a matter of placing the GDR under an obligation to ensure that land actually could be bought for job-creating investments when the treaty came into force. The leasehold arrangement with a right of first purchase, as hitherto envisaged by the GDR coalition, would not be enough to attract investors and provide them with opportunities of securing collateral for borrowing. It was only after very intensive consultations that we succeeded in finding a solution which, in my view, was of crucial significance for the ensuing period. We agreed – subject to the consent of Mr de Maizière – on a text which enshrined the GDR's commitment to provide pieces of land in industrial areas in sufficient number and size which could be acquired as property by investors to create industrial estates and for other job-creating investments (with a binding commitment to use the land for the agreed purpose). Furthermore, the state-owned land used previously by enterprises was to be transferred to the new incorporated enterprises. Deeds of sale for land were to include generally accepted market clauses on subsequent price reviews and any necessary adjustments. Consenting to this arrangement was not easy for Günther Krause, although he was fully convinced personally that these measures were necessary. This was because he had to win over not only the Prime Minister in his own government but also all the other groups who had stipulated a different arrangement in the coalition agreements. He therefore had no other choice than to accept this text only provisionally at first. Above all, he had to leave open the question of whether this wording should be included in the text of the treaty or in the later joint declaration on unsettled property claims.

After we had clarified this point within the small group, we studied and discussed the entire text of the treaty once more in the plenary session of the two delegations in a kind of final reading. Happily, we were able to note that we had achieved full agreement at expert level on the text of the treaty, apart from the final wording which still had to be decided of the environmental article, the two financial articles 27 and 28 (the negotiation of which was to be reserved for the ministers of finance), and the special political proviso on the acquisition of land. It was with satisfaction and sincere gratitude to all members of the delegation and staff members, some of whom had worked day and night, that Mr Krause and I were able to see the conclusion of our work early on Sunday morning. The ministers of finance would now have to conduct the final negotiations; and the governments would then have to take the overall political decisions. As we toasted the success of our work and expressed our common desire that this treaty, over and above the economic and monetary areas, would also be a crucial step towards political unity, all those involved on both sides of the table sensed that, together, we had collaborated on an historic task.

During the course of the day (Sunday, 13 May), I was able to inform the Chancellor of the conclusion of our talks and the results achieved. He was very pleased with the overall outcome and warmly expressed his gratitude for the excellent work as a whole. On the following Monday I flew to Berlin to take part in the finance ministers' discussion in the eastern part of the city.

In a preliminary discussion on the Federal German side under the chairmanship of the Federal Minister of Finance, Theo Waigel, together with the two Länder finance ministers, Mr Schleusser (North Rhine-Westphalia) and Mr Tandler (Bavaria), there was an exchange of views at the Permanent Representation of the Federal Republic of Germany in East Berlin on the general line to be adopted in the concluding financial negotiations. Mr Waigel presented his plans on the scale of financial assistance from the Federal Republic and on the subsequent allocation of the GDR budget debt, which met with the approval of the two Länder representatives. In the following discussion with Romberg, the GDR Minister of Finance, and his staff members in the office of the Ministry of Finance in East Berlin (in front of which a large number of representatives of the media had gathered), Professor Romberg's guarded attitude to the whole treaty again became apparent. It was quite obvious that he did not like the

idea that a great many of what he felt were the GDR's social achievements would now be thrown overboard. His ideas were evidently
directed first, more towards receiving much greater financial assistance from the Federal Republic than that offered by the Federal
Minister of Finance and, second, towards retaining greater autonomy
for fiscal and social policy in the GDR. Nevertheless, he ultimately
had no other choice than to reconcile himself to the plans submitted
by the West German representatives. As talks in Bonn were still to
take place – in particular, between the Federal Government and the
Länder – a definitive outcome was not yet possible on that day,
however. During this discussion, I once again became fully aware of
how important it was that the chairmanship of the expert talks on
behalf of the GDR had been in the hands of Günther Krause. In
contrast to him, Professor Romberg was obviously less convinced of
the urgent necessity of political reunification.

On the following day (15 May), the whole text agreed in our talks
was again submitted to the coalition meeting in Bonn for political
approval. In the meantime, the three points that still remained open
had been resolved to the extent that it was possible to incorporate
them into the text. First of all, the environmental article that had still
been unsettled up to that point had been reworded and approved by
East Berlin. Furthermore, Prime Minister de Maizière and the other
representatives of the GDR coalition had given their approval to the
text on the acquisition of land for industrial estates and other job-
creating investments as well as to adopting this text as an annex to the
treaty (Annex IX). Apart from that, the substance of the financial
Articles, 27 and 28, had been specified in the talks between the finance
ministers. The whole text – apart from the concluding negotiation on
the financial articles – was in its final form. I informed the coalition
meeting of the latest amendments to the text of the treaty itself and
pointed out that the bilateral talks on details of the provision on
fraud, as envisaged in Annex 1, Article 9 of the treaty, as well as on
the still-unsettled property questions would be continued, but that
their outcome was not to be included in the treaty. Following this
report, the coalition meeting gave its approval to the overall text
submitted and congratulated us on the outcome. The Chancellor
once again expressed his particular gratitude to all those involved
and stressed the historic significance of this work. Thus Waigel then
informed the cabinet meeting of his concrete plans for the ensuing
negotiations on the finance chapter. Among these, he mentioned the
establishment of a German Unity Fund, which had since been

discussed with the finance ministers of the Länder, and which was to
be financed by capital market funds, with half of its debt service to be
raised by the Federal Government and half by the West German
Bundesländer. There was no objection to this from the representatives
of the coalition parties who were present.

For the next day (16 May), the Chancellor had invited the prime
ministers of the Länder Governments so as to inform them of the
progress achieved in the negotiations. At this conference the Federal
Minister of Finance also presented his strategy for setting up the
German Unity Fund. The premiers gave their approval to this
arrangement, particularly as they saw this as a limitation of the
Länder share in funding assistance to the GDR. As far as the text
of the treaty itself was concerned, there were no substantive objections
on the part of the prime ministers at this conference. There were some
inquiries as well as critical comments (with regard to the rather vague
outlines of the structural adjustment measures and the formulation of
the Treuhand arrangement), but I am unable to recall any vehement
opposition.

On the afternoon of the same day there was a meeting of the
Bundestag Committee on German Unity. Seiters and I explained the
outcome of the negotiations up to that point and the overall thinking
behind the treaty. At that meeting, too, there were a number of
specific inquiries and critical comments; all in all, however, it was
possible to sense that the general assessment was a positive one.
Whereas the representatives of the coalition parties received the overall outcome in positive terms, the representatives of the opposition
parties were still very reserved. A heated debate was going on at that
time, especially within the SPD, on whether to approve the treaty or
not.

The official concluding discussion between the finance ministers
took place on 17 May at the Federal Ministry of Finance in Bonn.
Waigel once again presented the figures he had given in East Berlin a
few days earlier for the borrowing authorisations for the central,
regional and local authorities of the GDR and the Treuhand trust
fund for 1990 and 1991 and, at the same time, stated that he was
prepared to consent to the borrowing limits being exceeded in the
event of a clearly greater need, pursuant to Article 27. Furthermore,
on behalf of the Federal Republic, he announced that he was prepared
to place at the disposal of the GDR use-related cash transfers of
DM22 billion for 1990, and DM35 billion for 1991. In addition to
this, the Federal Republic would provide an initial injection of funds

for social security purposes. The GDR Minister of Finance, Professor Romberg, acknowledged the Federal Republic's generous transfers that were announced, but simultaneously made it clear that the need was likely to be greater. He nevertheless consented to the proposed draft of the finance articles, 27 and 28. With that, the last undecided point in the treaty text was finally settled. The two finance ministers were thus able to pass on the treaty texts for approval by the two cabinets.

On the morning of Friday, 18 May, the two cabinets in Bonn and East Berlin first of all gave their official approval to the texts of the treaty.

This was followed by the formal signing of the State Treaty at the Palais Schaumburg in Bonn on the afternoon of the same day. The GDR cabinet chaired by the Prime Minister, de Maizière, arrived by specially chartered plane in Bonn around midday. In the early afternoon, the treaty was signed by the two finance ministers before a large international press contingent and in the presence of the whole Federal Cabinet and the leading representatives of the Bundestag. Following this, the Chancellor first delivered a solemn declaration, in which he described the signing as 'an historic moment in the life of the German nation' and called upon all Germans in the east and in the west to create 'a united Germany in a united Europe'. Lothar de Maizière took up this idea in his declaration and stressed that on this day 'the actual achievement of Germany's unity' was commencing and that monetary, economic and social union would make the 'unification process irreversible'. The treaty was a 'good and well-balanced entity'. Both heads of government thanked their delegations and their leaders.

The concrete deliberations began the following week in the German Bundestag. At the request of the Chancellor, I assisted Seiters in the following weeks during the discussions in the Bundestag and with the Länder at numerous meetings. Despite political controversies, the overall concept of the treaty was being received in increasingly positive terms.

Besides this, in the weeks following the signing of the treaty, I dealt more intensively with the subject of the Treuhand trust fund. We had already touched on this subject repeatedly during our discussions and negotiations on the treaty. It had then become increasingly clear that this institution would have a key role to play in reorganising the GDR economy. The agency for administering state-owned property (Treuhand agency), which had been established by the Modrow government with effect from 1 March 1990, would have to have its range of responsibilities redefined and be given a new structure. Hitherto, it had been no more and no less than a central economic administrative body which had branched off from the ministries and which, moreover, was still largely managed by the ministries' former officials. Mr Krause and I readily agreed that the Treuhand agency would have to be radically reorganised with a primary remit to carry out privatisation. In the treaty itself, however, we were only able to enshrine the general thrust of the GDR's economic policy; for the time being its specific implementation remained a matter for the GDR. Mr Krause nevertheless asked us to assist the GDR government and him personally in the preparation of a new trust fund law. This was an awkward task given that there were still very different points of view within the GDR coalition at that time. The coalition agreement had contained the idea of retaining the Treuhand agency for the time being as a holding company for the GDR's enterprises and assets and, essentially, of privatising only this holding company by issuing free share certificates to the general public. We quickly reached agreement with the GDR delegation and with Mr Krause, in particular, that it would not be possible to create competitive and independently operating corporate structures in this way. Primarily, this could only be accomplished by privatising the individual enterprises. Even at that time, however, there were already many commentators who – at least in a number of cases – wanted to give priority in terms of timing to restructuring over privatisation.

At our delegation talks, we had agreed at the beginning of May that the responsible officials of the Federal Ministry of Finance and of the Federal Ministry of Economics would establish contact with their counterparts in the GDR ministries and assist them in preparing the legislative amendment needed to transform the Treuhand agency. In the second half of May, we then coordinated our proposals at permanent secretary level in a discussion in Bonn. Following this, several drafts for the revised version of the Treuhand law were sent to Mr Krause. It was evidently not easy, however, to get this new approach accepted in East Berlin. At all events, it took a few weeks before the new Treuhand law was finally passed in mid-June by the People's Chamber in East Berlin. Not long after the signing of the State Treaty, I informed the Chancellor that I would have to return to Frankfurt in the near future and therefore soon have to end my special advisory function. At the beginning of June I made a formal request to him to be relieved of my advisory duties as soon as possible so that I would be able to resume my work on the board of the

Bundesbank. Although he indicated that he would also like me to act as his adviser for the pending negotiations of European monetary union, he realised that neither this nor continuing my advisory duties for intra-German economic relations was compatible with my post in Frankfurt. After taking my official leave of him a few days later, I was able to resume my duties at the Bundesbank in Frankfurt in the second week of June. At the same time, the temporary office which had been set up in Bonn was closed.

All in all, it was not only the often hectic pace of work that characterised the 2 ½ months in Bonn and Berlin; it was also a period of great challenges and fascinating experiences. In a very short space of time, something was created with the State Treaty for which there had been no model, but which brought about the breakthrough for the political negotiations on the second State Treaty that soon followed. This achievement was only made possible by the great dedication with which all involved gave their whole energy. Working day and night, a treaty was prepared which – despite all its imperfections and even misjudgements – laid part of the essential groundwork for overcoming the division of Germany. The responsible politicians confined themselves to laying down its broad outlines, and left the formulation and negotiation of the details largely to the expert negotiations. I believe that this division of labour had a positive effect on the result. Certainly, it will still take some considerable time to overcome fully the more than 40 years of division and separation in Germany. This represents an enduring challenge and obligation for all Germans. The State Treaty on Monetary, Economic and Social Union established the initial legislative basis for this difficult process and laid the contractual foundations for the restoration of German unity in peace and freedom. The process of unification thus became irreversible.

Note

1. These are personal recollections which were written down largely from memory, using my appointments diary and selected texts.

Reference

1. Schäuble, W. (1991) *Der Vertrag – Wie ich über die Deutsche Einheit verhandelte* (*The Treaty – How I Negotiated on German Unity*), Stuttgart, p. 99 ff.

8 German Unification: A Personal View

Norbert Kloten

The offer came as a complete surprise. Until 6 February 1990, when the Federal Republic issued its offer to the GDR to form a monetary, economic and social union, both sides had assumed a step-by-step adjustment by East Germany, with the economic shock being cushioned by an appropriate exchange rate policy, and support from Bonn. Indeed, on the very day of the offer, when the heads of the Bundesbank and the GDR's National Bank (Staatsbank) were meeting in Berlin to discuss forms of monetary cooperation, and just before Bundesbank President Pöhl and his deputy Helmut Schlesinger learned of the offer, Pöhl dismissed a monetary union as 'premature and quite unrealistic'. A few hours before that, even the Federal Minister for Economic Affairs had been discussing a three-stage plan produced by his Ministry for a currency and economic union which envisaged 'tying the GDR Mark [M] to the Deutsche Mark [DM]' in the second phase and the creation of a 'common standard currency' only in the third. The Sachverständigenrat (Council of Economic Experts) warned Chancellor Kohl on 9 February that monetary union should not be placed 'at the head of the list'. But, as I myself pointed out in a cabinet meeting of the State Government of Baden-Württemberg on the evening of 5 February 1990, there was no alternative to a monetary union. The demand by the people of East Germany for the Deutsche Mark as a symbol of West German economic power and prosperity, combined with the breakdown of the East German regime's capacity to take any effective action, left no room for new reform programmes on the latter's part. Seen in this light, the Government's offer was clearly politically motivated.

Its acceptance by the Modrow administration of the GDR a few days later made it evident that East Germany's transformation to a market economy would be a unique one.[1] All the other former people's republics and successor states of the Soviet Union were compelled to change the inherited central planning system at their own discretion, with their own directives and on their own. The German

110

attempt, however, made the success of the monetary union and the process of unification a responsibility of the Federal Republic from the very beginning.[2] In this case, monetary union – a misleading term – signified nothing other than an expansion of the area in which the West German currency circulated as legal tender to include the GDR. The intention was to replace the East German Mark by the Deutsche Mark, maintaining unrestricted validity for all West German legal and institutional regulations. This required only the setting of a conversion rate between the two currencies along with the appropriate organisational and technical preparations, as well as efficient management of monetary policy by the Bundesbank.[3]

WHICH RATE?

The question of the appropriate conversion or readjustment rate was central to the public discussions from the start. However, finding this rate proved difficult. A joint commission of experts, with Helmut Schlesinger (then Vice-President of the Bundesbank) as its intellectual leader, proved unable to solve the problem. The East German parties at the negotiating table were willing to come half way, but saw themselves as representatives of a central bank which they expected to merge sooner or later with the German Bundesbank. Moreover, their arguments were influenced by the way of thinking and experience of life in the GDR. Some information was withheld, other items were glossed over.

Nevertheless, the commission managed to draw up a (much revised) draft of a 'Consolidated Balance Sheet of the GDR Credit System' before concluding its activities prior to the elections to the People's Chamber on 18 March 1990. The balance sheet reflected conditions in a centrally administrated economy. The National Bank of the GDR was at the same time a bank of issue, a refinancing institution for banking institutions, a centre of credit, the central computing agency of the economy, the organ responsible for monetary and lending policies, and a commercial bank (for example, it lent to industry and commerce).

The 'Consolidated Balance Sheet' included all assets and liabilities of the GDR's credit system. Some of its entries were surprising, notably the 'liability reserves for a slope coefficient' (*Rückstellungen für Richtungskoeffizienten*), about which nothing had previously been known in the West. The 'slope coefficient' was an exchange rate used for internal conversions between imports and exports. From 1988 onwards, importers had to pay a duty of M4.40 for every DM of imports (previously M2.20). On the other hand M4.40 were credited for each DM of export revenues.

In accord with the official exchange rate, the Deutsche Handelsbank (German Bank of Commerce) exchanged each Deutsche Mark required for imports against M1.00, and in the case of exports supplied M1.00 against each Deutsche Mark of export earnings. The difference of M3.40 received from importers appeared in the accounts of the Staatsbank as liabilities reserves and were then used to subsidise exports to the extent of M3.40 for each Deutsche Mark of export earnings.

Since imports from the West exceeded exports to it by an ever increasing margin, a countervailing item for foreign debt emerged in the GDR. In the final 'Consolidated Balance Sheet' of 31 May 1990 it was shown as M96.4 billion. In the decision-making about the conversion rate, however, this 'liability slope coefficient' for the readjustment rate did not really carry much weight. Other aspects predominated.

At first, it was thought that current exchange rates (either those which had been determined administratively or those which had been reached on the market) could be used as a guide. Upon closer inspection, however, they proved unusable. It was not clear what the value of credits extended to the GDR economy would be worth under the conditions of a market economy. The balance sheets of companies in Deutsche Marks were not yet available (and would provide innumerable shocks). Prices had been manipulated, and subsidies had distorted price structures. The GNP, about 10 per cent of West Germany's, reflected the general situation in COMECON; worker productivity was initially estimated at 40 per cent, then at 33 per cent, and before long at only 25 per cent of that in the West. Although an overhang of purchasing power clearly existed, it remained indefinable. The stock of real capital and the buildings and machines were superannuated.

A more or less arbitrary conversion rate was unavoidable, focused especially upon the market (real) value of the assets and liabilities of the Consolidated Balance Sheet. Most of the entries of this Balance Sheet would shift depending on the selected conversion rate. For instance, a conversion rate of two GDR Marks for one Deutsche Mark would mean a major cutback in credit extended to domestic borrowers (especially in the areas of 'enterprise' and 'housing'), while the same conversion rate would cut the value of current and savings accounts to half of their previous value. A more favourable conversion rate for these deposits would result in an asymmetrical rate for assets and liabilities and consequently in unsettled balances. A conversion rate for assets of M2: DM1 and for liabilities of GDR M1: DM1 – one of the alternatives discussed – would lead to an 'active countervailing position', requiring matching funds from the Federal Government.

The situation was further complicated by the fact that a change-over rate had to be found not only for stock variables but also for flow variables, such as wages and retirement pensions. Was it better to select one and the same rate, or to apply two different ones?

The goal was to limit the expense of readjustment for the Federal Republic, the legal successor to the GDR, and to make the increased stock of Deutsche Marks after the change-over consistent with the target of monetary stability. After deliberating with great thoroughness and much controversy, the Bundesbank's Central Bank Council finally recommended a single change-over rate of M2 : DM1 for both stocks and flows.

EXPERTS DIVIDED

The discussion inside and outside the Central Bank Council made it clear how little sound knowledge was available about conditions in the GDR and how poorly prepared the West (not to speak of the East) was to solve problems arising from a change to a new system within the former Socialist Bloc. The Academic Advisory Council of the Federal Ministry of Economics, of which I am a member and which had a far-reaching influence on the discussions on regulating inter-German relations with its bellwether report of December 1989 ('Economic Policy Challenges of the Federal Republic in Relation to the GDR'), also found itself deeply divided on the issue of the correct conversion rate. At the end of March 1990, the Council finally recommended by a majority vote, but with the greatest caution, a differentiated conversion rate of 2:1 for stock variables and 1:1 for flow variables.

THE CASE FOR A 1:1 CONVERSION RATE FOR FLOWS

With all due loyalty to the Bundesbank's Central Bank Council, I personally pleaded strongly and in direct contact with the Federal Chancellery that flows should be converted at par. With a conversion rate of 2:1, compensatory payments would have been unavoidable due to the intolerable results (as low as DM650 gross monthly pay for the vast majority of blue-collar and even white-collar workers). This was generally conceded even by those who advocated a 2:1 conversion rate. The results would have been incomprehensible to all concerned. Employees in the GDR would have felt that they had been 'taken to the cleaners'.

Moreover, wage levels would be determined in the employment market from day 'X' on. (In fact, after 1 July 1990, employers and workers struck agreements which very quickly drove wages up far beyond productive work levels). In my judgement, both economic and political considerations supported a 1:1 change-over.

MOST SAVINGS ACCOUNTS HELD BY SMALL SAVERS

Everything depended on the acceptance of the new order by the citizens of the GDR. This point of view, as well as demands of social justice, also prompted me to argue for a graduated conversion rate for stock variables. Statistics on the structure of savings deposits became available only at a very late point. They showed that some 70 per cent of accounts (having a 10 per cent share of total deposits) were in the form of small savings deposits, of up to M5000. Savings accounts with between M50 000 and M500 000 or more constituted only 2.1 per cent of the accounts but about 25 per cent of the total stock of savings deposits.

This indicated an enormous divergence in the formation of savings deposits, even remembering that many citizens of the GDR carried more than one savings account book in their pockets. In addition to advocating a partial change-over for savings balances (no monetary capital accumulation in the Western sense existed in the GDR), I also supported the view that freedom to dispose of larger Deutsche Mark deposits at will should be limited at first, and that part of the new deposit balances should also be linked as far as possible to a transfer of assets from the hands of the state into the private sector. As it later turned out, this would have been difficult to achieve.

A POLITICAL OPTION

Helmut Kohl, the Federal Chancellor, who was kept up to date on the controversy and the differences of opinion, had already recognised the political explosiveness of the conversion rate; he held out the prospect of a conversion rate of 1:1 for wages and for small savings deposits even before the campaign for the People's Chamber began. The international treaty of 18 May 1990 between the GDR under Lothar de Maizière and the German Federal Government under Chancellor Kohl set 1 July 1990 as the target date for the currency substitution and stipulated that all flow variables would be exchanged at a ratio of 1:1, and stock variables at a ratio of 2:1. Certain amounts of savings deposits were exempted from this and were scaled according to specific groups of persons at a rate of 1:1. The average conversion rate was 1.81:1, and in fact turned out to be only 1.6:1 after the elimination of pure accounting positions in the 'Consolidated Balance Sheet', in particular the liability reserve for a slope coefficient. The active countervailing item amounted to DM26.4 billion.

M3, defined by the Bundesbank as the money supply to be used for outlining its goals and consisting of the sum total of currency in circulation, demand deposits, time deposits with a duration of up to four years, and savings deposits with statutory periods of notice, rose by 14.7 per cent instead of the originally expected 10 per cent. However, a partial braking influence by the subsequent formation of money capital was anticipated, and this turned out to be the case.

AVALANCHE OF DEBT

Many financial burdens devolved upon the Federal Republic due to the conversion rates chosen; these, however, were mainly due to the desolate conditions prevailing in the GDR as well as to the enormous increase in wages and the rapid and open-handed transfer of West German social safeguards to the new federal states. An avalanche of new debts resulted from the enormous financial transfers from West to East Germany, from the initially nonchalant attitude of West German governmental units, particularly the Länder, toward their spending (as if there had been no such thing as reunification), and from the government's inability to bring the excessive federal subsidies under control. The total indebtedness of governmental agencies rose from about DM960 billion at the end of 1989 to more than DM2 trillion in 1995. State spending as a percentage of the national product via taxes levied by the federal government, the states, and the municipalities, as well as duties levied for social security (the so-called 'Staatsquote'), grew from around 46 per cent to just over 53 per cent (see Table 8.1a).

Financial transfers to the new federal states totalled, for example, DM640 billion between 1991 and the end of 1994. Revenue shortfalls were also incurred due to investment subsidies and special depreciation allowances. Tax returns are to be deducted from this.

Table 8.1a   German public sector deficit (DM billion)

Year	Revenue	% of GDP	Expen- diture	% of GDP	Deficit	% of GDP	GDP
1990*	1094.3	45.11	1124.4	46.35	−30.1	1.2	2426.0
1991	1343.5	47.08	1452.1	50.89	−108.7	3.8	2853.6
1992	1502.8	48.86	1621.1	52.71	−118.3	3.8	3075.6
1993	1564.5	49.54	1693.7	53.63	−129.2	4.1	3158.1
1994	1670.9	50.32	1775.9	53.48	−105.0	3.2	3320.4
1995	1737.5	50.25	1860.0	53.80	−122.5	3.5	3457.4
1996	1744.5	49.27	1879.0	53.06	−134.5	3.8	3541.0

*Former FRG (old Länder only)
Source*: Deutsche Bundesbank, *Monthly Report*, various issues.

Table 8.1b   The Credibility bonus: foreign financing of the deficit (DM billion)

Year	Net Borrowing Total	% of GDP	Net Borrowing from Foreigners	% of Total	% of GDP	GDP
1990*	111.9	4.61	15.1	13.49	0.62	2426.0
1991	106.3	3.72	50.9	47.90	1.78	2853.6
1992	106.8	3.47	73.3	68.64	2.38	3075.6
1993	154.6	4.89	109.0	70.51	3.45	3158.1
1994	85.8	2.58	−20.9	x	−0.63	3320.4
1995	97.6	2.82	58.3	59.70	1.69	3457.4
1996	124.2	3.51	54.1	43.56	1.53	3541.0

*Former FRG (old Länder only).
Source*: Deutsche Bundesbank, *Monthly Report*, various issues.

FALSE EXPECTATIONS OF RAPID GROWTH

The real situation stood in stark contrast to the overoptimistic expectations at the beginning of the reunification process. How is this to be explained?

First, many observers, especially neo-liberals, overestimated the strength of forces making for faster economic growth after the introduction of free market mechanisms. They took as their model the first months and years after the German currency reform (the work of the Allies) along with the suspension of economic controls in broad areas of the economy by Ludwig Erhard (June 1948). Premature analogies were used to create expectations of high growth rates, sharp increases in labour productivity, and a spontaneous dedication to productive work by the citizens of the GDR. In a study commissioned by the Federal Government (March 1990), for instance, the opinion was expressed that the transition to a free market economy would not necessarily involve 'painful sacrifices in prosperity'.

The hopes for a speedy recovery of the GDR's economy underrated – and this is the second major reason – the effects of the legacy of 'Real Socialism'. In 1990, when the Privatisation Trust Fund (*Treuhandgesellschaft*) was established, a privatisation surplus of DM60 billion was forecast. In fact, the Trust left DM250 billion in debt behind. Essentially, the economy of the GDR, like that of other Central and Eastern European economies, was on the brink of bankruptcy. As a result, both the extent and the duration of the required adjustments were underestimated.

This was aggravated by a third factor: for all practical purposes, the unique German strategy of transition made it impossible to prepare for the new situation in advance. The initiating factor in the processes of adjustment was the substitution of the Deutsche Mark for the GDR Mark, together with the simultaneous enthronement of West German prices and quality standards, as well as Western technical and economic norms.

On 'day X', 1 July 1990, fundamental economic realities were transformed practically overnight, together with the circumstances of each and every individual. The stock of real capital was largely invalidated, and hundreds of thousands of jobs became obsolete. Professional abilities, training and experience became more or less useless. The infrastructure was in a deplorable condition. Sins of the past against the environment could no longer be ignored. Hopelessly overstaffed public administrative organs found themselves confronted with tasks for which they were unprepared. Events then gained tremendous momentum and were not free from undesirable side-effects.

Well into the first months of the monetary union, Chancellor Kohl continued to put his confidence in the optimistic preliminary forecasts. This explains his assurances to his compatriots in the East that everyone would be better off after reunification. This also explains his repeated rejection of additional taxes as a prerequisite for reunification. He was supported in this position not least by organisations from the business community as well as by the German Council of Industry and Commerce (*Deutscher Industrie- und Handelstag*). There was a general reluctance to countenance any measures that might endanger the corporate tax reforms already approved by the coalition government in Bonn.

As early as the end of February 1990, in some publications and especially in a speech to the Chamber of Regional Industry and Commerce in Stuttgart on 6 March 1990, I called attention to the fact that 'massive support by West Germany will be required'; 'the temptation to rely on borrowing in order to close financial gaps must be resisted'; 'the Federal Government, the states and the municipalities should try to exercise extreme restraint in their own expenditures'. I said, 'I take it as a requirement of honesty that a tax increase should not be ruled out.' And: 'A temporary tax increase would in fact be a more solid form of financing than net borrowing in every respect.' The official reaction was straightforward: additional tax burdens were out of the question.

CONCLUDING REMARKS

The highly praised 'German Unification' fund (*Fonds 'Deutsche Einheit'*) of May 1990, with a balance sheet total of DM 115 billion (later increased to about DM160 billion), was financed primarily by borrowing (DM95 billion). In the *Stuttgarter Zeitung*, I criticised the fact that this fund was equivalent to following the path of least political resistance and was also quite incapable of meeting the impending financing burdens; moreover, the Länder were contributing too little to funding German reunification; subsidies were not being reduced; additional taxes were unavoidable in the long run. I also warned against the idea of shifting burdens from the present generation to the next.

It is well known how things turned out. The 'solidarity tax' has long been a reality, along with the ever more insistent reach of the Federal Government into the tax payer's pocket. At least today we can credit the German Federal Government for pursuing (since 1994) a determined policy of consolidating the finances of the Federal Republic. In the new Länder of former East Germany, the downward trend in the economy has been turned around. The process of closing the gap in productivity and living standards has developed a dynamic of its own, although it continues to require massive financial injections.

Notes

1. For the earlier pre-unification state of the GDR economy, see Frowen (1985).
2. In fact, Hans Tietmeyer, the former Secretary of State and now President of the Deutsche Bundesbank, was temporarily freed from his duties in the Bundesbank Directorate to be Chancellor Kohl's personal adviser during the German Treaty negotiations (see Tietmeyer, 1994).
3. On these issues, see also Kloten (1997a) and (1997b).

References

Frowen, S.F. (1985), 'The Economy of the German Democratic Republic,' in D. Childs, *Honecker's Germany*, London: Allen & Unwin, pp. 32–49.

Kloten, N. (1997a), 'The German Currency Union: Challenges for Both Parts of Germany', in S.F. Frowen and J. Hölscher (eds), *The German Currency Union of 1990 – A Critical Assessment*, London: Macmillan; New York: St. Martin's Press, pp. 177–99.

Kloten, N. (1997b), 'Der theoretische Hintergrund der deutsch-deutschen Währungsunion', in E.W. Streissler (ed.), *Studien zur Entwicklung der ökonomischen Theorie*, vol. XVI *Die Umsetzung wirtschaftspolitischer Grundkonzeptionen in die kontinentaleuropäische Praxis* des 19. und 20. Jahrhunderts, Part I, Papers of the Verein für Socialpolitik, new series, vol. 115/XVI, Berlin: Duncker & Humblot, pp. 171–233.

Tietmeyer, H. (1994), 'Erinnerungen an die Vertragsverhandlungen', in T. Waigel and M. Schell (eds), *Tage, die Deutschland und die Welt veränderten*, Munich: edition ferenczy at Bruckmann, pp. 57–117. Authorised English version in this volume entitled 'Recollections of the German Treaty Negotiations of 1990', pp. 68–109.

9 Ethics and Morals in Central Banking: Do They Exist, Do They Matter?[1]

Otmar Issing

HENRY THORNTON AND CENTRAL BANKING

Money and interest rates have always been discussed in an ethical and moral context. For a long time charging interest was considered disreputable, and at times liable to hard secular and ecclesiastical punishment. The second Lateran Council, for example, decided in 1139:

> Furthermore, we condemn that practice accounted despicable and blameworthy by divine and human laws, denounced by Scripture in the Old and New Testaments, namely, the ferocious greed of usurers; and we sever them from every comfort of the church, forbidding any archbishop or bishop, or an abbot of any order whatever or anyone in clerical orders, to dare to receive usurers, unless they do so with extreme caution; but let them be held infamous throughout their whole lives and, unless they repent, be deprived of a Christian burial.[2]

Even if those times are past, it remains questionable whether – to quote the well-known Austrian capital theorist Eugen von Böhm-Bawerk – charging interest has ever lost its 'moral stigma' completely. A central banker should therefore think three times before talking about questions of ethics and morals, as he or she represents an institution which not only lends money against interest but also compels its customers to hold interest-free deposits (at least where (non-interest-bearing) minimum reserves exist). Or is it thought to be less reprehensible if it is banks which are charged interest?

The authority of Henry Thornton shows a way out of this dilemma, as it was he who introduced interest rates into the theory of the monetary process and who cast the relations between money, prices and interest that are intuitively familiar to every banker into a scientific mould (Schumpeter, 1954, p. 707).

Henry Thornton personifies several elements which are of great significance for central bank policy. With his famous work *An Enquiry into the Nature and Effects of the Paper Credit of Great Britain* he ushered in a new era in the development of monetary theory (Hayek, 1962, p. 36). As a successful banker – one of his brothers was, incidentally, a director of the Bank of England and from 1799 to 1801 its governor – he knew the practical side of the money business, and as a Member of Parliament for 33 years he took great interest in the problems of monetary policy, particularly in connection with the financial crises caused by the war with France. His ideas challenge the monetary policy maker to this day (Hetzel, 1987, p. 15). Finally, Thornton was also a man who at times devoted six-sevenths of his considerable income to charitable purposes and who spent much time writing religious pamphlets: his 'Family Prayers', which appeared posthumously, were a sort of 'Victorian bestseller' (Laidler, 1987). An obituary characterised him as follows: 'A more upright, independent, and truly virtuous man has never adorned the Senate' (Hayek, 1962, p. 33).

Can there be a better platform for discussing issues of ethics and morals in connection with central bank policy than a lecture dedicated to his name? The following passage from his *Paper Credit* (p. 259) could be displayed in any central bank as a code for a policy of sound money even today:

To limit the total amount of paper issued, and to resort for this purpose, whenever the temptation to borrow is strong, to some effectual principle of restriction; in no case, however, materially to diminish the sum in circulation, but to let it vibrate only within certain limits; to afford a slow and cautious extension of it, as the general trade of the kingdom enlarges itself; to allow of some special, though temporary, increase in the event of any extraordinary alarm or difficulty, as the best means of preventing a great demand at home for guineas; and to lean to the side of diminution, in the case of gold going abroad, and of the general exchanges continuing long unfavourable; this seems to be the true policy of the directors of an institution circumstanced like that of the Bank of England. To suffer either the solicitations of merchants, or the wishes of government, to determine the measure of the bank issues, is unquestionably to adopt a very false principle of conduct.

ETHICS, ECONOMIC ETHICS, MONETARY ETHICS?

For years interest in 'ethics and morals' has been booming. Following a spate of conferences and publications, the subject matter is becoming increasingly complex, and in the process a multiplicity of ethical subdivisions is replacing general economic ethics in the area of research concerning ethics and economics. These subdivisions reflect both increasing specialisation and the opening-up of new areas of academic pursuit. (Schmitz, 1988, p. 374, differentiates, for example, currency ethics from monetary ethics and financial ethics.) The findings of general economic ethics or its various specialised forms are linked with a whole series of moral codes of behaviour; corporate ethics, for example, has given rise to published statements in which moral codes of conduct are formulated as a guide for management.

After all these efforts, is there really now a need for monetary ethics, and a moral dimension to central bank policy based on them? The answer seems somewhat banal: the consequences of decisions on currency issues and monetary policy are far-reaching, and are generally measured in more than just purely economic terms. No modern school of ethics can ignore the consequences of actions; the responsibility of central bankers therefore ends up in the interdependent web of technical regularities and explicit or implicit evaluations. Conversely, it is inevitable that this gives rise to an ethical dimension to central bank policy and to moral criteria governing the actions of monetary policy makers.

This chapter is not an attempt to establish and categorise a form of ethics for central bank policy and a moral code for central bankers (for a general overview see Homann and Hesse *et al.*, 1988, p. 13 ff.). Instead, it addresses the much less ambitious question of how far and in what way ethical and moral aspects could, or perhaps even should, play a role in central bank policy.

COMPETENCE VERSUS MORALITY?

The categories of ethical reflection and a moral way of thinking are associated exclusively with human nature. In his 'Nicomachean Ethics' (Book II, 1103b) Aristotle sets out the essential principles of ethics:

Since, then, the present inquiry does not aim at theoretical knowledge, like the others (for we are inquiring not in order to know
what virtue is, but in order to become good, since otherwise our
inquiry would have been of no use), we must examine the nature of
actions, namely how we ought to do them; for these determine also
the nature of the states of character that are produced, as we have
said. (*The Works of Aristotle*, Volume II, p. 349)

The morally worthy man stands over and above the competent
man:

the case of the arts and that of the virtues are not similar; for the
products of the arts have their goodness in themselves, so that it is
enough that they should have a certain character, but if the acts
that are in accordance with the virtues have themselves a certain
character it does not follow that they are done justly or temperately.
The agent also must be in a certain condition when he does
them ... These are not reckoned in as conditions of the possession
of the arts, except the bare knowledge; but as a condition of the
possession of the virtues knowledge has little or no weight ... Actions, then, are called just and temperate when they are such as the
just or temperate man would do; but it is not the man who does
these that is just and temperate, but the man who also does them as
just and temperate men do them. (Book II, 1105a ff, *The Works of
Aristotle*, Volume II, p. 350 f.)

That was how Aristotle treated the relationship between technical
knowledge and moral attitudes, and he clearly conceded priority to
morals. If I may be allowed to skip over 2000 years of philosophising
and venture to address the direct 'application' of this theory, I would
like to ask the following two questions: is placing morality before
ability justified in central bank policy, and is it right to choose the
morally virtuous man before the technically qualified man or even
instead of him?

Are professional competence and moral integrity in fact mutually
exclusive? Does Aristotle's maxim, rather, not tend to be based on a
construed, or artificial, conflict?

The general assumption sometimes made by advocates of public
choice, that a form of 'marginal morality' prevails on the way up the
ladder to success, with the result that the degree of morality in the
upper hierarchical levels is on average relatively low (Tullock, 1965,

p. 22), remains unaffected by this. According to this theory, Aristotle's postulate – which further develops the demand of his mentor Plato and which calls for the realisation of the ideal state by making philosophers king – could only be achieved if the morally virtuous but technically inept were appointed to managerial positions. Quite apart from the practical difficulty of finding such people with a certain degree of reliability – and of regularly checking to see whether or not their morality remains intact in this leading position – this approach leads to an irreconcilable contradiction since the highly virtuous people chosen will be absolutely unable to reconcile their moral principles with their responsibility for actions whose consequences they, as people unacquainted with the discipline concerned, can in no way foresee.

To develop this idea just one stage further, this means to qualify a lack of the relevant technical knowledge in a position of responsibility as immoral. But it is not easy to define the technical competence necessary for any given job in a complex world as any one person never possesses more than a certain share of the available knowledge. Consequently, the highly qualified expert who trusts her own (limited) ability and knowledge exclusively but has little respect for the opinion of others could actually represent a particular danger when she can make or at least influence decisions which are important for other people.

This is a serious objection in a world which is dominated by uncertainty, not only with respect to the correct analysis of a given situation, but even more so with respect to assessing the future effects of monetary policy measures. (For addressing the problem in general, see Rawls, 1971, p. 56ff.). There has always been a broad spectrum of opinion in academic circles, and making a compulsory selection based on absolute and unquestionable superiority seems to be possible only for the person who is immune to critical reflection. If, like F. Hahn, one believes that monetary theory as a basis for a scientifically oriented central bank policy is more of a framework than a completed building, it will be difficult to avoid moral concepts when absolute, one-sided dogmatic positions are to be assessed. On the other hand, the central bank policy maker cannot delay making decisions until academics have reliably solved all the problems: decisions always have to be made in advance of a full understanding of the real problems. Under moral aspects, such an acknowledgement, of course, is no excuse for arbitrary deliberations and decisions.

In a world of uncertain knowledge, technical demands and moral categories become fused in a mixture which is not easy to unscramble, if it can be done at all. Standing Aristotle's sequence on its head makes the morals of the expert an essential but subordinate condition relative to his technical ability. However, is the moral attitude more than just an appendage, which is to be welcomed in individual cases, but which, in the end, is unnecessary – and under certain conditions actually detrimental – to the satisfactory functioning of society?[3]

From the point of view of utilitarianism – in the sense of teleological ethics or so-called consequentialism – this conflict disappears, for it judges actions by their consequences, and not by their motives or intrinsic qualities (Brittan, 1983, p. 334). In the specific case of central bank policy the question is: must – or at least should – policy makers possess moral qualities in addition to their technical knowledge? If they must or should, how are these qualities to be defined? Is a moral attitude, as such, actually essential?

PERSONS OR RULES?

In the numerous well-known works on the history of individual central banks persons often stand in the foreground. For example, large sections of David Marsh's book on the Deutsche Bundesbank and its predecessors constitute a series of biographical impressions prefaced, for good reasons, by a list of the *dramatis personae* (Marsh, 1992, p. 7). In his official history of the Bank of England John Fforde sees in its long history a reason for the significance of events which reflect the influence of persons: 'For reasons lying deep in British habits of self-satisfaction, these circumstances of prolonged birth were widely presumed to endow the result with a special virtue, enhanced with a flavour of prestige, power, expertise and mystery' (Fforde, 1992, p. 4). This may be illustrated by a rather curious incident: in his negotiations with the government Montagu Norman, the dominant figure in the twentieth century, was anything but over-scrupulous in his methods; this man, who was 'ever the master of ambiguity' once sank unconscious into the arms of the Chancellor of the Exchequer, 'thus literally disarming the opposition' (King, 1993, p. 8).

A certain bias towards the personality story is no doubt to be expected from the journalist. Nevertheless, the theory of the striking significance of individual persons cannot simply be dismissed. For example, the policy of the Reichsbank under Hjalmar Schacht serves time and again as proof of the personality theory (Müller, 1973). And in a study of monetary policy in the USA, Sherman Maisel (1973, p. 107) comes to the conclusion: 'Monetary policy does not merely reflect monetary doctrine; it is strongly influenced by the personalities in the Federal Reserve System and by their interaction, as well as by their responses to external suggestion and pressures.'

This list could probably be extended almost indefinitely in both time and place. If, however, individual people with their individual opinions are actually to the fore in monetary policy, is it not the inner attitude, the morals of central bankers, which is essential? If this is true, what is this moral attitude, and what provides it with monetary policy relevance? Considerations of this nature result, on the one hand, in a quest for the motives of the people concerned; and on the other hand, they give rise to the query as to whether the personal attitude is of any relevance to the outcome of policies. For example, Milton Friedman emphasises in his commentary on the attitude of Schacht and Norman, to which he adds Benjamin Strong of the Federal Reserve and Governor Moreau of the Banque de France (to whose memoirs he refers), that they were convinced that they were acting in everyone's interest and were capable of working together to solve the underlying economic problems of the Western world. In discussing this point of view, Friedman wrote: 'Though of course stated in obviously benevolent terms of doing the "right thing" and avoiding distrust and uncertainty, the implicit doctrine is clearly dictatorial and totalitarian' (Friedman, 1962, p. 229).

Irrespective of whether Friedman was actually right or wrong in his assessment of the moral aspect, this would on no account definitively answer the question concerning concrete monetary policy results in an institutional arrangement in which individuals and, in particular, 'such' individuals possessing powers of this kind. Moreover, an individual may be sufficiently stigmatized by such adjectives, but may nevertheless fail to be fully characterised regarding his or her 'moral position'.

However, we may have had enough of this – at best anecdotal – approach. There is little to be gained from a closer look at the relevant individual cases and from the ensuing problem of generalisation, principally because the various individuals concerned have acted under quite different conditions, or, to be more precise, under very different constraints.

If more is involved than the degree of fame of persons with whom institutions are often identified in public, and if the question arises as to the content of monetary policy, the individuals initially take a back seat in the analysis, and the monetary policy regime concerned and its institutional determinants move into the foreground.

As in other cases, however, positive statements and normative demands often overlap here, too. Thus, many constraints on central bankers' individual room for manoeuvre are conceivable, in the extreme case of which, monetary policy decisions are strictly linked to objective factors. The classical gold standard can be taken as the most important example of an institutional arrangement in which the course of monetary policy was essentially set by the obligation to exchange currency for gold, despite all the flexibility which individual authors had been at pains to devise (see, for example, Bloomfield, 1959).

However, normative points of view come to the forefront in the case advocated by the Chicago School. In his work 'Rules versus Authorities in Monetary Policy', Simons (1948) deals with a whole programme, namely the call for the replacement of dangers to the liberal order in general and to the monetary system in particular, caused by individuals and their preferences, by proposing that policy be guided by clear and binding rules. Milton Friedman takes up this idea in his *Program for Monetary Stability* and establishes his k per cent rule which, in its demand for as steady a monetary growth as possible, even over very short periods, is designed to prevent any discretionary room for action whatsoever.

Persons and their attitudes have no place in this system. According to the advocates of strict rules, it would also be much too risky if a society had to rely on the knowledge and morals of central bankers and grant them appropriate discretionary room for action. Karl Brunner's vision of central bank policy makers (1981, p. 18 ff.) is of people who have always been surrounded by a peculiar and protective political mysticism, which in turn is expressed in an essentially 'metaphysical approach' to monetary policy. Central bank policy is presented as an esoteric art in which only the initiated can participate. Such an attitude, he argues, is, first, dangerous because it exposes monetary policy to almost limitless exploitation for political purposes; and second, this arrangement is all the more questionable as the choice of incumbents is (in his judgement), at best arbitrary, and the filling of executive posts with competent people is the exception rather than the rule.

These criticisms have been supplemented by the contribution of public choice, according to which it should be assumed that self-interest has precedence in the case of central bank executives, too.

The result is that, where a choice has to be made, personal gain, such as increased prestige, will come before public welfare (Chant and Acheson, 1973). This line of investigation therefore provides a further argument for the view that, wherever possible, such an important task as monetary policy should not be entrusted to the discretion of 'personalities'.

Rules which are binding are therefore the better alternative – particularly according to the findings of the public choice theory – as they replace the 'rule by men' (Friedman, 1962, p. 235) with the 'rule by law' (Hayek, 1971, p. 185 ff.) in an important policy area. Simons (1948, p. 169) elevates established rules somewhat excessively when he actually endows them with 'moral qualities':

> In a free-enterprise system we obviously need highly definite and stable rules of the game, especially as to money. The monetary rules must be compatible with the reasonably smooth working of the system. Once established, however, they should work mechanically, with the chips falling where they may. To put our present problem as a paradox – we need to design and establish with the greatest intelligence a monetary system good enough so that, hereafter, we may hold to it unrationally – on faith – as a religion, if you please.

Accordingly, in the extreme, monetary policy is to be entrusted to a fully anonymous mechanism; while in a somewhat less rigorous form it requires the expert (or technocrat, in the positive sense of the term) to operate the 'apparatus' in line with clear instructions. The internal acceptance by the expert of the standards prescribed from outside still does not establish any moral quality (Kliemt, 1985, p. 240 f.). Nevertheless, one will not be able to deny the 'operator', who is comparable with the pilot of an aircraft, personal characteristics and therefore possibly a professional ethos beyond his professional qualities. The significance of those, however, in the case of monetary policy remains a moot point.

The reason for establishing monetary policy rules is to achieve the actual objectives of monetary policy by first limiting or, indeed, eliminating room for the discretionary action of individuals. From that point of view any rule is all the more attractive, the more it increases the probability that major goals will actually be realised. The extent of the demands made by Simons (1948, p. 181 f.) on such a set of rules may again be seen in the following quotation:

To assure adequate moral pressure of public opinion against legislative (and administrative) tinkering, the monetary rules must be definite, simple (at least in principle), and expressive of strong, abiding, pervasive, and reasonable popular sentiments. They should be designed to permit the fullest and most stable employment, to facilitate adjustment to such basic changes (especially in technology) as are likely to occur, and, secondarily, to minimize inequities between debtors and creditors.

If any monetary policy rule could actually meet such demanding criteria, it would be quite irresponsible not to put this proposal into practice. It is particularly the advocates of public choice who expect such irresponsible opposition from central bankers, because the establishment of strict rules would rob the latter of any aura of technical experts and reduce them to the status of semi-automatons. If, when the status quo of room for discretionary action was being subsequently defended even under such conditions, individual interests were seen to be given priority over those of the public at large, such an attitude must immediately be described as 'immoral'.

By analogy, this reproach would have to be levelled at the advocate of the unconditional application of rules if the implementation of her suggestion is not only unable to deliver the forecast results and, consequently, the more or less 'promised' improvement, but possibly raises the risk of instability. At any rate, hardly anyone would identify herself today with the claim made by Simons.

Friedman's demand for a rule which would legally commit the central bank to increasing the money stock annually by a constant percentage and, what is more, at as steady a rate from month to month as possible, essentially promises – much more modestly – protection from major monetary disturbances and a marked reduction in short-term monetary uncertainty and instability (Friedman, 1960, p. 99). If, for the moment, one disregards the institutional prerequisite which Friedman considers essential for the absolute control of the money stock, not the least of these preconditions being the complete restructuring of the entire banking system, there is sufficient evidence today to show why the money stock rule could not produce the results claimed. This objection is justified, first, by the heated debate over the 'right' definition of the money stock which has prevailed among monetarists since then and, second, by the fact that unforeseeable financial innovations can decisively change the economic content of a statutorily fixed growth rate for a money stock aggregate laid down a very long time in advance.

It is not surprising that, under these circumstances, scholars have progressively turned their backs on the idea of simple rules. At first, relatively makeshift safety valves in the form of proviso clauses were used which, in the case of serious deviations – for example, exceeding particular unemployment rates – are to permit or even demand a departure from the prescribed path.

Later, interest was increasingly focused on so-called feedback rules, whose fundamental idea is that the appropriate form of action dictated to the central bank in the sense of an endogenous flexibility be amended by a number of automatic feedbacks, thus continuing to deny central bank management its discretionary scope. Approaches of this kind hardly go beyond the level of academic seminars and therefore form a basis on which the implementation of statutory regulations could not conceivably be substantiated.

TIME INCONSISTENCY AND CONSERVATIVE CENTRAL BANKERS

Friedman, to mention just the best known monetarist, identified a major problem but was unable to offer a satisfactory solution. There can hardly be anyone left who doubts that the ideal rule has still not been found (see also Loef, 1993, p. 153 f.).

Is, then, our only hope with the paper standard that a responsible central banker will make the right decisions in the interest of the common welfare? There are hardly any convincing reasons for relying on this mixture of resignation in the search for the effective institutional arrangement and of confidence in the selection of the right people. First, monetary policy makers who have been granted full powers of discretion are not in a position appropriately to evaluate the flood of frequently contradictory information and accurately to assess the time-lags before the measures taken begin to work. Second, monetary stability in a monetary policy regime of this kind will fail if only because in the long run the central bank will hardly be able to resist the pressure from political groups who seek 'generous' monetary expansion to accommodate their own inflationary behaviour.

Finally, monetary policy makers who fully reserve decisions over future action to their own discretion fall into the trap of time inconsistency. Under these conditions economic agents will expect that a central bank will, for example, later compromise pay agreements which were agreed on the basis of expected price stability, so as to exploit the potential gains in employment realisable by monetary policy expansion. In this scenario, which is interesting under aspects of game theory, inflation will be higher than it would be in the case of a strict, though unavailable, rule without there being any improvements in output and employment because the economic agents have anticipated corresponding action on the part of the central bank.

Some authors have thought to overcome this dilemma by appointing 'conservative central bankers' (Rogoff, 1985). Such a person attaches more importance to monetary stability than does society as a whole. This approach fits into the principal-agent model in which society (the principal) transfers the fulfilment of a task to be performed in its interests to persons (agents) chosen for the purpose (Fratianni, von Hagen and Waller, 1993).

The model of the 'conservative central banker' must, however, be seen as an almost futile attempt to revive the 'personality theory'. The solution even to the question of how one is reliably to find the person with the desired qualities must remain just as unsatisfactory as any supposed guarantee of protection against the *ex post* opportunism of a person once he has been selected. This is especially the case if a long term of office and protection against dismissal are among the basic institutional preconditions of a regime in which one expects central bank management to defend the value of money in situations of real or imaginary conflict between price stability and other economic policy objectives.

Incidentally, with the figure of the conservative central banker, a quality of person is meant whose relationship with moral categories is not to be overlooked. If, in a process which is difficult to operationalise effectively, society somehow chose the person with the right convictions, it would be morally essential that subsequent actions fulfilled this expectation. However, whether this expectation is justified, at least *ex ante*, would probably not, or at least not only, be based on the great preference for monetary stability which the person concerned had previously announced in one way or another. Instead, it would have to be concluded from that individual's entire personality structure. Should and could one place the fate of a country's monetary policy on this supposition alone?

However, the model of the conservative central banker which has emerged in textbooks can, on closer analysis, be even less easily dismissed as no more than theoretical conjecturing than it was at first sight; time and again demands are openly voiced in political circles for this or that opinion to be given greater emphasis in monetary policy. However, the objections already mentioned apply to every attempt to make the real (or, more likely, alleged) preferences of the persons involved the basis of monetary policy decisions.

If moral issues in the widest sense were made the criteria of selection, monetary policy decisions would inevitably also be morally evaluated. One can easily imagine how, for example, in times of recession or of a trade-off – albeit only a short-term one – between inflation and unemployment, central bank policy would inevitably be drawn into the political struggle with ideological dimensions: does the 'social conscience' announced in an expansionary policy or the determination to preserve monetary stability earn a higher moral rating? Is there, shall we say, also a 'moral' trade-off between these two types of behaviour?

IMPOSED GOAL AND INDEPENDENCE

Monetary stability as a public good has no advocate in the everyday pursuit of politics and differing interests. The idea of entrusting the fulfilment of this task to the selection of the right persons alone is unconvincing for the reasons already mentioned, especially as the question arises as to why the political authorities which for opportunist reasons are not themselves in a position to defend monetary stability should transfer the important instrument of their monetary policy to persons whose decisions could result in conflicts with their own objectives and, in extreme cases, the loss of their own (government's) powers.

Evidently a more stable institutional arrangement is required, one which can also function with the 'wrong' people in emergencies. If a society thinks the objective of monetary stability is important, although always under threat in the political process, the only solution is to be found in an arrangement which takes the monetary system out of the political sphere as far as possible. If the fixed link of the creation of central bank money to a naturally scarce asset, as under the gold standard, is ruled out because of the known disadvantages, and if a strict monetary rule cannot produce the desired stability either, there is only one way left: that is, to transfer responsibility for monetary policy to an independent central bank and at the same time to commit the latter to the clear objective of maintaining monetary stability (Issing, 1993).

Advocates of public choice, and all those economists who, following the enlightenment of Scottish origin, support the programme of 'economising on virtue', declare they are dissatisfied with this system. They believe that the independence of the central bank is reconcilable with the condition of democratic control only if there are sanctions for central bankers who do not pursue the objectives they were appointed to observe (Vaubel, 1990, p. 945). This approach endeavours to link the pursuit of a public mandate with that of the individual's interests; that is, it establishes the appropriate incentives (Neumann, 1992). Conceivable here would be, for example, a mixture of a threat of punishment up to and including dismissal for failure, on the one hand, and bonuses for achievement of the objective of price stability, on the other.

This model was implemented in New Zealand in 1990 (see Issing, 1993, p. 26 ff.). The central bank was committed to the goal of price stability; in an agreement between the finance minister and the central bank governor, the exact modalities are laid down before the governor is appointed. If the governor does not fulfil the stipulated mandate, he or she can be prematurely dismissed at the request of the minister.

The appeal of this regulation is obvious, not least because there is no need to waste time thinking about the moral conduct of the person concerned: under such a regime one can expect that anyone, regardless of individual qualities, will try to achieve the prescribed macroeconomic objective.

Unfortunately, an arrangement of clear objectives, independence in implementing policy, and the threat of sanctions in the case of failure, which is so attractive at first sight, loses a great deal of its simplicity and therefore persuasiveness on closer analysis. It is reasonable to say that punishments only make sense if the person concerned can actually be shown to be responsible for undesirable developments. From the central bank's point of view, however, major influences on the price level – such as increased indirect taxes, deteriorations in the terms of trade or inflationary wage agreements – represent exogenous factors. Only in a world of completely flexible prices could one expect monetary policy to compensate immediately for such effects through restrictive pressures. In the real world such an undertaking would not only be futile – that is, the rise in the price level could in no way be prevented by monetary policy – but the overall economic costs would also be unbearably high. With the inclusion of proviso clauses for exogenous factors – which, incidentally, has also been done in the case of New Zealand – the arrangement loses its intended unambiguous character. The failure to meet the target becomes subject to interpretation and is therefore hardly 'litigable'. This is all the more true as the allocation of responsibility for monetary policy decisions has to take account of the sometimes considerable time-lags before measures take effect.

As with the strict monetary rule, it is the intention of the public choice approach to establish the right incentives to eliminate all risks to an objective in the public interest which can arise from personal preferences. However justified one may think the approach in principle, one can have little hope of finding an arrangement which is absolutely 'crisis-proof'. As in all institutions, persons are likely to play a role in central banks, too; their attitude, or their 'morals', if you like, will always influence the measures taken and, consequently, the outcome of monetary policy (see also Hausmann and McPherson, 1993, p. 672 f.).

This attitude or these morals can, admittedly, also change under the influence of the institution. In connection with the model of the conservative central banker, the danger of moral hazard was described above: that is, a person prior to his appointment to the central bank board could pretend to be more stability-minded than is consistent with his actual inclinations and his subsequent conduct in practice. The converse is, of course, also conceivable. Under the influence of the institution and its past, his personal preferences may change in favour of a greater priority for monetary stability. What personal predisposition is required before a 'Becket effect' of this kind actually materialises is a moot point, as is the question of how resistance to the influence of the institution and its functions is to be morally defined.

CENTRAL BANK CONSTITUTION AND CENTRAL BANK POLICY

Ethical categories and moral aspects are expressed, first, at the level of the central bank constitution and, second, at that of the individual and collective behaviour within the prescribed institutional framework.

In looking for the best possible institutional arrangement it is 'the ethics of forming an appropriate opinion in matters of constitutional political economics' that is involved, and 'not ethical questions concerning the content' (according to a commentary by H. Kliemt). The competent authority in this sphere is not the central bankers themselves but the legislator and, initially, politicians. One cannot deny that there is an ethical-moral dimension to considering the intention of reserving recourse to the banknote printing presses, and the transfer of monetary policy responsibility to an independent central bank. This certainly does not only apply whenever one – like Glucksmann (1993) – elevates, say, the preference of the Germans for a stable currency to the rank of a 'currency religion'.

If the ideal of a perfect regulatory system, which precludes any discretionary latitude and leads in a more or less automatic process to the desired results, remains barred, success will always depend on the persons responsible. It would then be naive and, in view of the possible consequences, too risky simply to count on the central bankers' 'morals'. On the other hand, scepticism that – through appropriate incentives – the known defects of adhering to rules could be successfully overcome, more or less through the back door, by 'subduing selfish interests' will probably be difficult to avoid. However, the public choice approach probably falls short in any case by assuming an all-too-simple motivation structure, and in underestimating the influence of the institution (see also Simon, 1993). In a concluding résumé of his deliberations, North (1991, p. 140) says that the public choice approach cannot be the complete answer as informal restrictions inevitably also play a role. Our knowledge of the interaction between culturally based standards of behaviour and formal rules may still be rather limited. This probably also applies to the sphere of central bank policy.

Notes

Originally given as the Henry Thornton Lecture at the City University, London, on 23 November 1995.

1. My first approach to this topic can be found in Issing (1994) and (1995). I would like to thank Geoffrey E. Wood for valuable suggestions.
2. Decrees of the Ecumenical Councils, Vol. One, Nicaea I to Lateran V, edited by N.P. Tanner, SJ, London, 1990, p. 200.
3. Sen (1992, p. 2 ff.) refers to the two different substantiations of economics. One approach deals with matters of ethics, the other (engineering) with the functioning of the economy. Developments in modern theory have largely driven the ethical approach into the background, to the detriment of economics and ethics. Bringing the two closer together again promises substantial 'rewards' (Sen, 1992, p. 88 f.).

References

Aristotle, 'Nicomachean Ethics', *The Works of Aristotle*, Volume II, Chicago: Encyclopædia Britannica, Inc., 1952.

Bloomfield, A.J. (1959), *Monetary Policy under the International Gold Standard: 1880–1914*, New York: Federal Reserve Bank of New York.

Brittan, S. (1983), 'Two Cheers for Utilitarianism', *Oxford Economic Papers*, 35, pp. 331–50.

Brunner, K. (1981) 'The Art of Central Banking', in H. Göppl and R. Henn (eds), *Geld, Banken und Versicherungen (Money, Banks and Insurance Enterprises)*, Königstein: Athenäum, pp. 14–38.

Chant, J.F. and K. Acheson (1973), 'Mythology and Central Banking', *Kyklos*, 26, pp. 362–79.

Fforde, J. (1992), *The Bank of England and Public Policy 1941–1958*, Cambridge Cambridge Univ. Pr.

Fratianni, M., J. von Hagen and C. Waller (1993), 'Central Banking as a Political Principal-Agent Problem', Centre for Economic Policy Research, London, Discussion Paper Series, no. 752.

Friedman, M. (1960), *A Program for Monetary Stability*, New York: Fordham Univ. Pr.

Friedman, M. (1962), 'Should there be an Independent Monetary Authority', in L.B. Yeager (ed.), *In Search of a Monetary Constitution*, Cambridge, Mass: Harvard Univ. Pr., pp. 219–43.

Frowen, S.F. and F.P. McHugh (eds.) (1995), *Financial Decision-Making and Moral Responsibility*, London: Macmillan; New York: St. Martin's Press.

Glucksmann, A. (1993), 'Lieber die Mark als noch einmal Hitler' ('Better the Mark than another Hitler'), *Rheinischer Merkur*, 3 September.

Hausman, D.M. and M.S. McPherson (1993), 'Taking Ethics Seriously: Economics and Contemporary Moral Philosophy', *Journal of Economic Literature*, 31, pp. 671–731.

Hayek, F.A. (1962), 'Introduction' in H. Thornton, *An Enquiry into the Nature and Effects of the Paper Credit of Great Britain* (1802), edited by F.A. v. Hayek, London: Cass, pp. 11–63.

Hayek, F.A. (1971), *Die Verfassung der Freiheit (The Constitution of Liberty)*, Tübingen: Mohr.

Hetzel, R.L. (1987), 'Henry Thornton: Seminal Monetary Theorist and Father of the Modern Central Bank', Federal Reserve Bank of Richmond, *Economic Review*, 73, 4, pp. 3–16.

Homann, K., H. Hesse *et al.* (1988), 'Wirtschaftswissenschaft und Ethik' ('Economics and ethics'), in H. Hesse (ed.), *Wirtschaftswissenschaft und Ethik (Economics and Ethics)*, Schriften des Vereins für Socialpolitik, new series, vol. 171, Berlin: Duncker & Humblot, pp. 9–33.

Issing, O. (1993), *Central Bank Independence and Monetary Stability*, Institute of Economic Affairs, London, Occasional Paper 89, London.

Issing, O. (1994), 'Ethik der Notenbankpolitik – Moral der Notenbanken' (Ethics of Central Bank Policy – Morals of Central Banks), in H. Hesse and O. Issing (eds.) *Geld und Moral* (Money and Morals), Munich.

Issing, O. (1995), 'The Role of the Central Bank and its Responsibility', in S.F. Frowen and F.P. McHugh (eds.) *Financial Decision-Making and Moral Responsibility*, London: Macmillan; New York: St. Martin's Press, pp. 15–26.

King, M. (1993), 'The Bundesbank: A view from the Bank of England', in Deutsche Bundesbank, *Auszüge aus Presseartikeln* (press excerpts), No. 25 (2 April), pp. 1–5.

Kliemt, H. (1985), *Moralische Institutionen* (*Moral Institutions*), Freiburg, München: Alber.

Laidler, D. (1987), 'Thornton, H.' in J. Eatwell, M. Milgate, P. Newman (eds), *The New Palgrave, A Dictionary of Economics*, London: Macmillan, pp. 633–635.

Loef, H.-E. (1993), 'Zwei Geldbasisregeln im Vergleich – Möglichkeiten für eine regelgebundene Geldpolitik in Europa?' ('Comparison of two rules for a monetary base – opportunities for a rule-based monetary policy in Europe?'), in D. Duwendag and J. Siebke (eds), *Europa vor dem Eintritt in die Wirtschafts- und Währungsunion* (*Europe Prior to Entry into Economic and Monetary Union*), Schriften des Vereins für Socialpolitik, new series, vol. 220, Berlin: Duncker & Humblot, pp. 97–158.

Maisel, S.J. (1973), *Managing the Dollar*, New York: Norton.

Marsh, D. (1992), *The Bundesbank, The Bank that Rules Europe*. London: Heinemann.

Müller, H. (1973), *Die Zentralbank – Eine Nebenregierung* (*The Central Bank – A Subsidiary Government*), Opladen: Westdeutscher Verlag.

Neumann, M.J.M. (1992), 'Bindung durch Zentralbankunabhängigkeit' ('Linkage through central bank independence'), in H. Albeck (ed.), *Wirtschaftsordnung und Geldverfassung* (*Economic Order and Monetary Constitution*), Göttingen: Vandenhoeck & Ruprecht, pp. 62–73.

North, D.C. (1991), *Institutions, Institutional Change and Economic Performance*, Cambridge etc.: Cambridge Univ. Pr.

Rawls, J. (1971), *A Theory of Justice*, Cambridge, Mass.: Harvard Univ. Pr.

Rogoff, K. (1985), 'The Optimal Degree of Commitment to an Intermediate Monetary Target', *The Quarterly Journal of Economics*, 100, pp. 1169–189.

Schmitz, W. (1988), 'Währungsethik – eine tragende Säule der Wirtschaftsethik' ('Monetary ethics – a mainstay of economic ethics'), in H. Hesse (ed.), *Wirtschaftswissenschaft und Ethik* (*Economics and Ethics*), Schriften des Vereins für Socialpolitik, new series, vol. 171, Berlin: Duncker & Humblot, pp. 373–400.

Schumpeter, J.A. (1954), *History of Economic Analysis*, New York: Oxford Univ. Pr.

Sen, A. (1992), *On Ethics and Economics*, Oxford: Blackwell.

Simon, H.A. (1993), 'Altruism and Economics', *The American Economic Review*, Papers and Proceedings 83, 2, pp. 156–61.

Simons, H.C. (1948), 'Rules versus Authorities in Monetary Policy', reprinted in Simons, H.C., *Economic Policy for a Free Society*, Chicago: Univ. of Chicago Pr., pp. 160–83.

Thornton, H. (1802), *An Enquiry into the Nature and Effects of the Paper Credit of Great Britain*, edited by F.A. v. Hayek, London: Cass 1962.

Tullock, G. (1965), *The Politics of Bureaucracy*, Washington, D.C.: Public Affairs Pr.

Vaubel, R. (1990), 'Currency Competition and European Monetary Integration', *Economic Journal*, 100, pp. 936–46.

10 The Evolution of the Deutsche Mark as an International Currency

Carola Gebhard

INTRODUCTION

The Deutsche Mark is one of the major currencies in the international monetary system. It is the principal reserve currency after the US dollar and a very attractive currency for domestic and foreign investors. Increasingly the world's trading and financial relationships are structured around the three pillars of the US dollar, Deutsche Mark and Yen.

In 1999 the Deutsche Mark is expected to be replaced by the new European single currency. This chapter will examine the evolution of the Deutsche Mark as an international currency and give a better understanding of what might happen with the proposed Euro.

HOW THE DEUTSCHE MARK BECAME AN INTERNATIONAL CURRENCY

Since its introduction on 20 June 1948, the Deutsche Mark has developed into the most stable currency in Europe and has even become a measure for the performance of the world's number one currency, the US dollar.[1] The Deutsche Mark was launched in extremely unfavourable conditions. Right up to the day of the currency reform, which later turned out to be the key date signalling the start of the German economic miracle, the Reichsmark remained the legal tender, although it was increasingly repudiated as a means of exchange as a result of severe suppressed inflation. With Germany under the control of four foreign powers and with uncertainty about the political and economic future, every economic initiative was paralysed. According to the saying 'money is what money does', some 'pseudo currencies' had developed in Germany, including a 'cigarette-currency' or a 'brandy-currency' (Köllner, 1972, p. 91). The creation of a new monetary system with a new currency was therefore inevitable and had to start from scratch. This required a functioning central bank, something which did not exist at the time. Thus the Allies decided to set up a new two-tier central banking system.[2]

This central bank structure, modelled on the federal structure of the Federal Reserve System, consisted of the legally independent Landeszentralbanken (Land Central Banks) and the Bank deutscher Länder (the federal central bank) in Frankfurt am Main. Based on the general recognition that it is neither sufficient nor necessary to back note issue with gold or foreign exchange in order to maintain the value of a currency, the Deutsche Mark was a pure 'paper currency' from the beginning. The crucial thing is to keep the money supply under control.[3]

The two-tier central banking system was abolished in 1957 and the Bank deutscher Länder was replaced by the Deutsche Bundesbank. The Landeszentralbanken were no longer independent as they became part of the Bundesbank, but they still have independent powers in some matters.[4] The stability-oriented policy of the Bank deutscher Länder was continued by the Deutsche Bundesbank, supported by several features of the German economic and political situation. One of these was a special awareness among the German population of the importance of price stability: within a single generation they had lost their savings in two major inflations (1923 and 1947/48: see Nölling, 1993, p. 37).[5]

Furthermore, the German central bank made every effort to promote popular understanding and support for its policy of price stability which was also necessary as a sound base for the central bank's independence. After two adverse experiences of a central bank subject to directives from the government, there was a consensus after the Second World War that the central bank must be independent (Emminger, 1986, pp. 26–7). And thus, among all important central banks of the world, the Bundesbank is the most independent, followed by the Swiss National Bank and the Austrian Central Bank.[6]

The growing importance of the Deutsche Mark was reinforced by Germany's integration into the world economy, the growing competitiveness of German industry and Germany's low inflation rate. This relative stability continued into the 1980s and 1990s. The average annual inflation rates for Germany, the USA, the UK, Japan, France, Italy and Switzerland since 1980 show that Germany has been outstanding in maintaining a stable internal value for its currency, but, admittedly, so has Japan without an independent central bank (see Table 10.1).[7]

Table 10.1 Inflation rates of selected countries based on consumer price indices, 1980–95 (per cent)

Country	1980	1985	1987	1988	1989	1990	1991	1992	1993	1994	1995
Germany*	+5.4	+2.0	+0.2	+1.3	+2.8	+2.7	+3.5	+4.0	+4.1	+3.0	+1.8
USA	+13.5	+3.6	+3.7	+4.0	+4.8	+5.4	+4.2	+3.0	+3.0	+2.6	+2.8
UK	+18.0	+6.1	+4.1	+4.9	+7.8	+9.5	+5.9	+3.7	+1.6	+2.5	+3.4
Japan	+7.8	+2.0	+0.1	+0.7	+2.3	+3.1	+3.3	+1.7	+1.3	+0.7	−0.1
France	+13.3	+5.8	+3.3	+2.7	+3.5	+3.4	+3.2	+2.4	+2.1	+1.7	+1.8
Italy	+21.2	+9.2	+4.7	+5.1	+6.3	+6.4	+6.3	+5.2	+4.5	+4.0	+5.3
Switzerland	+4.0	+3.4	+1.4	+1.9	+3.2	+5.4	+5.8	+4.1	+3.3	+0.8	+1.8

* 1980–93: West Germany only; 1994: unified Germany.
Source: IMF, *International Financial Statistics* (1995 and June 1996).

Gradually, the credibility of the Bundesbank due to its consistent monetary policy led to the Deutsche Mark becoming the *anchor currency* within the EMS. It is second only to the US dollar as a reserve currency and is also a very attractive currency for domestic and foreign investors. The growing importance of the Deutsche Mark is also reflected in its weighting in the SDR basket. This weighting, which is revised every five years, broadly reflects the relative importance of these currencies in international trade and finance. It is 'based on the value of the exports of goods and services of the members issuing these currencies and the balances of their currencies officially held by members' of the IMF.[8]

Table 10.2 shows the changes in the weighting. Since 1981, the Deutsche Mark has been the second most important currency. The Deutsche Mark has increased its weight in the SDR basket further in

Table 10.2 Currencies and weights in the SDR basket (per cent)

Currency/Weight	1981–85	1986–90	1991–95	1996–
US dollar	42	42	40	39
Deutsche Mark	19	19	21	21
Yen	13	15	17	18
French franc	13	13	11	11
Pound sterling	13	13	11	11

Sources: IMF, *International Financial Statistics* (1995); IMF, *Survey* (9 October 1995).

the past 10 years, and the Yen has increased its weight strongly, while the weightings of the US dollar, the French franc and the pound sterling have all declined.

On 1 July 1990 the Deutsche Mark became the sole legal tender in both East and West Germany via the extension of the area of the Deutsche Mark to the GDR (König, 1997, p. 15).

THE DEUTSCHE MARK IN INTERNATIONAL TRADE

One major factor in determining whether a country's money is used as an international currency is the country's share of world trade and the amount of trade invoiced in its currency. The specific patterns influencing the choice of an invoicing currency have been analysed in a number of empirical studies: see, for example, Grassmann (1973), Scharrer (1978) and Tavlas (1991). Summarising these results, it can be said that the larger a country's share of world exports, the more its exports tend to consist of specialised manufactured products, and the more it exports to developing countries, the more likely it is that the exporter's currency will be used as a currency in which invoices and transactions are denominated and paid (that is, as the invoicing vehicle) (Tavlas, 1991, p. 8). To understand the Deutsche Mark's evolution and its use in international trade, the following assesses briefly Germany's share of world exports, its trading partners and major exports in comparison to its major counterparts.

Germany's Trade Patterns

The shares of leading industrial countries in world trade (see Table 10.3) shows that Germany ranked first from 1986 to 1988

Table 10.3   Share of world exports (percentage of world's total)

Country	1985	1986	1987	1988	1989	1990	1991	1992	1993*	1994	1995
Germany	9.8	11.9	12.2	11.8	11.6	11.9	11.5	11.7	10.4	10.3	10.4
USA	11.5	10.6	10.3	11.5	12.1	11.5	12.1	12.0	12.3	12.1	11.7
UK	5.2	5.0	5.3	5.2	5.0	5.4	5.3	5.1	4.8	4.9	4.9
Japan	9.2	10.0	9.3	9.4	9.1	8.4	9.0	9.2	9.8	9.5	9.0
France	5.2	5.8	5.9	5.9	5.8	6.2	6.1	6.3	5.7	5.6	5.7

* Up to 1993, data refers to West Germany only.
Source: OECD, *Economic Outlook* (June 1996).

and in 1990, followed by the USA. Since 1991 Germany has switched to second place.

As a country's share in world exports has been found to be an important determinant of invoicing behaviour, the potential of the Deutsche Mark as an invoicing vehicle appears to have been enhanced during the 1980s and was not really weakened, even in recent years, when the country bore the tremendous economic burden of Germany's reunification.[9]

Currency Denomination in German Exports

Most German exports are invoiced in Deutsche Mark and the proportion has not changed much in recent years (see Table 10.4). During the last fifteen years the proportion of German exports invoiced in Deutsche Mark is high, at an average of 78 per cent.

Table 10.4: Currency denomination of German exports* (per cent)

Currency	1980	1985	1989	1990	1991	1992	1993	1994	1995
Deutsche Mark	82.5	79.5	79.2	77.0	77.3	77.0	74.1	76.4	74.8
US dollar	7.2	9.5	7.5	6.5	7.8	7.3	10.4	9.8	n/a
French franc	2.8	2.7	3.4	3.9	3.3	3.4	3.3	2.9	n/a
Pound sterling	1.4	1.8	2.6	2.7	2.4	3.2	2.6	2.4	n/a
Lira	1.3	1.5	1.8	2.2	2.0	2.2	2.0	1.7	n/a
Yen	x	0.4	0.4	0.4	0.4	0.6	0.8	0.7	n/a
Other	x	4.6	5.1	7.3	6.8	6.3	6.8	6.1	n/a

* = Only West Germany; all currencies = 100%.
Sources: Deutsche Bundesbank, *Monthly Report* (November 1991 and January 1995) and data supplied by Deutsche Bundesbank (1995 and 1997).

Nevertheless, as shown in Table 10.5, the US dollar also plays a role in exports to other non-European countries (12 per cent). However, the table also shows that the US dollar has lost its role as a means of payment and unit of account in German trade within Europe.

Although the significance of other European currencies in German invoicing has been growing in recent years, they still have little importance compared with the huge amounts exported to these countries and invoiced mainly in Deutsche Mark.

Table 10.5:   Structure of German foreign trade by currencies and by
regions in 1989 (per cent)

Country/country group	Deutsche Mark	US dollar	other
Exports			
Europe*	80	2	18
USA	62	37	1
other countries	82	12	6
all countries	79	8	13
Imports			
Europe*	60	11	29
USA	14	67	19
other countries	46	37	17
all countries	53	22	25

There is only data for 1989 available; * = Western Europe.
Source: Deutsche Bundesbank, *Monthly Report* (November 1991).

Currency Denomination in German Imports

The Deutsche Mark plays a smaller role in German imports than in
exports, but it is increasing (see Table 10.6). Between 1980 and 1994
the proportion invoiced in Deutsche Mark grew by around 10 percentage points to 53 per cent, whereas the US dollar proportion decreased
by about 14 percentage points to 18 per cent (see Table 10.6). This
shows that more of Germany's trading partners[10] are using the
Deutsche Mark for invoicing their exports to Germany.

Table 10.6:   Currency denomination of German imports* (per cent)

Currency	1980	1985	1989	1990	1991	1992	1993	1994	1995†
Deutsche Mark	43.0	47.8	52.6	54.3	55.4	55.9	54.1	53.2	51.3
US dollar	32.3	28.1	22.3	20.9	20.4	18.4	18.7	18.1	n/a
French franc	3.3	3.8	4.1	3.6	3.0	3.1	3.0	3.2	n/a
Pound sterling	3.4	3.0	2.6	2.5	2.3	2.2	2.2	2.2	n/a
Lira	2.4	1.5	1.8	1.9	1.8	1.7	1.5	1.1	n/a
Yen	x	1.8	2.0	1.8	2.0	1.7	2.0	1.7	n/a
Other	x	14.0	14.6	15.0	15.1	17.0	18.4	20.4	n/a

* From July 1990 imports of the former DDR are included.
†Figures for 1995 consider only first half of 1994.
Sources: Deutsche Bundesbank, *Monthly Report* (November 1991 and January 1995) and data supplied by Deutsche Bundesbank (1995 and 1997), all
currencies = 100 %.

Comparison with Currency Denomination of Foreign Trade in Other Countries

The role of the Deutsche Mark becomes even more obvious by comparing it with the currency denomination of foreign trade in other countries.[11] The figures in Table 10.7 and Table 10.8 show that a similar pattern is found only for the US dollar. Focusing first on exports, the exporter's currency is dominant in all countries considered (excluding Japan), but only in the case of the USA does the home currency dominate more in its trade than the Deutsche Mark in German trade.

Table 10.7:   Currency denomination of exports in other countries (per cent)

Country	Deutsche Mark		US dollar		French franc		Pound sterling		Lira		Yen	
	1980	1987	1980	1987	1980	1987	1980	1987	1980	1987	1980	1987
Germany	82.5	81.5	7.2		2.8	2.5	1.4	1.8	–	1.7	–	0.5
USA	1.0	2.0	97.0	94.0	1.0	1.0	1.0	1.0	–	1.0	–	1.0
France	9.4	10.2	13.2	11.8	62.5	61.5	3.2	3.6	–	3.9	–	0.4
UK	3.0	4.0	17.0	7.0	2.0	2.0	76.0	78.2	–	–	–	–
Italy	14.0	18.0	30.0	7.4	8.0	9.0	–	–	36.0	38.8	–	–
Japan	1.9	2.0	61.5	63.6	–	–	0.9	1.0	–	–	32.7	33.4

Sources: Page (1981), Black (1989), Tavlas (1991), Deutsche Bundesbank, *Monthly Report* (November 1991), Central Statistical Office (1989). US figures for 1987 are Black's estimates.

Table 10.8   Currency denomination of imports in other countries (per cent)

Country	Deutsche Mark		US dollar		French franc		Pound sterling		Lira		Yen	
	1980	1987	1980	1987	1980	1987	1980	1987	1980	1987	1980	1987
Germany	43.0	52.4	32.3	22.0	3.3	3.9	3.4	2.6	2.4	1.6	–	2.5
US	4.1	*8.0	85.0	80.0	1.0	*2.0	1.5	*3.0	1.0	*2.0	*1.0	*2.0
France	12.8	15.3	33.1	18.7	34.1	46.5	3.8	2.8	3.0	4.4	1.0	1.2
UK	9.0	14.0	29.0	20.0	5.0	8.0*	38.0	38.0	–	*2.0	–	*2.0
Italy	14.0	19.0	45.0	28.0	9.0	9.0	*5.0	*5.0	18.0	27.0	–	–
Japan	2.0	*2.0	93.0	84.0	1.0	*1.0	2.0	*1.0	–	–	2.0	10.6

*= Black's estimates.
Sources: Page (1981); Black (1989); Tavlas (1991); Deutsche Bundesbank, *Monthly Report* (November 1991); Central Statistical Office (1989).

On the import side, the Deutsche Mark also plays a role internationally. More than 50 per cent of German imports are invoiced in Deutsche Mark, whereas the main currency used in Japan's and Italy's imports is the US dollar. Only France comes close to the German figure, with 46.5 per cent of French imports invoiced in French francs (see Table 10.8)[12].

The data in Tables 10.7 and 10.8 also show that the use of the US dollar in trade between the major European trading countries has declined. Although the dollar is the most widely used currency in world trade, within Europe most traders use the currencies of their trading partners. The increase in use of the importer's currency was apparently at the expense of the US dollar.

Measures of the Use of the Deutsche Mark as a Vehicle Currency in Foreign Trade

A vehicle currency is used for denominating and executing trade between parties, none of whom is based in the area where the currency is legal tender (Tavlas, 1991, p. 5). A vehicle currency will emerge whenever indirect exchange costs (such as costs of information, search, uncertainty and enforcement) through the vehicle are lower than direct exchange costs between two other non-vehicle currencies (Black, 1989, p. 5).

Commodities which have a world market and a world market price are normally denominated in a single currency, in most cases the US dollar. In such markets, using a currency with which most participants are familiar as a numéraire (that is, unit of account) minimises the transaction costs, since it is more efficient to transmit price information about homogeneous products in a single currency than through many currencies (Page, 1981, p. 62).

There is little data on the use of the Deutsche Mark as a vehicle currency in trade between third countries. Clearly, the primary vehicle currency is still the US dollar. International trade in raw materials, crude oil and gold are all denominated in US dollars (Gerhardt, 1984, p. 53). International statistics and comparisons are expressed in US dollars or, to a smaller extent, in SDRs. However, there is some evidence that the Deutsche Mark is being used to a small extent as a vehicle currency in third countries' trade: some non-German customers[13] of British exporters do generally expect to be invoiced in Deutsche Mark, especially in eastern Europe (Small Business Research Trust, 1993).

Another study conducted by Patrick Anckar (1994) found out that there are only two currencies, the US dollar and the Deutsche Mark, which are used to a notable amount in invoicing Sweden's, Finland's and the USA's exports.[14] The two major reasons for choosing these currencies were global acceptability and broad forward markets.[15]

To sum up, taking the German statistics as a base, about 14 per cent of world trade is denominated in Deutsche Mark. This is due to the dominance of the Deutsche Mark in Germany's bilateral trade, and especially to the huge amount of German imports invoiced in Deutsche Mark. There is no data from other central banks on their country's use of currencies in payment in foreign trade by country of destination. It is very probable that trade of other countries invoiced in Deutsche Mark is trade with Germany, as the amount of trade with Germany of the countries in Tables 10.7 and 10.8 is in each case greater than the share invoiced in Deutsche Mark. However, there is some evidence that if there is another vehicle currency in addition to the US dollar, it is the Deutsche Mark.

The circulation of the Deutsche Mark abroad

Another indicator of a currency's use is whether or not it is held abroad in the form of notes. As the circulation of Deutsche Mark denominated notes outside the banking system has increased since the 1950s, Seitz (1995) analysed in a recently published study the circulation of the Deutsche Mark abroad to find evidence of foreign demand for it.[16] The results show that at the end of 1994 between 30 per cent and 40 per cent of the total currency issue was probably held abroad. This means in absolute terms DM65 billion to DM90 billion, respectively. Deutsche Mark banknotes[17] circulating abroad are held for transaction purposes as well as a store of value. This reflects the international strength, stability and acceptance of the Deutsche Mark. Furthermore, it reflects the fact that the Deutsche Mark is a potential substitute for the US dollar and is used as a parallel currency, especially in eastern European countries. It is very likely that the Deutsche Mark is widely used in these countries, since the demand for cash increased even more with the opening of eastern Europe.[18]

The growth of foreign holdings of the Deutsche Mark abroad is clearly an indicator of its growing international role. Similar studies for the USA reported that 70 per cent of the US dollar issue circulates abroad. However, despite the big gap between it and the US dollar, the Deutsche Mark's use for transaction purposes and as a store of value in third countries is substantial.

THE DEUTSCHE MARK IN INTERNATIONAL CAPITAL AND MONEY MARKETS

To understand the Deutsche Mark's role in international financial markets, its importance in the foreign exchange markets and the quantity of foreign investment denominated in Deutsche Mark need to be considered in detail. But first, the development of Germany's financial market official policy and regulations in which this role has developed will be explained.

Official Policy and Regulations

Official policy has matured as the Bundesbank's attitude towards the increasing role of the Deutsche Mark has changed. Between the late 1960s and the early 1980s, the Bundesbank attempted to limit the international use of the Deutsche Mark, especially its use as a reserve currency, as it was afraid that this could interfere with domestic stabilisation, particularly at times of speculative expectations of an appreciation of the Deutsche Mark (Unger, 1991, pp. 96–8).

The special fear was that if foreign investors and central banks[19] invested their money in the German capital market, the domestic money supply would increase and disturb domestic price stability. The Bundesbank could have followed a restrictive monetary policy to control commercial bank liquidity, but this would have increased interest rates and thus attracted even more foreign investment. The Bundesbank's fear was that it would not be able to fulfil the role which German legislation has assigned to the Bundesbank: '[to regulate] the quantity of money in circulation and of credit supplied to the economy, with the aim of safeguarding the currency, and providing for the execution of domestic and external payments (Bundesbank Act, section 3)' (Boeck and Gehrmann, 1974, p. 39).[20]

Furthermore, increasing investment in the Deutsche Mark increases demand for the Deutsche Mark which would then appreciate. Thus it was feared that the Deutsche Mark foreign exchange rate would not correspond any more to Germany's domestic and foreign economic performance and thus hurt Germany's economic growth (Boeck and Gehrmann, 1974, p. 39).

German restrictions on capital movements were directed primarily at inflows. The most important restriction placed on capital inflows in 1968 was known as the 'gentlemen's agreement' between the Bundesbank and the German banks. This agreement stipulated that only German banks could lead syndicates to issue bonds denominated in Deutsche Mark. At that time, foreign Deutsche Mark bonds had become very popular, and thus, as Germany's capital market was still very narrow, large issues of these bonds 'had an adverse effect on Germany's capital market'.[21]

The problem of unwanted capital imports eased considerably with the end of the Bretton Woods system, as the squaring of the balance of payments now took place largely without central bank intervention. After the ban on the payment of interest on non-residents' deposits with domestic banks had been abolished in September 1975, there was a large degree of freedom in capital imports, but the purchase of money market paper and bonds (with remaining maturities of up to four years) continued to require authorisation:

> This was mainly due to a desire to limit somewhat the continuously increasing significance of the Deutsche Mark as a reserve currency. Nevertheless, the building up of Deutsche Mark reserves by foreign countries could not be prevented, not least because the Euro-Deutsche Mark market offered enough attractive investment opportunities for non-residents.[22]

Otmar Emminger (1986, pp. 44–5), a former President of the Bundesbank, named four major reasons for this desire.

1. As long as the Deutsche Mark was the 'switch over currency' for the US dollar, the Deutsche Mark was affected by every difficulty of and loss of confidence in the dollar.
2. The existence of another accepted currency as a substitute for the US dollar enhanced instability within the international currency system by making it possible to shift currency reserves around.
3. At the time, when Germany was running surpluses in its balance of payments, surpluses of foreign exchange increased, caused by other countries diversifying their foreign exchange currencies. The Bun-

desbank had to intervene as this behaviour enhanced the tendency to overvalue the Deutsche Mark and to undervalue the US dollar, respectively, which caused an unwanted extension of the domestic German money stock.

4. The capacity of the German money and capital markets was limited compared with that of the USA.

Another argument against the use of the Deutsche Mark as an investment and reserve currency had been that if Germany ran a balance of payments deficit in the longer run, private and official investors would exit from the small German financial market and the Deutsche Mark which would put even more pressure on Germany's economic policy than a 'normal' deficit would do. Moreover, there was no wish to give large Deutsche Mark holders the option of using the threat of the withdrawal of their Deutsche Mark deposits as a political tool (Boeck and Gehrmann, 1974, p. 40).

By the early 1980s, the Bundesbank's position had changed substantially, as the following statement shows: 'In view of the international role of the Deutsche Mark, Germany cannot shut itself off from the trend which is now under way, since the Deutsche Mark must remain competitive against the international investment currencies.'[23]

Although Germany had current account deficits in 1980 and 1981 and had thus a real interest in obtaining foreign investment to finance these deficits, the level of development that the German financial markets had reached, as well as the general efforts of liberalisation, were probably more significant in bringing about that change of heart.

The last capital controls were lifted in 1981. This was the abandoning of the authorisation requirement for purchases of domestic bonds with a (remaining) maturity of up to one year, and of money market paper by non-residents. The division between the market for Deutsche Mark bonds of domestic issuers and the market for foreign Deutsche Mark bonds ended in 1984 with the abolition of the 'coupon tax', a withholding tax on foreign investors' interest income from domestic bonds, and encouraged foreign demand for Deutsche Mark assets. In 1985, the Bundesbank allowed the German-based subsidiaries of foreign banks to undertake the lead management of issues of foreign Deutsche Mark bonds.[24]

Since 1990, there have been no restrictions (except those due to minimum reserve policy) on bonds denominated in foreign currencies or ECU being used in Germany or by residents.[25]

Furthermore, German stock market legislation has undergone many changes in recent years. The Act Amending the Stock Exchange Act of 1989 and the abolition of the securities transfer tax in 1991, which imposed a considerable burden on the secondary market, were very important for Germany's international competitiveness as a financial centre. These two obstacles impeded the move towards a securitised money market.[26]

All these developments and changes within the German official policy and regulations show major changes in the Bundesbank's attitude towards the international role of the Deutsche Mark. It evolved from aversion into passive observation and ended up being supportive of foreigners holding investments in Deutsche Mark. In the opinion of the Bundesbank, the major reason for the growing international role of the Deutsche Mark is confidence in German monetary policy and its stability.[27] This bonus of confidence has been kept, and has indeed been a help in financing Germany's reunification.

Some regulations have been retained. Foreign securities denominated in Deutsche Mark have to have a minimum maturity of two years, so that the minimum reserve policy of the Bundesbank will not be in danger. Otherwise, German banks would be able to issue paper through addresses abroad, and thus avoid minimum reserve requirements, whereas minimum reserves would have to be maintained if the paper were issued in Germany.[28] The Bundesbank continues to insist on Deutsche Mark denominated issues being launched only under the lead management of a credit institution domiciled in Germany which is referred to as 'the anchor principle'. Nevertheless, this may now also include the branch office of a foreign credit institution located in Germany.[29]

With recent changes (1994) in the Securities Trading Act, which is a part of the Second Financial Market Promoting Act, the supervisory system for securities transactions has been adapted to international standards. The major points were the establishment of a Federal Supervisory Office for Securities Trading and the introduction of an effective market and securities trading supervision system on the stock exchanges. The goal of these measures has been to safeguard the viability of the capital market and to improve investors' protection.[30] These changes 'are likely to contribute to enhancing Germany's international competitiveness and attractiveness as a financial centre'[31] and show the strong effort now being made to improve Germany's competitiveness as a financial centre. Moreover, at the end of 1995 the

German minister of finance has announced a law to encourage financial markets by extending investment possibilities in Germany. It mostly focuses on investment funds (Norman, 1995, p. 20). However, compared with other major countries, some of the changes came quite late.

Foreign Deutsche Mark Denominated Investment

With this background, we can appraise the international role of the Deutsche Mark from the viewpoint of international investors. Two different kinds of analysis have to be made.

First, the development of foreign Deutsche Mark denominated investment in Germany has to be considered. This consists of funds invested for both the short and the long term in German banks, in the private sector (enterprises and individuals), and in the public sector.

Second, the currency distribution of external bond issues put the Deutsche Mark's role in an international context. Euro- banks also have large liabilities in Deutsche Mark but, according to the Bundesbank, a large amount which can only be estimated has to be excluded because of double-counting due to Euro-banks' borrowing in Germany and inter-bank transactions within the Euro-Deutsche Mark market. Thus foreign-owned assets in Germany should, when combined with international Deutsche Mark denominated bonds held by non-residents (amount based on estimates of the Bundesbank), account for the largest part of foreign investment in Deutsche Mark.

Foreign Deutsche Mark Denominated Investment in Germany

At the end of June 1996, the total amount of foreign short-and long-term financial assets in Germany was DM1217 billion. Compared with the stock at the end of 1990 this amount has more than doubled (for all figures mentioned, see Table 10.9).

Since the abolition of the coupon tax on interest received by non-residents from domestic securities in 1984, investment in securities has become more popular.[32] In 1984, only about 26 per cent of foreign investment was held in securities, while this amount had increased to 61 per cent in June 1996. The amount invested in public promissory notes has declined since 1984 and thus represented at the end of the reviewed period only 3.8 per cent of the total. As this instrument had been coupon tax-free it lost with the abolition of the coupon tax a

Table 10.9   Foreign Deutsche Mark denominated investment in Germany*
1980–June 1996 (year-end level or end-of-month level in DM billion)

Position	1980	1984	1986	1988	1990	1992	1994	June 1996
German banking system	117.1	142.6	177.4	193.5	265.7	345.7	463.8	566.8
Private sector	58.1	102.7	159.0	145.3	184.7	192.6	230.0	260.2
of which financial loans	6.1	10.9	9.1	10.0	14.4	16.8	22.4	n/a
of which equities[†]	19.7	43.8	100.3	86.0	111.9	103.5	143.1	n/a
of which bonds[‡]	3.1	4.3	14.4	15.5	14.7	16.8	14.7	22.9
Public sector	41.5	104.1	160.9	186.2	219.0	336.0	499.4	573.2
of which promissory notes	29.5	77.4	72.8	50.6	44.1	40.9	42.5	53.6
of which bonds[§]	11.7	25.5	88.0	135.5	174.0	293.4	451.3	515.1
Others	9.0	6.2	6.9	8.8	10.4	11.1	12.0	16.3
Total	225.7	355.6	504.2	533.7	679.8	885.4	1205.2	1416.4
of which long-term (%)	59.3	64.9	76.2	75.3	71.8	75.0	79.1	n/a
of which securities (%)	19.4	26.2	47.1	49.0	48.0	55.2	60.4	61.1

Please note that 1996 figures are not strictly comparable as the sub-categories in the latest report have slightly changed.
*excludes direct investment, trade credits, credit relations between foreign and domestic enterprises and individuals, real estate and other equity holdings.
[†]includes investment in German bank shares.
[‡]includes bond issues of the Federal Post Office and until 1993 of the former Federal Railways.
[§]1994 includes bond issues of the former Federal Railways.
Sources: Deutsche Bundesbank: *Zahlungsbilanzstatistik* (May 1995) and *Monthly Report* (April 1997).

major advantage compared with the more liquid government bonds.[33] Foreign investment in the public sector took place mainly in fixed income government bonds. The amount invested in this kind of paper has trebled between 1990 and June 1996 to DM515 billion. It was thus 36 per cent of the total foreign investment in Germany. In 1990 the amount of foreign investment grew only slightly. At the beginning of that year, German monetary union had been announced. This caused uncertainty and fear of inflation among foreign investors. But in the end the Bundesbank's consistent policy of stability maintained confidence in the stability of the Deutsche Mark. Thus foreign investors helped to a large extent to cover the funding needs of the reconstruction of the economy in East Germany.[34]

Overall, the Deutsche Mark amount invested in the domestic public sector increased about 160 per cent from 1990 to June 1996 to DM573 billion. The public sector's Deutsche Mark indebtedness to non-residents is now greater than that of any other domestic borrower. About 28 per cent of its total debts was raised from non-residents and even 47 per cent of the securitised debt was held by non-residents.[35]

The smallest sector of foreign investment is the private sector. It accounted only for DM260 billion. One reason for this is that two items important for corporate financing (direct investment and trade credits) do not count as financial Deutsche mark denominated external assets in this context.[36]

This whole development describes the growing role and interest of foreign investors in the Deutsche Mark. However, to consider its international role, a comparison of international statistics is necessary.

The Role of the Deutsche Mark in the International Bond Markets

In the international bond market, the role of the Deutsche Mark may be tackled in two ways: firstly, the proportion of Deutsche Mark denominated bonds issued in the international market; secondly, its share of bond issues held by foreigners.

The increase in Deutsche Mark denominated bonds in 1992 and 1993 (see Table 10.10) has been due to the fact that European governments borrowed in order to rebuilt their foreign exchange reserves (which had been exhausted in their efforts to defend the parities in the EMS against speculative attacks in 1992) and that German regional governments increased their use of international bond markets.[37]

Table 10.10:   Currency distribution of international bonds issues 1985–96
(per cent of total issue)

Currency	1985	1986	1987	1988	1989	1990	1991	1992	1993	1994	1995	1996
Deutsche Mark	6.8	7.5	8.3	10.4	6.4	8.0	6.6	10.4	11.8	7.8	15.5	14.0
US dollar	60.6	55.0	36.2	37.2	49.6	34.8	31.1	36.9	35.9	37.5	39.5	42.9
Pound Sterling	n/a	4.8	8.3	10.5	7.7	9.2	8.4	7.6	10.8	8.8	5.9	8.8
Yen	7.7	10.4	14.7	10.0	9.3	13.4	13.4	11.2	9.6	13.3	12.6	8.8
Swiss franc	8.9	10.2	13.4	11.6	7.3	10.1	6.5	5.8	6.1	4.8	5.6	3.3
ECU	4.1	3.1	4.1	4.9	4.9	7.8	10.6	6.8	1.6	2.0	1.7	0.7
Other	11.9	9.0	15.0	15.4	14.8	16.7	23.4	21.3	24.2	25.8	19.2	21.5

Sources: OECD: *Financial Market Trends* (June 1995 and March 1997).

The increase in the share of the D-Mark, especially during 1992 and 1993 can be explained by two factors – first the D-Mark borrowing by European governments to rebuild their foreign exchange reserves (which were exhausted after the ERM crises of those years), and

Figure: 10.1   International Deutsche Mark denominated bonds held by non-residents, 1980–June 1996.

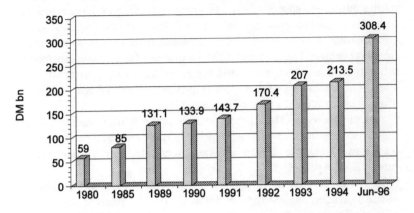

Sources: Deutsche Bundesbank, *Monthly Report* (May 1991) and (April 1997), calculated on the basis of total issues outstanding (face values) and estimated domestic holdings.

second, the increased use of the international bond markets by German regional governments (International Monetary Fund, 1994, p. 70).

The total value of D-Mark international bond issues in 1996 reached DM150.7 billion, a large increase from the DM103.5 billion recorded in 1995. Although in a rapidly increasing international bond market this represented a fall in total share, it maintained the D-Mark's position as the second most important currency for denomination of international bonds (OECD, 1997, p.52). Since 1980 the total holding of international D-Mark denominated bonds abroad has increased tremendously, from DM59.0 billion to DM308.4 billion in June 1996.[38]

The Deutsche Mark in the Foreign Exchange Market

Every three years, 26 central banks conduct a survey of their foreign exchange markets focusing on the size and structure of these markets. The BIS then aggregates the data from each central bank to produce aggregate data on the international market. The last survey was conducted in April 1995.[39] In the following section the key findings of the surveys with respect to the Deutsche Mark in Germany, Japan, the UK and the USA will be pointed out.[40]

In Germany, the Deutsche Mark was traded against the US dollar in roughly every second business transaction. As the Bundesbank points out, it is a special feature of German foreign exchange dealings that the domestic currency is used in direct trading against other currencies to a considerably greater extent than in almost any other financial centre. The trading of the Deutsche Mark against currencies other than the dollar accounted for more than one-quarter of turnover. The exchange of US dollars against other foreign currencies took place in almost every other case.

In London, US$/DM trading dominates the market and accounted for 22 per cent of transactions (April 1995). The overall proportion of trades involving the Deutsche Mark accounted for 33 per cent of turnover in April 1995.

In Tokyo the amount traded in the Deutsche Mark is smaller and it is basically traded against the US dollar (US$/DM account for 11.7 per cent of all transactions, 3.7 per cent are traded in DM/Yen).

The Federal Reserve Bank of New York reported that virtually all foreign exchange trades involved either the US dollar, Deutsche Mark or Yen. The most traded currency pairs have been the US$/DM, with 30 per cent of turnover volume, followed by the US$/Yen with 20 per cent of turnover volume.

A notable development since the last survey has been the rapid growth of transactions in the French franc, other[41] European Union and emerging market currencies. The growth of transactions in these currencies has created a demand for greater use of direct trading in non-US dollar trades, which means transactions that do not go through the US dollar as a vehicle currency.[42] The use of the dollar as the vehicle currency in foreign exchange transactions has in fact declined, a development due in particular to the increased use of the Deutsche Mark: most of the direct trades were concentrated in Deutsche Mark transactions and the most actively traded currency pair was the DM/FF with 3.5 per cent of the turnover volume. This development is evident in the higher share of DM/non-$ trades, which increased from 10 per cent in 1992 to 13 per cent in 1995. Simultaneously the share of $/DM trades fell from 33 per cent to 30 per cent while the US$/non-DM transactions remained unchanged at 57 per cent.

This development has parallels in financial history: at the time when the US dollar replaced the pound sterling as the principal unit of account and medium of financing international trade, the US dollar also replaced the pound sterling as the vehicle currency in the foreign exchange market (Einzig, 1970, pp, 305–6). Of course, a 13 per cent share for the Deutsche Mark in the US foreign exchange market as a vehicle currency is not yet sufficient grounds to talk about replacement, but nevertheless, it shows that the Deutsche Mark is increasingly used as a substitute for the US dollar.

It is not really possible to give a clear ranking of investment currencies, because investment considerations are based on facts which are changing very fast as they are also based on speculation. Thus a bigger part of the increased Deutsche Mark volume is due to speculation and not related to foreign trade transactions. But overall, the Deutsche Mark has been one of the most attractive investment currencies.

Even Germany's reunification could not weaken the Deutsche Mark's position as an international investment and reserve currency as König pointed out in a recently published book edited by Frowen and Hölscher (König, 1997). Due to Germany's credible and consistent policy of monetary stability the Deutsche Mark kept its external position also after 1989.

THE DEUTSCHE MARK AS A RESERVE CURRENCY

Having examined the role of the Deutsche Mark as a trading currency, investment currency and its use in the foreign exchange market, we turn now to its role as a reserve currency.

During the past 25 years, major changes in the world's currency system, such as floating exchange rates and other exchange rate arrangements, including the introduction of the EMS, have resulted in the development of a multicurrency system.

Since the end of the Bretton Woods system the Deutsche Mark has become the second most important reserve currency after the US dollar, accounting for 15.3 per cent (1995) of the world's total reserves (see Table 10.11).

It is worth mentioning that the international role of the Deutsche Mark started with its role as a reserve currency. According to the Bundesbank, the Deutsche Mark had probably already replaced the pound sterling as the second most important reserve currency by the beginning of the 1970s (at that time, only fragmentary statistical information was available).[43] This was long before the Deutsche Mark became the anchor of stability in the EMS and an important investment currency. Since 1975, when data first became available, industrial countries have been the major holders of foreign exchange reserves denominated in Deutsche Mark. In 1994 they held 58 per cent of the total amount of foreign exchange reserves held in Deutsche Mark (see Figure 10.2).

Table 10.11: Shares of major currencies in total foreign exchange reserves 1975–95 (per cent)

End of period	US dollar	Deut- sche Mark	Yen	Ster- ling	Private ECU	French franc	Swiss franc	Dutch guilder
1975	78.2	8.8	1.8	2.8	–	1.8	2.2	0.9
1976	77.6	9.3	2.2	1.7	–	1.5	2.1	0.8
1977	77.9	9.0	2.1	1.6	–	1.2	2.0	0.7
1978	76.2	10.7	3.1	1.5	–	1.2	2.0	0.8
1979	73.7	11.8	3.5	1.8	–	1.2	2.4	1.0
1980	69.7	14.7	4.2	2.9	–	1.7	3.2	1.3
1981	71.9	12.7	4.1	2.1	–	1.3	2.7	1.1
1982	71.2	12.0	4.6	2.4	–	1.2	2.7	1.1
1983	72.4	11.2	4.7	2.5	–	1.0	2.3	0.8
1984	70.7	11.8	5.4	2.9	0.2	1.0	2.0	0.7
1985	66.0	14.1	7.4	2.9	0.5	1.2	2.2	0.9
1986	69.1	13.5	6.9	2.5	0.8	1.1	1.7	1.0
1987	67.8	14.6	7.7	2.2	0.9	0.7	1.8	1.1
1988	64.6	15.7	7.9	2.5	2.1	0.9	1.9	0.9
1989	60.4	18.7	7.9	2.5	3.0	1.3	1.7	1.0
1990	56.4	19.1	9.0	3.1	4.6	2.1	1.7	1.0
1991	57.3	17.0	9.5	3.3	4.5	2.5	1.6	1.0
1992	62.0	14.8	8.6	3.1	2.7	2.2	1.3	0.6
1993	61.7	16.0	9.2	3.1	2.6	2.1	1.3	0.6
1994	61.0	15.5	8.9	3.2	2.7	2.0	1.3	0.4
1995	60.0	15.3	8.2	3.1	2.5	2.0	1.2	0.5

Sources: Data supplied by Deutsche Bundesbank (1995 and 1997)

The oil exporting countries[44] moved in the opposite direction. Beginning in 1980, the amount they held in Deutsche Mark decreased substantially, and in 1994 they only held 2.5 per cent of the total Deutsche Mark holdings (in 1970 they held 30 per cent). In absolute terms this means that they have more than halved the amount they held in Deutsche Mark.

Non-oil developing countries demonstrated a different attitude. Their percentage share of total Deutsche Mark holdings stayed more or less stable, between 25 and 30 per cent, but in absolute terms the amount held in 1994 is almost 10 times higher than 1974. As developing

Figure 10.2   Foreign exchange reserves held in Deutsche Mark by country group 1975–94

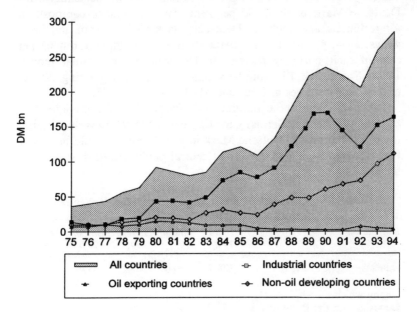

Source: Data supplied by Deutsche Bundesbank (1995).

countries have sizeable foreign debts denominated in US dollars (according to the World Bank, 38.3 per cent of their long-term debt was denominated in US dollars in 1992), they prefer to hold the major part of their foreign reserves in that currency. Reflecting the point that a country's foreign reserves mirrors its debt structure, the Deutsche Mark only plays a more significant role in developing countries in Europe and Central Asia and accounts for 11 per cent of the total.

The domination of industrial countries holding Deutsche Mark reflects the strong position of the Deutsche Mark in Europe.

According to IMF statistics, the Yen plays a more important role than the Deutsche Mark as a reserve currency in Asian countries. In the East Asian and Pacific region, the Yen is also a major currency in which long-term debts are denominated (28.6 per cent in 1992), which indicates a higher profile in these countries' foreign reserves.[45]

The confidential nature of information on the currency composition of central banks' reserves makes it very difficult to evaluate clearly which countries are holding Deutsche Marks in their portfolio. However, the Reserve Bank of Australia, for example, has most of its currency reserves in non-dollar currencies and its benchmark for Deutsche Mark is about 30 per cent. The benchmark composition for Indonesia also includes Deutsche Mark (Nijathawom and Senivongs, 1994, p. 36). The Netherlands Bank is holding about 63 per cent of their currency reserves in Deutsche Mark (annual report, 1996). Taking all EU countries together, they are holding 20 per cent of their reserves in Deutsche Mark (Masson, 1997).

Table 10.12 shows the amount of Deutsche Mark denominated foreign reserves held in Germany for the years 1990–94. Less than half of the total amount of Deutsche Mark in world reserves could be identified; apparently, most deposits of central banks are held with Euro-banks.

Table 10.12   Location of Deutsche Mark denominated foreign reserves

DM billion	End of 1990	End of 1991	End of 1992	End of 1993	Mid-1994
Deutsche Mark assets of monetary authorities, among which:	229.7	220.6	203.2	258.4	258.5
Deposits with the Bundesbank	*51.7*	*41.1*	*26.0*	*22.8*	*18.3*
Identified deposits with:					
Banks in Germany	7.5	6.0	5.5	5.1	6.2
Euro-banks	65.1	49.9	46.9	36.9	45.6

Source: Data supplied by the Deutsche Bundesbank (1995), deposits with the Bundesbank do not include Bundesbank liquidity paper (Bulis).

THE DEUTSCHE MARK AS A REFERENCE CURRENCY

Finally, we consider the role of the Deutsche Mark as a standard or measure of other countries' exchange rate policies. A reference currency is used to express exchange rate relationships and thus a currency is called a reference currency if other countries use it to orient their monetary policy. As such, it is clearly one of the channels through which the economic and even political influence of major economic powers is transmitted to other countries. Foreign governments wishing to peg their currencies to a stable currency have to give up a large part of their monetary autonomy. They do so voluntarily in order to import economic and financial stability. They then focus on an exchange rate target and not on the money supply.

When many other currencies are pegged to one another the effect is the same as if most of a country's exports and imports are invoiced in its own currency: this is an advantage for an economy as far as price stability is concerned. Exchange rate fluctuations do not occur and do not distort competition and thus trading is much easier.

The Deutsche Mark's Role in Europe

In the course of the Deutsche Mark's rise as an international currency, the Deutsche Mark also became the anchor-currency in Europe.

The development of the Deutsche Mark's weighting in the ECU basket also clearly shows this growing importance. In absolute terms the Deutsche Mark's weighting has declined, but this was only necessary to maintain the balance within the basket as the Deutsche Mark has appreciated. For the same reason it has been necessary to give the weaker, depreciating currencies a stronger weighting (see Table 10.13).

Table 10.13   Currencies and weights in the ECU basket

Currency	As of 13 March 1979	As of 17 September 1984	As of 21 September 1989
Deutsche Mark	0.828	0.719	0.6242
Pound sterling	0.0885	0.0878	0.08784
French franc	1.15	1.31	1.332
Lira	109.00	140.00	151.8
Dutch guilder	0.286	0.256	0.2198
Belgian franc	3.66	3.71	3.301
Luxembourg franc	0.14	0.14	0.130
Danish krone	0.217	0.219	0.1976
Irish pound	0.00759	0.00871	0.008552
Greek drachma	–	1.15	1.440
Spanish peseta	–	–	6.885
Portuguese escudo	–	–	1.393

Source: Deutsche Bundesbank, *Devisenkursstatistik* (November 1995).

The Deutsche Mark in the European Monetary System

The dominant role of the Deutsche Mark in Europe and within the EMS was not planned at the EMS's start in 1979. The original idea of the EMS was to have a system without a leading key-currency. After the end of the Bretton Woods system, the member countries were no longer willing to follow another central bank's monetary policy (Unger, 1991, pp. 107–24).

However, the Bundesbank's monetary policy, which has made the Deutsche Mark into an exceptionally stable currency and thus the European anchor of stability, resulted in the 1970s and 1980s in the use of the Deutsche Mark as the effective currency peg or reference currency in the EMS. Another reason for that behaviour was the fact that the economies of the following countries are tied strongly to Germany and thus stable exchange rates are an advantage: the Netherlands, Belgium\Luxembourg and Denmark. These countries export between 20 and 30 per cent of their total exports to Germany and about 39 per cent of Austrian exports also go to Germany (Saunderson, 1993, pp. 45–6).

Austria is one exception as it has held the Schilling since the late 1970s within a tight divergence band of less than 1 per cent against the Deutsche Mark without official agreement. After becoming a member of the European Union on 1 January 1995, and thus having joined the ERM of the EMS on 9 January 1995, it declared that it would continue to keep the Schilling's external value consistent against the Deutsche Mark.[46]

As Unger points out, there is another incentive for Austria to peg the Schilling to the Deutsche Mark, as they hold a large amount of their foreign debts in Deutsche Mark (about 37 per cent in 1988), with the rest mainly in Yen (about 23.5 per cent) and Swiss franc (about 34.5 per cent). The US dollar counts for less than 1 per cent. Being pegged to the Deutsche Mark guarantees that a large part of Austrian foreign debts is hedged against foreign currency risk.

Even if the EMS countries peg their currencies to the Deutsche Mark by following the Bundesbank's interest rates, officially membership of the ERM commits them to maintaining the spot exchange rates between their currencies and the currencies of the other participants within margins of 15 per cent[47] above and below the cross rates based on the central rates expressed in ECUs.

The Netherlands is the only country within the EMS whose currency is officially more tightly pegged to the Deutsche Mark, since it is only permitted to fluctuate within 2.25 per cent of the Deutsche Mark.

The special role played by the Deutsche Mark can also be seen from its increasing use for interventions in the EMS:

> The share of the DM interventions in the EMS rose from about one-quarter at the beginning of the 1980s to almost 60% towards the end of the 1980s. In addition, the Deutsche Mark has become the main intervention currency of countries linked to the EMS.

Viewed against this background, it comes as no surprise that the Deutsche Mark has virtually the same weight as the US dollar in the reserves of European central banks (excluding the Bundesbank). (Issing, 1993)

Every key and reserve currency becomes at some point a major intervention currency. The Deutsche Mark has become also an intervention currency for the USA, due to its key role in Europe, and therefore the USA has accumulated sizeable Deutsche Mark reserves (Tietmeyer, 1991). The USA's currency reserves are now confined entirely to Deutsche Mark and Yen (51 and 40 per cent, respectively).

The Importance of the Deutsche Mark in Central and Eastern Europe

With the ongoing changes in central and eastern Europe, the importance of the Deutsche Mark has been growing further as Germany has crucial trading relationships with these countries.

Several Eastern European countries have pegged their currency to the Deutsche Mark or to a currency basket which is in most cases dominated by the Deutsche Mark:

- Estonia pegged its Kroon, created in June 1992, to the Deutsche Mark; the Federal Republic of Serbia and Montenegro has pegged its Dinar to the Deutsche Mark (Pringle, 1996, pp. 51 and 178);
- the Czech Koruna is pegged to the Deutsche mark (*Financial Times*, 27 May 1997, p. 2);
- the Slovak Koruna is fixed to a currency basket consisting of 60 per cent Deutsche Mark and 40 per cent US dollar (Saunderson, 1993, p. 47);
- the Deutsche Mark is the anchor currency for the Bosnian dinar;
- finally, the Polish Zloty targets a basket of five currencies which consists of the Deutsche Mark (35 per cent), the US dollar (45 per cent), the pound sterling (10 per cent), French franc (5 per cent) and the Swiss franc (5 per cent).[48]

The Deutsche Mark and Other Reference Currencies

The number of countries pegged to the US dollar has steadily declined. From 1974 to 1990, the percentage of developing countries pegged to the US dollar declined from 62.2 to 25.8. At that time, there were no currencies left pegged to the former reserve currency, sterling, although some currency baskets included a small amount of sterling (Pringle, 1991, p. 19).

Currently, only the Deutsche Mark has a growing (regional) importance for other countries who want to orient their monetary policy to another country's currency.[49] Although the Yen is a reserve currency in Asia, no currency is pegged to it formally or informally. Some currencies are linked to a basket, which contains the Yen, but this is also true of the Deutsche Mark.[50] Unlike the situation in Europe, where countries are linked to the Deutsche Mark, the currencies of Japan's smaller neighbouring countries are pegged predominantly to the US dollar. The Asian-Pacific region remains part of the dollar area.

Looking at the three major reserve currencies in the world, it is only the dollar and the Deutsche Mark which are at the centre of a regional or global currency system.

CONCLUSION: THE EVOLUTION OF THE DEUTSCHE MARK AS AN INTERNATIONAL CURRENCY

The Deutsche Mark has emerged as one of the three key currencies in the multicurrency monetary system, along with the US dollar and Yen.

Given the factors determining the international use of a currency, the main determinants of the expanding role of the Deutsche Mark have been Germany's relatively low rate of inflation and the confidence in the Deutsche Mark's value, which are the result of the credibility of the Bundesbank's monetary policy.

The evolution of the Deutsche Mark has followed a different pattern from that of the pound sterling or US dollar. These two currencies developed their role out of their use as trading and investment currencies and gradually became in each case the dominant reserve currency. Their functions as reference and intervention currencies were then a natural accompaniment to their use by private sector traders and investors.

The Deutsche Mark: A New Model of an International Currency

The Deutsche Mark started the other way round: in spite of the fact that the significance of the Deutsche Mark as an international transaction currency remained limited, its use as a reserve currency was sufficient to give it the status of an international currency. Moreover, its evolution was initially driven largely by official institutions, including central banks, rather than by the needs of foreign traders. The Deutsche Mark became the currency of choice of many foreign official bodies which needed reserves which keep their value. Already at the beginning of the 1970s, the Deutsche Mark had replaced the pound sterling as the second most important reserve currency. Over time, it also became a very attractive store of value for foreign investors. Today, the volume of Deutsche Mark denominated financial assets held by foreign private investors are many times larger than official Deutsche Mark reserves.

On the other hand, the fact that Germany is today the world's second most important net creditor surely underpins the international status of its currency. Both the UK and the USA were big creditors at the time their currencies acquired the status of international currencies. Through international lending and investing German companies provide a supply of Deutsche Mark to international markets. The growing use of Deutsche Mark denominated assets as a store of value for foreign official and private holders is its main claim to be a true international currency.

Traditionally, it has been thought that to be a real international transaction currency, a currency should be used widely in third country trade. In this area, the Deutsche Mark is still relatively underdeveloped in comparison to the US dollar. Although 14 per cent of world trade is denominated in Deutsche Mark, this is mostly due to Germany's strong position in international trade. The Deutsche Mark's use in the trade of third countries is still limited. There is no evidence that the Deutsche Mark will make any significant inroads into the dominance of the dollar as the dominant transaction currency.

The fact remains that traders in the world market tend to use one currency as a numéraire because it is more convenient and less expensive. In this aspect of a currency's role, 'inertia' and the degree to which a currency's usefulness depends on the extent to which it is already widely used and accepted count even more than, for example, its use as an investment currency. At least as far as a global unit of account is concerned the world thinks in terms of dollars and, despite the Deutsche Mark's strong position in Europe, it would be a considerable surprise if, for example, a large international financial institution decided to present its statistics in Deutsche Mark. Barring a catastrophic event, the US dollar will remain the currency of choice for such international accounting purposes, simply because everybody is used to it. Consequently, there can be only one 100 per cent internationally used currency in a world monetary system performing as a unit of account, means of payment and store of value. But as this system is changing, offering substitutes for many uses, it is less important than formerly to have one major currency which fulfils every criteria.

A currency's role in investment is determined by different factors from those influencing its role as a transactions currency. In this field the relative importance of currencies changes more often reflects, for example, changes in expected rates of return to investors. This is also seen in the wide variations seen in the significance of a currency at different times in international investment as demonstrated earlier. Table 10.14 summarises the interna-

Table 10.14   The international role of the Deutsche Mark at a glance

Function	Sector	
	Private	*Official*
Unit of account	• Dominating in German trade. • Use of the Deutsche Mark in invoicing exports to Germany.	• Anchor currency in the EMS • Dominates many currency baskets, especially in central and eastern Europe. • Reference currency
Means of payment	• 14 % of world trade is denominated in Deutsche Mark. • Minor but growing role as a vehicle in third countries trade. • Potential substitute for the US dollar in countries using an 'unofficial' parallel currency.	• Leading intervention currency in the EMS. • Growing importance as a intervention currency for the USA. • Growing importance as vehicle currency in the foreign exchange market.
Store of value	• Attractive currency for foreign investors. • Second rank in international bond issues in 1995.	• World's second most important reserve currency.

Source: own composition of the discussed key findings (1995).

tional role of the Deutsche Mark as a unit of account, means of payment and store of value.

Into a European Currency?

The present study may help to clarify the conditions necessary for the Euro, the planned single EU currency, to assume a full international role. Nobody knows whether the single currency will be able from the beginning of EMU to replace the Deutsche Mark as an international investment and reserve currency. Investors in long-term Deutsche Mark bonds are uncertain whether they will be repaid in a currency that may be worth substantially less than the Deutsche Marks they had invested. Thus, in 1995 there were some reports of a move by investors from Deutsche Mark to Swiss francs; certainly, the yield on long-term German government bonds rose above those on long-term US Treasury issues.

The much smaller size of the Deutsche Mark financial markets in comparison to the USA is perhaps the main reason why the Deutsche Mark by itself will clearly not overtake the role of the US dollar in the foreseeable future. But, if the new currency unit is introduced at the beginning of 1999, and if this currency gradually acquires the same credibility as the Deutsche Mark, then the world scenario could change again. While it is not very likely that the Euro will replace the US dollar in the short or even medium term, it will help to develop a competitive European investment and reserve centre.

The US dollar is far from fulfilling all the conditions necessary for a full and stable international currency. The experience of previous dominant currencies, such as sterling, shows that the markets can and do develop alternatives if the incentive is big enough. Clearly, a currency that depreciates persistently over many years will over that time lose its attractions as an investment and vehicle currency. Equally, a combination of the Deutsche Mark's strength as a store of value with London's money market could greatly enhance the world role of a new European currency.

The Multicurrency System

The new multicurrency system was responsible for the changing role of reserves. Today, demand for reserves is partly dependent on countries' access to capital markets. Central banks need reserves which keep their value, and in a system with three major reserve currencies this creates competition, too. The dollar's decline, if continued, will erode its reserve currency role, but it may still be used as a vehicle currency. Consequently, the Euro and the Yen will became more and more significant. With time, other currencies, such as those of emerging markets, may qualify for at least some of the tasks of an international currency and expand the multicurrency system. In this competitive system, certain currencies will dominate particular regions of the world economy; the world no longer needs one currency dominating in all the roles performed by dominant currencies in the past.

Notes[51]

1. See Deutsche Bundesbank (1988), p. 13.
2. See Deutsche Bundesbank, *Monetary Policy* (March 1994), p. 10.
3. Ibid., p. 11.
4. Ibid., p. 12.
5. The first collapse of the German currency (the Mark, established as a gold coin standard under the Kaiserreich) was in 1923 and was replaced by the Reichsmark in 1924. During the Third Reich, monetary policy was forced into the service of armaments financing and later the war economy. Even if price controls suppressed inflationary pressure, the real value of the currency was eroded (see Deutsche Bundesbank, *Monetary Policy* (March 1994), p. 8).
6. This is based on a ranking conducted by MMS International Inc. in August 1995.
7. After the end of the Bretton Woods system, the Bundesbank began in December 1974 to set an annual monetary target to keep the value of the currency stable. In its opinion, a stable, medium-term orientation for monetary policy provides credibility, lowers inflationary expectations, reduces uncertainty and contributes to a climate conducive to capital formation (see Deutsche Bundesbank, *Monetary Policy* (March 1994), pp. 110–20).
8. See IMF (9 October 1995), p. 308.
9. In the long run, of course, the enlargement of the economy following reunification may allow it to increase its share of world trade further.
10. Especially Germany's European trading partners, as the amount of German imports from European countries is very high (60 per cent; see Table 10.5).
11. Figures concerning the currency denomination of other countries' foreign trade are only available for 1980 and 1987. They still allow a comparison, as invoicing behaviour, and trade practices in general, need a long time to change. The British Central Statistical Office, for example, did several surveys on currency used in invoicing British trade. The idea was to see if there was any shift in the currencies used in

invoicing, as a result of the move towards the Single European Market. They stopped the surveys in 1989 because they found little change in the mix of currencies used in invoicing British trade.

12. Which is most likely due to its close link in trade with its former colonies whose currency, the Franc CFA, is pegged to the French franc.

13. Customers in France, Italy, USA, the Netherlands, Spain, Eastern Europe, Latin America, Japan/East Asia.

14. The Deutsche Mark is used as a vehicle currency for about 27% and the US dollar for almost 66% of these countries' exports.

15. See Anckar (1994), pp. 178–84.

16. This trend could not be explained by referring to domestic transactions alone or to cash holdings of enterprises, domestic hoarding and the shadow economy. (In October 1995, the cash circulation of the Deutsche Mark excluding the cash balances of credit institutions, was about DM225.8 billion.) But estimates of the circulation of the Deutsche Mark abroad have been very difficult, as only the total amount of currency circulating outside German banks is known and not the geographical breakdown of this total.

17. In this context, the circulation of the Deutsche Mark coin is insignificant.

18. The current president of the Bundesbank Hans Tietmeyer had already mentioned a couple of years earlier that 'the substantial amounts of D-Mark notes circulating in these countries...has in some cases reached the proportions of a parallel currency.'; Tietmeyer (4 May 1991).

19. Central banks could also keep their reserves with the Bundesbank, but with less profit.

20. Deutsche Bundesbank (March 1994), p. 17.

21. See Deutsche Bundesbank, *Monthly Report* (July 1985), p. 14.

22. Ibid., p. 17.

23. Ibid., p. 14.

24. See Deutsche Bundesbank, *Monthly Report* (May 1991), p. 23.

25. See Deutsche Bundesbank, *Monthly Report* (March 1992), p. 25.

26. Ibid., pp. 26–8.

27. See many of its statements, e.g., Deutsche Bundesbank, *Annual Report* (1994), p. 56, and *Monthly Report* (May 1988), p. 22.

28. See Deutsche Bundesbank, *Monthly Report* (March 1992), p. 25.

29. See Deutsche Bundesbank, *Monetary Policy*, (March 1994), pp. 50–1.

30. See Deutsche Bundesbank, *Annual Report* (1993), p. 87.

31. Deutsche Bundesbank, *Annual Report* (1994), p. 94.

32. See Deutsche Bundesbank, *Monthly Report* (April 1991), p. 23.

33. See Deutsche Bundesbank, *Monthly Report* (May 1991), p. 25.

34. See Deutsche Bundesbank, *Monthly Report* (April 1991), pp. 25–6.

35. See Deutsche Bundesbank, *Monthly Report* (April 1997), p. 22.

36. Ibid., p. 22.

37. See IMF (September 1994), p. 70.

38. See Deutsche Bundesbank, *Monthly Report* (May 1991), p. 31, and (April 1997), p. 25.

39. At the time this study was completed, only data on individual central banks was available. The BIS's analysis of the size of the global market

in 1995, adjusted for double counting, will be available in 1996. Products included in the survey are foreign exchange spot, forward and swaps.

40. See press releases from 19 September 1995 from the Bank of England, Bank of Japan, Deutsche Bundesbank and Federal Reserve Bank of New York.

41. Other = other than DM, FF and £.

42. The fact that a currency is traded directly and that no vehicle currency is necessary to trade it reduces transaction costs substantially and this, in turn, makes the currency more likely to be traded. The lower the transaction cost, the more the currency is used in international transactions.

43. See Deutsche Bundesbank, *Monthly Report* (January 1990), p. 41.

44. Algeria, Indonesia, Iran, Iraq, Kuwait, Libya, Nigeria, Oman, Qatar, Saudi Arabia, United Arab Emirates, Venezuela.

45. So recently, the central banks of Malaysia and Thailand started increasing their holdings of the Yen as a proportion of their total reserves, and the central banks of Singapore and Taiwan shifted some of their foreign reserves out of US dollars into Yen: see Terazono (1995), p. 6 and Baker (1995), p. 19. The benchmark for the Philippines foreign exchange reserves is about 70 % in US dollar and 30 % in Yen: see Nijathawom and Senivongs (1994), p. 36. About 30 % of the Philippines long-term debts were denominated in Yen in 1992.

46. See IMF: *Annual Report on Exchange Arrangements and Exchange Restrictions* (1995), p. 29.

47. Since 2 August 1993.

48. See IFM: *Annual Report on Exchange Arrangements and Exchange Restrictions* (1995), p. 395.

49. However, in some other parts of the world, some smaller developing countries have pegged their currencies to those (Australian dollar, Indian rupee, Italian lira, South African and or Russian rouble) of their larger neighbours: see IMF: *Annual Report on Exchange Arrangements and Exchange Restrictions* (1995).

50. The Chilean Peso is pegged to a basket consisting of 0.45 US dollar, 0.4691 Deutsche Mark and 24.6825 Yen; the Icelandic Króna is pegged to a basket consisting of ECU, Yen and US dollars; Israel's New Shekel is defined in relation to a basket consisting of the Deutsche Mark, French franc, Yen, pound sterling and US dollar see IMF: *Annual Report on Exchange Arrangements and Exchange Restrictions* (1995).

51. Page references of Deutsche Bundesbank, *Monthly Reports,* refer to German editions.

References

Anckar, P. (1994), *Currency Choice in Exporting*, Helsingsfors, Swedish School of Economics and Business Administration.

Baker, G. (1995), 'Benefits of building a bloc', *Financial Times*, 17 August, p. 19.

Bank of England (1995), press release, 19 September.
Bank of Japan (1995), press release, 19 September.
Black, S. (1989), 'Transactions Costs and Vehicle Currencies', *International Monetary Fund Working Paper*, No. 89/96, Washington, DC.
Boeck, K. and Gehrmann, D. (1974), *Die Deutsche Mark als internationale Reservewährung*, Hamburg, Weltarchiv.
Central Statistical Office (1989), *Currency of Invoicing*, London, HMSO.
Deutsche Bundesbank, *Annual Reports* (various years).
Deutsche Bundesbank (1985), 'Freedom of Germany's capital transactions with foreign countries', *Monthly Report*, July, Frankfurt, pp. 13–24.
Deutsche Bundesbank (1988), 'Forty years of the Deutsche Mark', *Monthly Report*, May, Frankfurt, pp. 13–23.
Deutsche Bundesbank (1990), 'The long-term trends in global monetary reserves', *Monthly Report*, January, Frankfurt, pp. 34–55.
Deutsche Bundesbank (1991), 'Germany's securities transactions with non-residents in the second half of the eighties', *Monthly Report*, April, Frankfurt, pp. 14–27.
Deutsche Bundesbank (1991), 'Non-residents' Deutsche Mark assets and liabilities at the end of 1990', *Monthly Report*, May, Frankfurt, pp. 23–31.
Deutsche Bundesbank (1991), 'The significance of the Deutsche Mark as an invoicing currency in foreign trade', *Monthly Report*, November, Frankfurt, pp. 40–4.
Deutsche Bundesbank (1992), 'Financial centre Germany: underlying conditions and recent developments', *Monthly Report*, March, Frankfurt, pp. 23–31.
Deutsche Bundesbank (1994), *The Monetary Policy of the Bundesbank*, Frankfurt.
Deutsche Bundesbank (1995), 'Monetary demand and currency substitution in Europe', *Monthly Report*, January, Frankfurt, pp. 33–49.
Deutsche Bundesbank (1995), 'Zahlungsbilanzstatistik', *Statistisches Beiheft zum Monatsbericht* 3, May, Frankfurt.
Deutsche Bundesbank (1995), press release, 19 September.
Deutsche Bundesbank (1995), 'Devisenkursstatistik', *Statistisches Beiheft zum Monatsbericht* 5, November, Frankfurt.
Deutsche Bundesbank (1997), 'The role of the Deutsche Mark as an international investment and reserve currency', *Monthly Report*, April, Frankfurt, pp. 17–30.
Einzig, P. (1970), *The History of Foreign Exchange*, 2nd edn, London, Macmillan.
Emminger, O. (1986), *Deutsche Mark, Dollar, Währungskrisen*, Stuttgart, Deutsche Verlagsanstalt. Federal Reserve Bank of New York (1995), press release, 19 September.
Financial Times (1995): 'International bonds: Deutsche Mark and Yen lift nine-month totals', 9 October, p. 5.
Financial Times (1997), 'Czechs abandon currency link with US dollar', 27 May 1997, p. 2.
Gerhardt, W. (1984), 'Der Euro-DM-Markt. Marktteilnehmer, Zinsbildung und geldpolitische Bedeutung', *Veröffentlichungen des HWWA-Instituts für Wirtschaftsforschung*, Hamburg, Weltarchiv.

172   *Evolution of DM as International Currency*

Grassman, S. (1973), 'A Fundamental Symmetry in International Payments Patterns', *Journal of International Economics*, No. 3, (May), pp. 105–16.

IMF (September 1994), *International Capital Markets. Development and Prospects*, Washington, DC.

IMF (1995), *Annual Report on Exchange Arrangements and Exchange Restrictions*, Washington, DC.

IMF (1995), *International Financial Statistics, Yearbook*, Washington, DC.

IMF (9 October 1995), *Survey*, Washington, DC.

IMF (June 1996), *International Financial Statistics, monthly edition*, Washington, DC.

Issing, Otmar (1993), 'Prospects of the international monetary order', Speech at the EFMA convention in Monte Carlo on 19 March 1993.

Köllner, Lutz (1972), 'Chronik der Deutschen Währungspolitik 1871–1971', *Taschenbücher für Geld und Wirtschaft*, Vol. 61, Frankfurt, Fritz Knapp.

König, R. (1997), 'The Deutsche Mark Exchange Rate Impact', in S.F. Frowen and J. Hölscher (eds), *The German Currency Union of 1990: A Critical Assessment*, London, Macmillan, pp. 13–33.

Masson, P.R. (1997), 'Characteristics of the Euro, the Demand for Reserves, and Policy Coordination and EMU', Seminar on EMU and the International Monetary System in Washington, DC, 17–18 March.

Netherlands Bank (1996), *Annual Report*, Amsterdam.

Nijathawom, Bandid and Chirathep Senivongs (1994), 'International Use of Currencies: Evidence in the East Asia and Pacific Region', *Paper on Policy Analysis and Assessment*, No. 2537, Bangkok, Bank of Thailand, pp. 30–9.

Nölling, Wilhelm (1993), *Unser Geld: der Kampf um die Stabilität der Währungen in Europa*, Berlin, Ullstein.

Norman, Peter (1995), 'Germany to extend investment choices', *Financial Times*, 20 October, p. 20.

OECD (June 1996), *Economic Outlook*, Paris.

OECD (1997).

OECD (various issues), *Financial Market Trends*, Paris.

Page, S.A.B. (1981), 'The Choice of Invoicing Currency in Merchandise Trade', *National Institute Economic Review*, No. 98, pp. 60–72.

Pringle, Robert (ed.) (1991), *Morgan Stanley Central Bank Directory*, 1st edn, London, Central Banking Publications.

Pringle, Robert (ed.) (1996), *Morgan Stanley Central Bank Directory*, 5th edn, London, Central Banking Publications.

Saunderson, Allan (1993), 'The Expanding DM Area', *Central Banking*, Vol. IV/2, pp. 45–50.

Scharrer, H.-E. (1978), 'Währungsrisiko und Währungsverhalten deutscher Unternehmen im Außenhandel', *Veröffentlichungen des HWWA-Institut für Wirtschaftsforschung*, Hamburg, Weltarchiv.

Seitz, F. (1995), 'Der DM-Umlauf im Ausland', *Diskussionspapier No. 1 der Volkswirtschaftlichen Forschungsgruppe der Deutschen Bundesbank*, Frankfurt, Deutsche Bundesbank.

Small Business Research Trust (1993), *The Royal Bank of Scotland Quarterly Survey of Exporters*, vol. 1/3, Milton Keynes.

Tavlas, G.S. (1991), 'On the International Use of Currencies: the Case of the Deutsche Mark', *Essays in International Finance*, No. 18, Princeton.

Terazono, E. (1995), 'Yen's fall keeps everyone guessing', *Financial Times*, 15 August, p. 6.

Tietmeyer, H. (1991), 'The Role of the Deutsche Mark in the New Europe', Speech at the Financial Symposium of the Graduate School of Management of the University of California in Berlin, 4 May, 1991.

Unger, S. (1991), Die Deutsche Mark als internationale Reserve- und Anlagewährung: Ursachen, Entwicklung und Folgen der internationalen Verwendung der deutschen Währung, Konstanz, Hartung-Gorre.

11 Profiles of Bundesbank Presidents

HANS TIETMEYER, BUNDESBANK PRESIDENT SINCE OCTOBER 1993

Hans Tietmeyer's is, perhaps, the most acute and concentrated intelligence which has dominated the German and international political, economic and monetary scene in his various capacities as Secretary of State in Bonn, as leader of the German Treaty Negotiations of 1990 establishing the German Economic, Monetary and Social Union (GEMSU), and since then as President of the Deutsche Bundesbank.

Hans Tietmeyer read economics at the Universities of Münster, Bonn and Cologne, graduating in 1959 and obtaining his doctorate in 1961. He was Manager of the Cusanuswerk from 1958 until 1962 when he entered the German civil service, taking up a position with the Federal Ministry of Economics in Bonn for the next 20 years.

In 1982 he was appointed Secretary of State in the Federal Ministry of Finance, a position he held until the end of 1989, when he joined the Board of the Bundesbank before becoming Deputy President and finally President on the retirement of Helmut Schlesinger on 1 October 1993, and a year later became Chairman of the G10 Group of Central Bank Governors.

In the Ministry of Economics, Hans Tietmeyer spent many years as Secretary of the Department responsible for basic principles (*Grundsatzabteilung*) and became its Head with the rank of a *Ministerialdirektor* when his predecessor Otto Schlecht was appointed Secretary of State. Tietmeyer played a constructive role in the preparation of the Werner Report in 1970. He also prepared the 'Lambsdorff Paper' that in 1982 led to important political changes from the Social Democratic/Liberal coalition to a coalition under Chancellor Kohl. In the Federal Ministry of Finance he played a vital role in managing international monetary issues. During the negotiations leading to German unification, Hans Tietmeyer was the personal adviser to Chancellor Kohl and for this purpose was temporarily freed from his duties in the Directorate of the Bundesbank and the Central Bank Council. (For his recollections of the German Treaty negotiations of 1990, see pp. 68–109 in this volume).

Hans Tietmeyer has a brilliant analytical mind and not surprisingly a long list of publications, mainly in the form of papers, to his name. He always remained close to scholarship and made a point of maintaining an excellent relationship with both the Academic Economic Advisory Council to the Federal Ministry of Economics and the German Council of Economic Experts (*Sachverständigenrat*). At the same time he has a sound understanding of, and feeling for, politics that made him predestined for looking after the Bundesbank's external affairs.

Profissor Tietmeyer firmly believes that the stability of the value of money is the prerequisite for a high level of both economic growth and employment, and must be defended at all costs – not least on ethical grounds. These views he strongly expressed to a packed audience at the annual Von Hügel Lecture at the University of Cambridge in 1992 while still Deputy President. As President he has given ample proof of his determination to put this belief into practice.

Despite his political background and expertise, he has always been a firm defender of the independence of the Deutsche Bundesbank and central banks generally and, in particular, the independence of the proposed ESCB. He is content that the seat of the Bundesbank is in a city not too close to the seat of the Federal Government, as he sees a distinct advantage in geographical distance. Today he enjoys a strong hold over monetary policy as Bundesbank President, a position he rightly treasures.

Tietmeyer's attitude towards a single European currency is a favourable but cautious one, though he himself is the last person who is likely to rush into any irreversible act in this direction as long as conditions for a Euro as stable as the Deutsche Mark are not met.

Stephen F. Frowen

HELMUT SCHLESINGER, BUNDESBANK PRESIDENT 1991–SEPTEMBER 1993

Helmut Schlesinger, the born scholar, spent virtually his entire career with the Deutsche Bundesbank. Born in 1924 he graduated from Munich University in 1949, receiving his doctorate in 1951. After a short spell in industry and with the influential Ifo-Institute (Institute of Economic Research) in Munich, he joined the Bundesbank in 1952 at the age of 28. From 1964 to 1972 he was in charge of the Economics and Statistics Department and became a member of the Directorate of the Bundesbank and (*ex officio*) of the policy-making Central Bank Council in 1972 while remaining in charge of the department. A further promotion came in 1980 when he was appointed Deputy Governor (*Vize-Präsident*), a position he held until 1991 when, on the sudden and unexpected resignation of Karl Otto Pöhl, he was made President of the Bundesbank. This position he held until his retirement on 30 September 1993 at the age of 69.

Professor Schlesinger's presidency – far from being a stop-gap appointment until Hans Tietmeyer, then Deputy President, was ready to take over – proved to be among the most challenging of all Bundesbank presidencies, his relatively short term of office as President falling into an exceedingly turbulent time both domestically and internationally. On the domestic front, he was faced with the traumatic macroeconomic consequences of German unification and the formation of a Monetary, Economic and Social Union with the former GDR. Finding an appropriate readjustment rate for the conversion of the East German Mark into Deutsche Marks proved a rather complex task. It was Helmut Schlesinger who soon (while still Deputy President) became the intellectual leader of a joint committee of experts to solve this problem, but political influences proved stronger.

On the international front, Helmut Schlesinger established himself as a tough negotiator. Part of the foreign press, especially in the UK, put at least some of the blame for the ERM breakdown in September 1992 on Schlesinger. The impression given by the press was that he lacked flexibility as well as political expertise and subtlety. In reality, it would have been difficult for him to act differently from the way he and his fellow members of the Central Bank Council did, being bound by the principal mandate of the Bundesbank (that is, to safeguard the stability of the Deutsche Mark). Throughout his four decades with the Bundesbank, Schlesinger had built up the reputation of a hardliner over the issue of a stable Deutsche Mark, and his views and actions were not going to change while President, whatever the circumstances. He proved right in the end and, when he retired as Bundesbank President, he was justly acclaimed at home and abroad as one of the great central bank governors with an expertise in the conduct of monetary affairs not easily surpassed.

It is scarcely surprising that in his retirement from official duties, he remains in constant demand as Visiting Professor first at Princeton University and more recently at the Humboldt University of Berlin, as well as on a permanent basis at the University of Speyer. He has published widely on monetary theory and monetary policy and has been awarded honorary doctorates by the Universities of Frankfurt/ Main, Göttingen and St Gallen.

Stephen F. Frowen

KARL OTTO PÖHL, BUNDESBANK PRESIDENT 1980–91

Karl Otto Pöhl, born in 1929, was Deputy President of the Deutsche Bundesbank from 1977 to 1979 and President from 1980 until his sudden resignation over policy matters in 1991.

After graduating in economics at the University of Göttingen in 1955, he was engaged in economic research at the Munich Institute of Economic Research (Ifo-Institute) from 1957 to 1960, was a financial journalist (partly with the weekly *Volkswirt*) from 1961 to 1967), joined the management of the Bundesverband des privaten Bankgewerbes (1968–70) and from then on spent seven years in Government service. He was first *Ministerialdirektor* (Ministerial Director) in the Ministry of Economics (1970–1) then Economic Adviser to Chancellor Willy Brandt (1971–2), until finally he became Secretary of State in the Ministry of Finance in 1972, a position he held until being appointed Deputy President of the Deutsche Bundesbank in 1977 and finally President in 1980.

It is scarcely surprising that with his political background, his presidency was marked more by the international role he played in monetary affairs than by his domestic policies. Thus as Deputy President of the Bundesbank, he was also President of the Monetary Commission of the EU 1976–7, and as Bundesbank President he became Chairman of the Committee of Central Bank Governors of the Group of Ten (1983–9). At that time, Margaret Thatcher, then the UK's Prime Minister, considered President Pöhl to be strongly hostile to any serious loss of monetary autonomy for the Bundesbank and, according to her autobiography *The Downing Street Years*, she placed great hope in him to prevent the emergence of the Delors Report giving momentum to EMU. To express her opposition to an ECB, she again used arguments from an article by Pöhl, illustrating all the difficulties in the way of such an institution, at the Hanover European Council meeting in June 1988; but this did not prevent the Delors Committee from being set up.

Karl Otto Pöhl certainly had the political know-how and charisma to play a major role on the international scene in monetary affairs, a part he obviously enjoyed. His views on domestic monetary matters were not always unopposed within the Central Bank Council, the body responsible for monetary decision-making, although as Chairman of the Council his voice carried considerable weight. Perhaps there is some truth in the belief that at times he tended to soften under international pressure when other Council members preferred a consistent policy against inflation at home.

Pöhl was quite clearly more a man of subtle political calculation rather than of monetary analysis. He left the Bundesbank in 1991 to become a Partner with personal liability in the private bank Sal. Oppenheim Jr & Cie in Cologne.

Stephen F. Frowen

OTMAR EMMINGER, BUNDESBANK PRESIDENT, 1977–9

Otmar Emminger exercised a powerful influence over Bundesbank policies for almost a quarter of a century.

Emminger joined the Bank deutscher Länder – predecessor of the Bundesbank – as Head of the Economics and Statistics Department in 1953, at the age of 42. He was soon put in charge of managing relations with international organisations, notably the IMF, and he quickly built up a department on international monetary policy. It was the field that he was to make his life's work, and over the years he amassed an encyclopaedic knowledge of every aspect of international finance: a knowledge he was not reluctant to display, or use to correct other people's mistakes. He also became Germany's executive director at the IMF, but did not reside permanently in Washington, preferring to commute from Frankfurt when necessary.

Emminger played a key role in the formulation and implementation of Germany's exchange rate policy from the end of the 1960s onwards. His main contribution perhaps was made during the early 1970s, when he was an early convert to the need for flexible exchange rates. In 1972, when a majority of the Central Bank Council backed Klasen in persuading the government to impose exchange controls rather than let the exchange rate float, Emminger was in favour of flexibility. Like the Finance Minister, Karl Schiller, Emminger realised that exchange rate flexibility offered the best and perhaps only means of protecting Germany from imported inflation (this was a period which witnessed massive speculative flows out of the dollar into the Deutsche Mark, swelling Germany's money supply). He was proved right.

Emminger had a short spell as president (retiring some months after the statutory retirement age of 68) but was a member of the Central Bank Council from the establishment of the Bundesbank in 1957. Indeed, his membership of the top policy-making committee has been exceeded only by Leonhard Gleske, who served for more than 25 years.

Emminger has been variously described as 'peppery', 'schoolmasterly' and 'didactic', and he was not one to suffer fools gladly. He was certainly one of the cleverest central bankers of recent times. His mastery of his craft gave him the self-confidence to talk much more openly to journalists than most central bankers of his generation, and he took those he trusted fully into his confidence. Many journalists will recall late-night sessions at hotel bars with Emminger during IMF meetings or other international gatherings; for a young economic commentator, listening to him expound some topical issue in international monetary policy was an education in itself. In short, his acerbic personality did not endear him to all his counterparts in other central banks – or even to all his colleagues at home – but one wishes more central bankers were as accessible, as confident or as clever.

Robert Pringle

KARL KLASEN, BUNDESBANK PRESIDENT, 1970–7

Klasen headed the Bundesbank during a turbulent decade of radical economic change. In the early 1970s, dollar and sterling crises rocked the Bretton Woods international monetary system, which in 1973 was replaced by a system of floating exchange rates. The first oil crisis fuelled inflation world-wide. In Germany, too, the rate of price increase accelerated sharply. The fact that it was possible to hold the inflation rate in Germany to a single figure, and then to halve it again to around 3.5 per cent by the time Klasen retired from office as President of the Bundesbank, was essentially due to a firm monetary policy.

Klasen was born in Hamburg, the son of a shipping company employee. He studied law and aimed for a career in the judiciary.

As a young law student in the early 1930s he joined the Social Democratic Party, because, he said, he wanted 'to do something against the rise of Hitler'. Once the Nazis came to power it was impossible for him to become a judge and he decided to switch to a career in banking, joining Deutsche Bank in 1935 as a legal consultant, a job he held until 1948, when he was chosen as President of the newly established Land Central Bank in Hamburg. He thereby also became a member of the Central Bank Council of the Bank deutscher Länder.

During his time as President of the Land Central Bank in Hamburg Klasen developed a close friendship and working relationship with two leading SPD politicians from Hamburg: Professor Karl Schiller, who was to become Minister for Economic and Financial Affairs, and Helmut Schmidt, the future Chancellor. It was on Professor Schiller's initiative that Klasen was appointed to succeed Karl Blessing as President of the Bundesbank. In the meantime Klasen had returned to Deutsche Bank, had been appointed to its board in 1952 and was elected joint spokesman of the board in 1967.

His stamina and ability to achieve his objectives were remarkable. Klasen had indeed never been a theoretician; he thought rather in pragmatic political terms and his insights were the fruit of his experience and many and varied contacts. He formed his opinion above all in conversation with friends and people he trusted. It is also against this background that we have to see Klasen's clash in June 1972 with his friend Schiller, his opposite number at the Ministry for Economic and Financial Affairs. Schiller wanted to counter the speculative capital inflows with flexible exchange rates. However, on Klasen's recommendation and against Schiller's advice, the government decided to introduce exchange controls, which led to Schiller's resignation. Subsequent developments were to show that Schiller, not Klasen, had been right on this important question.

Klasen firmly believed that a monetary system which had worked well for many years should not be abandoned prematurely, but should be defended at least for a time, even with unconventional means, as long as there remained a chance of re-establishing the conditions for it to operate more efficiently. When, with the change-over to flexible exchange rates the following year, the Bundesbank regained its room for manoeuvre to pursue a stabilisation policy, Klasen made vigorous and determined use of it.

Leonhard Gleske

Index

Abbreviations used

DM   Deutsche Mark
EMS European Monetary System
EMU European Monetary Union
ERM Exchange Rate Mechanism of
       European Monetary System
FBSO Federal Banking Supervisory Office
FRG Federal Republic of Germany
GDR German Democratic Republic
GMU German Monetary Union
IMF   International Monetary Fund
PM   Prime Minister

Acts of Parliament refer to Federal Republic of Germany.

Acheson, K., 128
Act to Promote Economic Stability
  and Growth (1967), 52
Albeck, H., 137
Alesina, A. 43n 4, 48, 169 n15
Allied military powers
  reformed German currency, 116,
    140
  set up central banking structure,
    11, 14
Anckar, Patrick, 147
Arestis, P., 10, 44
Aristotle, 122–5
audit of credit institutions, 59, 64–5
Australia, Reserve Bank of, 160
Austria, policy on exchange rates of,
  160
Austrian Central Bank, 140

Baker, G., 170 n 45
Bank deutscher Länder, 11–12, 14,
  140, 178
Banking Act (1961), 56, 57, 58–9,
  63–4
banks
  deposit guarantee schemes of, 63, 65
  external audit of, 59, 64–5

  supervision of, 56–64, 65–6
  see also Bundesbank; Land Central
    Banks
Basle Committee on Banking
  Supervision, 57, 66
Becker, Jürgen, xii, **56–67**
Belgium, economic ties with
  Germany of, 162
Black, S., 145–6
Blüm, N., 79
Blumfield, A. J., 127
Boeck, K., 148, 150
Böhm-Bawerk, Eugen von, 120
Bretton Woods exchange rate
  system, 3–4, 34, 47, 149, 179
Britain, *see* UK
Brittan, S., 125
Brunner, Karl, 127–8
Bundesbank (Deutsche Bundesbank)
  advises Federal Government, 5,
    6–7, 50–1, 68
  agree to second Tietmeyer to chair
    GMU negotiations, 68, 69
  as bank of issue, 48–9
  branches, 18–19, 58
  Central Bank Council of, *see*
    Central Bank Council

changed policy on international
 role of DM, 148–50
credibility within Germany, 9–10,
 48, 140
criticisms of policy, 2, 24–5
Bundesbank (*Contd.*)
 Directorate, 12, 14–15, 16
 and exchange rate policy, 46–7
 federal structure of, 12–13, 140
 and Germany's membership of
  IMF and EMS, 53–4
 independence of, ix–x, xx, 5, 13–14,
  33, 45, 49, 140
 instruments of monetary policy,
  41–3
 Lombard policy 41–2
 minimum reserve policy, 42–3
 as model for European central
  banking system, 45
 monetary policy decided by
  Central Bank Council, 13
 monetary policy after GMU, 23–7
 monetary targeting, x, 27–30,
  34–40
 open market policy, 42
 presidents of, 174–180
 primary objective is stability of
  currency, ix–x, 3–4, 32–3, 50
 rediscount policy 41–2
 relations with Federal
  Government, 13, 45, 49–52
 role in negotiations on GMU, 70,
  73, 74, 85, 110, 111
 to set up organisation in GDR, 77,
  92–3
 staff, 17–19
 success of, xix–xx, 164
 supervision of credit institutions
  by, 58–9, 62, 63
 supports EMU, 2–3
Bundesbank Act (1957)
 established Central Bank Council,
  14
 established federal structure, 12
 established independence of
  Bundesbank, 3, 13, 46
 grants government right to defer
  Central Bank Council decisions,
  52

obliges Bundesbank to safeguard
 currency, 3, 32–3, 148
regulates relations between Federal
 Government and Bundesbank,
 49–51
regulates responsibilities of
 Bundesbank Directorate and
 Land Central Banks, 16–17
safeguards Central Bank Council
 from political manipulation, 15
Bundesrat, 15
Bundestag
 celebrate breakdown of Berlin
  Wall, 69–70
 committee on conflict between
  Federal Government and
  Bundesbank, 52
 discuss GMU treaty, 107
 informed of German treaty
  negotiations, 98, 106
Business Cycle Council for the Public
 Sector, 52

Caesar, R., 43 n2
central bank, independence of, 132–4
Central Bank Council of
 Bundesbank
 composition and functioning of,
  12, 13, 14–15
 in ERM crisis, 176
 in 1972 exchange rate crisis, 178
 formation of monetary policy by, 48
 in GMU negotiations, 68, 73–4,
  77, 113
 in Maastricht negotiations, 6–7
 members of Federal Cabinet may
  attend meetings, 50–1
 unanimity on EMU, 3
central banking, ethics and morals in,
 125–35
Chant, J. F., 128
Childs, D. 119
Chicago School, 127
CMEA (Council for Mutual
 Economic Assistance) countries,
 76, 86, 97
'conservative central banker', 131–2
Council of Economic Experts, 71, 110
Cukierman, A., 48

Delors, Jacques, 76
Delors Committee on EMU, 177
Denmark, economic ties with
  Germany of, 162
Deutsche Bundesbank, *see*
  Bundesbank
Deutsche Mark (DM)
  anchor currency in EMS, x, 25, 32,
    141, 161–3
  has become international currency,
    164–8
  conversion rate of GDR Mark
    into, 111–15
  critics of external strength, 2
  in ERM crisis, 25–7
  extension of currency area to
    include GDR, 20, 75, 97–8, 111,
    142
  in international financial markets,
    148–57
  in international trade, 142–8
  as reference currency, 160–4
  as reserve currency, 157–60, 164–5
  stability since introduction, ix, 139
Deutscher Industrie- und Handelstag,
  117
Dregger, A. 79, 96
Dresden, 70
Duwendag, D., 44, 137

Eastern European states
  change from centralised planning
    in, 110–11
  importance of DM in, 146, 147, 163
  refugees from, 69
Eatwell, J., 137
ECBS, *see* European System of
  Central Banks
ECU (European currency unit), 47, 54
Einzig, P., 156
Emminger, Otto, 140, 149
  profile, 178–9
EMS, *see* European Monetary
  System
EMU, *see* European Monetary Union
Erhard, Ludwig, 4, 75, 94, 116
ESCB, *see* European System of
  Central Banks
ethics, economics and 122

Eucken, W., 43 n1
Euro, *see* European single currency
European Central Bank (ECB)
  Bundesbank prepares way for, 37,
    43
  future independence, 47–8
  future role in exchange rate policy,
    54
  Thatcher opposed to, 177
European Central Banking System,
  see European System of Central
  Banks
European Monetary System (EMS)
  Bundesbank contracting party, 54
  Deutsche Mark dominant
    currency, 161–3
  ERM crisis in, 25–6, 176
  widening of exchange rate
    margins, 47
European Monetary Union (EMU)
  Bundesbank supports, 2–3, 8–9
  economic basis required, xi
  future success of, 55
  single currency, x–xi, 2, 47, 167, 168
  uncertainties of, 37
European single currency, x–xi, 47,
  167, 168
European System of Central Banks
  (ESCB)
  Bundesbank acts as model for, xx,
    45
  Bundesbank involved in preparing,
    3
  primary objective is to maintain
    price stability, 4, 55
European Union (EU) (formerly
  Community)
  consulted *re* German monetary
    union, 76
  Council of Ministers, 8, 54
  Monetary Committee of, 6
exchange rate policy, possible
  conflicts with monetary policy,
    46–7

Federal Accounting Office, 14
Federal Banking Supervisory Office
  (FBSO)
  established, 56

cooperates with Bundesbank, 17, 58
powers and instruments of, 60–4
responsibilities of, 58–9
Federal Chancellery, 73, 85
Federal Foreign Office, 79–80
Federal Government of Germany
Bundesbank advises, 5, 6–7, 50–1,
68
borrowing increased on monetary
union, 115–16, 117–19
Chancellery, 73, 85
charged with task of establishing
central bank, 48–9
choice of federal banking structure
by, 12
Foreign Office, 79–80
as member of IMF, 53–4
Ministry of Economics, *see*
Federal Ministry of Economics
Ministry of Finance, *see* Federal
Ministry of Finance
Ministry of Justice, 74
Ministry of Labour and Social
Affairs, 74, 84–5
offers GDR monetary, economic
and social union, 71, 110
powers in banking supervision,
59–60
relations with Bundesbank, 13, 45,
49–52
Federal Ministry of Economics
delegates in German treaty
negotiations, 74
in discussions on conversion of
GDR Mark, 84–5, 113
proposes 'guiding principle' law in
treaty negotiations, 75
rights and powers of Minister, 51
Tietmeyer at, 73, 174
Federal Ministry of Finance
in discussions on conversion of
GDR Mark, 84–5
draft treaty on GMU prepared by,
73, 79
in German treaty negotiations, 73,
74, 86, 96, 102, 106–7
represented in 'expert talks' on
monetary union, 72
rights and powers of Minister, 51, 60

Tietmeyer at, 69, 174
see also Waigel, Theo (Minister of
Finance)
Federal Ministry of Justice, 74
see also Kinkel, K.
Federal Ministry of Labour and
Social Affairs, 74, 84–5, 101–2
Federal Republic of Germany
(FRG), *see* Germany
Federal Supervisory Office for
Securities Trading, 151
Fforde, John, 125
financial markets
deregulation of, 35
DM in, 148–57
internationalisation of, 56, 66
Finland, use of DM in trade by,
147
France, xx, 140–1
Fratianni, M., 131
Friedman, Milton, 126–7, 129, 130
Frowen, Stephen F. xii, **xix–xxi**,
10 n2, 44, 119 n1, 136–7, 157,
172, **174–8**

Gaddum, J.-W., 92
Gawel, E., 31 n1
GDR Mark
conversion to Deutsche Mark,
21–3, 73–4, 78, 79, 84–5, 89, 90,
111–15
Modrow government seeks
stabilisation of, 71
Gebauer, W., 44
Gebhard, Carola, xii, **139–73**
Gehrmann, D., 148–9
Genscher, H. D., 79, 93
Gerhardt, W., 146, 150
Gerlach, S., 44 n6
German Council of Industry and
Commerce, 117
German Democratic Republic
(GDR)
coalition agreement on
three-dimensional union, 75–6,
77, 78, 83
currency conversion, 21–3, 73–4,
78, 79, 84–5, 89, 90, 111–15
free elections in, 72, 77

implications for economy of conversion to DM, 81–2, 87, 98, 99–100
initial resistance to relinquishing sovereignty, 70–1
Kohl offers monetary, economic and social union to, 20, 68–9
social and political breakdown, 69–70
in treaty negotiations, 82–107 *passim*
German Monetary Union (GMU)
Bundesbank advises Federal Government on, 6
constitutional implications of, 94
effect on Bundesbank's monetary policy, 23–4, 28–9, 37
effect on economies of former GDR and FRG of, 115–19, 153–4
environmental protection under, 99
fiscal administration under, 102
GDR demands social union, 75–6
initial offer and 'expert talks', 70, 71–2, 110
ownership problems arising from, 80–1, 87–9, 94, 103–4, 105
pressures for speed of, 20, 72, 73, 77
safeguards against currency fraud during, 96, 105
social security, health and pension arrangements under, 80, 95, 101
see also German treaty negotiations
German political reunification, 92, 93
German treaty negotiations, 68–109
aim to provide for future economic system of GDR, 75
working paper prepared by Federal Ministry of Finance, 79, 82, 83
first round, 82–3
second round, 83–4
third round, 85–90
fourth round, 91–5
fifth round, 98–104
final draft approved by FRG, 105, 107
Treaty signed, 107

second State Treaty, 109
German Unity Fund, 105, 106, 117–18
Germany (prior to 1990 refers to West Germany only)
banking system in, 11–19, 140
consensus on importance of stable currency, 1
constitutional implications of GMU, 94
constitutional provision for central bank, 47–8, 48–9
currency reforms, 11, 32–3, 48, 139–40
external audit of credit institutions in, 59, 64–5
foreign investment in, 152–4
inflation in, ix, 11, 140–1, 179
internal monetary stability having priority over exchange rate stability, 3–4
international trade of, 142–6
stock market legislation in, 151
unemployment in, 30
unification of, *see* German Monetary Union
see also Federal Government of Germany
Gleske, Leonhard, xiii, **11–19**, 178, **179–80**
Glucksmann, A., 135
Göppl, H., 136
Grabley, P., 82
Grassman, S., 142

Hagen, J. von, 131
Hahn, F., 124
Häuser, K., 44
Hausman, D. M. 134
Hayek, F. A., 121, 128, 137
Hefeker, C., 31 n4
Henn, R., 136
Herstatt Bank, 56
Hesse, H., 122, 137
Hetzel, R. L., 121
Hitler, economic policies under, 11
Hölscher, J. 119, 157, 172
Homann, K., 122

IMF (International Monetary Fund),
    Germany's membership of, 53–4
Indonesia, 160
inflation
    in Germany, ix, 11, 140–1
    revival of debate on relation to
        unemployment of, 1, 33
Issing, Otmar, xiii, 44 n6, **120–38**, 163
Italy, xix, 140–1, 146

Jagoda. B., 74, 87, 101
Japan
    currency used in trade, 145, 146
    inflation in, 140–1

Karakitsos, E., 10 n2
Kaufhold, P., 82
King, M., 125
Kinkel, K., 74, 81, 88, 94, 96–7
Kirche und Staat (Church and State),
    70
Kittel, W., 74
Klasen, Karl, 178
    profile 179–80
Klemm, P., 74, 102
Kliemt, H., 128, 134
Kloten, Norbert, xiv, **110–19**
Kohl, Helmut, 10 n1, 119 n2
    briefs Tietmeyer on German treaty
        negotiations, 68–9, 73, 74
    on Bundesbank policy, 10
    chairs coalition talks on GMU, 74,
        90
    informs Länder governments of
        progress towards union, 106
    makes GDR offer of monetary,
        economic and social union, 20, 71
    opinion on conversion rate of
        GDR Mark, 115
    pleased with outcome of GMU
        negotiations, 104, 105
    rejects additional taxes on
        reunification, 117
    at signing of State Treaty, 107
    wants to extend Federal pension
        system to former GDR, 80
    wants Tietmeyer as personal adviser
        in EMU negotiations, 109
Köhler, H., 72, 74

Köllner, L., 140
König, R., xiv, **20–30**, 142, 157
Krause, Günther
    leads GDR delegation in treaty
        negotiations, 82–105 *passim*
    in preliminary discussions on
        German monetary union, 78
    on reorganisation of Treuhand
        agency, 107–8
Krenz, Egon, 70

Laidler, D., 121
Lambsdorff, Otto Graf, 79
Land Central Bank of Hamburg,
    179–80
Land Central Banks
    established, 11, 140
    main offices of Deutsche
        Bundesbank, 12
    management of, 15–16
    presidents of, 14–15
    reorganised after GMU, 12
    responsibilities of, 16–17, 62
    sponsor branches in GDR, 93
Länder governments
    contribute little to cost of
        reunification, 115, 118
    financial planning by, 52
    informed of treaty negotiations,
        84, 98
    postwar banking supervision by, 56
Lautenschlager, H. W., 74
Liquidity Consortium Bank, 65
Loef, H.-E., 130
Ludewig, J., 73, 76, 77–8, 96
Luxembourg, economic ties with
    Germany of, 162

Maastricht Treaty on European
    Union
    Bundesbank advises on, 6–7
    Bundesbank supports road to
        EMU in, 2
    independence of central bank
        under, 45, 48, 49, 54–5
    provides for permanent stability
        union, 3, 4
Maisel, Sherman, 126
Maizière, Lothar de

elected PM of GDR, 72
government's first policy
  statement, 79
opens treaty negotiations, 82
at signing of State Treaty, 107
talks with Tietmeyer before treaty
  negotiations, 77, 81–2, 83
Mark (GDR currency), *see* GDR
  Mark
Marsh, David, 125
Masson, P. R., 160
McHugh, F.P., 136–7
McPherson, M. S., 134
Milgate, M., 136
Modrow government
  accepts offer of German monetary,
    economic and social union,
    110–11
  established Treuhand agency,
    107–8
  formed, 70
  not prepared to relinquish
    sovereignty, 71
monetary ethics, 122
monetary stability
  as public good, 33, 132
  recent questioning of importance
    of, 1–2
  and social equity, 4
morals and expertise, 123–5
Moreau (Governor of Banque de
  France), 126
Müller, H., 125

Netherlands, economic links with
  Germany, 162
Netherlands Bank, 160
Neumann, M.J.M., 133
New Zealand, monetary policy in,
  133
Newman, P., 136
Nijathawom, B., 160, 170 n45
Nölling, W., 140
Norman, Montagu, 125–6
North, D.C., 135

Olson, M., 43 n3

Page, S.A.B., 145–6

Plato, 124
Pöhl, Karl Otto, 68, 72, 110
  profile, 177–8
Pringle, Robert, xiv, **xix–xxi**, 164,
  178–9

Rawls, J., 124
Reichenbach, Klaus, 78
Reichsbank, 11, 17, 125
Reichsmark, 139
Rogoff, K., 131
Romberg, W., 82, 104–5, 107

Saunderson, A., 163
Schacht, Hjalmar, 125–6
Scharrer, H.-E., 142
Schäuble, W., 79, 81
Schell, M., 119
Schiller, Karl, 4, 178, 180
Schlesinger, Helmut, 44 n7
  delegate in German treaty
    negotiations, 74, 84–5, 91, 96, 98
  in informal discussions prior to
    treaty negotiations, 73
  learns of offer of GMU, 110
  profile, 175–6
Schleusser, H., 104
Schmid, Peter, xiv–xv, **32–43**
Schmidt, Helmut, 180
Schmidt-Bleibtreu, Bruno, 73
Schmitz, W., 122
Schumpeter, J.A., 121
Seiters, R., 73, 75, 79, 84, 91, 106,
  107
Seitz, F., 147
Sen, A., 135 n3
Senivongs, C., 160, 170 n45
Siebke, J., 137
Siegert, Walter, 82, 102
Simon, H.A., 135
Simons, H.C., 127–9
Staatsbank (State Bank of GDR), 77,
  91–2, 93, 110, 111
State Treaty on Monetary, Economic
  and Social Union, 109
  see also under German treaty
    negotiations
Stoll, W., 82, 92
Stolpe, M., 70–1

Streissler, E.W., 119
Strong, Benjamin, 126
Summers, L.H., 43 n4, 48
Supranowitz, S., 82
Sweden, use of DM in trade of, 147
Swiss National Bank, 140
Switzerland, inflation in, 140–1

Tandler, G., 104
Tanner, N.P., 135 n2
Tavlas, G.S., 142, 145–6
Terazono, E., 170 n45
Thatcher, Margaret, 177
Thornton, Henry, 120–1
Tietmeyer, Hans, **ix–xi**, xv, **1–10,
    68–109**, 119 n2, 163, 169 n18
    profile, 174–5
Tödter, K.-H., 44 n6
Treuhand agency, 90, 96, 102, 106,
    107–8, 116
Tullock, G., 123

UK (United Kingdom)
    Bank of England, 18
    Central Statistical Office, 168 n11
    delinked currency from DM, xix
    inflation in, 140–1
unemployment
    in Germany, 30
    revival of debate on relation to
        inflation, 1
Unger, S., 148, 162
US (United States) dollar
    declining as reference currency, 163

in international trade, 146–8,
    165–6, 167
lost dominant role in European
    trade, 143–4
traded against DM in foreign
    exchange markets, 155–7
USA (United States of America)
    central bank in, 18–19
    inflation in, 140–1
    monetary policy of, 126
    see also US dollar
USSR (Union of Soviet Socialist
    Republics) and German
    reunification, 76, 97–8
usury, religious objections to,
    120

Vaubel, R., 133

Wahlig, Bertold, xv–xvi, **45–55**
Waigel, Theo, 68, 71, 72, 73, 102,
    104, 119
Waller, C., 131
Wenzel, S., 82
Willeke, Caroline, xvi, **20–30**
Wood, G.E., 135 n1
Würzen, D. von, 74

Yeager, L.B., 136
Yen, use in international trade and
    investment of, 156, 159, 162,
    163, 164

Ziel, Alwin, 82, 86